GOD'S GRANDEUR

GOD'S GRANDEUR

THE ARTS AND IMAGINATION IN THEOLOGY

David C. Robinson, S.J.
Editor

THE ANNUAL PUBLICATION
OF THE COLLEGE THEOLOGY SOCIETY
2006
VOLUME 52

ORBIS BOOKS
Maryknoll, New York 10545

Published by Orbis Books, Maryknoll, New York 10545-0308.
Manufactured in the United States of America.

Library of Congress Cataloging-in-Publication Data

God's Grandeur : the arts and imagination in theology / David C. Robinson, editor.
    p. cm. — (The annual publication of the College Theology Society ; 2006, v. 52)
  ISBN-13: 978-1-57075-694-8
  1. Christianity and the arts. 2. Christianity and art. I. Robinson, David, 1930-
  BR115.A8G65 2007
  261.5'7—dc22
                                                        2007003057

Contents

v

PART III
LITERARY ARTS

PART IV
AESTHETICS AND EDUCATION

PART V
CONTEMPORARY FORMS

Introduction

David C. Robinson

Within the evolving history of any academic or intellectual society, many threshold moments help clarify its identity, community, and potential. The 2006 annual meeting of the College Theology Society on the theme of *God's Grandeur: The Arts and
Imagination in Theology* could certainly be viewed as such a moment. The theme itself marks a notable variation from more traditional topics related to the historical, systematic, scriptural,
ecclesial, or even social-scientific dimensions of the theological
enterprise.

At the conclusion of the convention, a practical consideration
indicated its significance for me as editor. I received numerous submissions for the annual volume (indeed, the largest number ever)
covering a highly diverse range of issues in the arts and aesthetics,
and faced the task of finding two qualified reviewers for each essay as part of the selection process. A detailed examination of the
membership of the College Theology Society revealed a surpris-
ingly small community that identified areas within the arts as the
primary foci of their scholarship and personal interest. An e-mail
to the wider constituency of the Catholic Theological Society of
America harvested additional potential readers. However, the editorial process revealed an interesting phenomenon. Virtually every
article elicited at least a modest polarization of opinion regarding
its virtues and needs as a *theological* presentation. Of course, editors usually face a diversity of views, whatever the subject under
consideration, but the range of responses left me pondering the
larger implications of our corporate undertaking. Was the CTS
community experiencing a potential transition in its understanding of the parameters and purposes of theological investigation?
Was the theme of "The Arts and Imagination in Theology" point-

ing us to more foundational reflections on the nature and direction of our common enterprise?

This led me to ponder the unique qualities of our endeavor. Tom Lucas's opening plenary address, treating indigenous iconography in the reconstruction of the windows of the Shanghai cathedral, provided me with a useful metaphor—namely the symbolic qualities of the rose, and its hybridization as both a physical entity and a cultural icon. As horticulturalists have known for generations, hybrids provide an effective means for maximizing assets or minimizing perceived defects in a given tree, plant, or flower. Hybrid roses have made available boutique colors, shapes, and sizes. However, with these adaptations have come limitations—are these new products "natural" in some culturally accepted sense? What do we sacrifice for the change—scent, or texture, or simple familiarity?

It does not seem too reckless a stretch to apply this hybridization metaphor to twenty-first-century theological thought. The original "seeds" of the endeavor in liturgical practice, catechetics, community narratives, and so on have expanded with the passing centuries through interaction with Western philosophical thought, anthropology, psychology, sociology, historical theory, and a seemingly endless lineage of intellectual conversation partners. Each of these partners has added a unique dimension to what is perceived as constitutive of theological methodology. In more recent generations, the role of the arts and aesthetics has begun a shift in its own "genetic morphology" within theological discourse.

Emerging from its earlier status as a pre-literate medium for catechesis, or a handmaid of devotion, or a product of religious patronage, art as a manifestation and interpretation of the Christian community's identity evolved dramatically during the twentieth century. Its place as an intellectual step-child of "higher" disciplines has been replaced by a more experimental understanding of the spiritual role of art and artist in believing (or even agnostic) communities. As a result, the theological import of such artworks has also begun to shift. Whether literary, aural, visual, or performative, an artistic creation embraces an expanded meaning-base beyond any connection to a particular tradition. Specifically theological implications of any given artwork have begun to move beyond the rubrics of accepted methodological paradigms. To recreate a stock phrase—the medium is the method.

I have personal experience of this emerging hybridization of disciplines. As one who has explored a variety of graduate programs in literature, theology, hermeneutics, and music, I have not experienced cognitive dissonance in connecting them within an individual confessional and intellectual identity. Rather, they have formed a hybridized perspective, or an interlinked web of disciplinary tools. Theology does not "explain" music as a religious phenomenon, for example. Music is simply another potential theological voice inside a complex harmony of concepts and symbols. As philosophers from Ricoeur to Lakoff have informed us, human meaning expands through the evolutionary development of metaphors (whether literary or not). The arts not only highlight new "metaphors" for theological methods, they also invite us to explore the ways in which our conceptual methods are themselves metaphors for more fundamental dimensions of human religious questions.

Our communal experience of gathering, reflecting, and then aggregating a variety of perspectives may point to a possible threshold moment for our various theological departments and associations in the future. As psychology and sociology have helped to reconfigure approaches to spirituality and ecclesiology, and feminist critiques have nuanced our appropriation of scripture, perhaps literature and the visual arts may provide the same creative impulse to the ways in which we construct so-called theological texts and narratives. Following the historical model of the rose, we may well forward the creation of a disciplinary "hybrid" that holds the form of the tradition, while significantly altering the "color and scent" of the organic entity we name theological discourse. Naturally, every discipline, whether spiritual, aesthetic, or academic, has its own evolutionary trajectory, and none exists in isolation from the others. However, our attentiveness to the ways in which the arts can help to hybridize the outcomes of more standard approaches may foster the next creative dimensions of theological reflection.

The preceding observations are certainly not the product of solipsistic occurrences within the orbit of the College Theology Society. On a global scale, interactions are underway that engage artistic and theological disciplines in profound dialogue. The extent to which such interactions are meta-systemic—pointing to a hybridized disciplinary future—is highly variable. Nonetheless, the seeds of change are being planted, and invite our cultivation. We need only look to contemporary graduate programs linking theology and the arts, such as those at St. Andrews University in Scotland, the Graduate Theological Union at Berkeley, Union Theological Seminary in New York, and Fuller Theological Seminary in Pasadena, to see the variety and possibility of future cross-fertilization.

In addition, a number of scholars and artists have been plumbing the relationships between the arts, religious practice, and theology. Thomas M. Lucas, S.J., has promoted the intersection of indigenous iconography and contemporary church architecture. Sandra Bowden and Terrence Dempsey, S.J., have been major proponents of an emerging twenty-first-century arena for the visual arts as interpreters of the spiritual and religious currents of an allegedly post-modern planet. Don Saliers and Richard Viladesau have opened new horizons to explore musical practice and phenomenology as theological voices in confessional communities and in the academy. More focused discussion of the intersection of the arts and theology as mutually reinforcing and recreating academic/intellectual disciplines can be found in the dialectical collections brought forth by Kimberly Vrudny and Wilson Yates (*Arts, Theology, and the Church: New Intersections*) and Jeremy Begbie (*Sounding the Depths: Theology Through the Arts*).

It is perhaps not yet viable to propose a "state-of-the-conversation" summary of these many contributing and competing opinions at play. Nonetheless, the forces of ferment are often the most profound sources of discovery. We can look forward with eager anticipation to the coming decades of interaction and cooperation that contain the promise of new hybrids and new adventures within the theological community.

Each of the three plenary speakers was provided with a theme or "controlling metaphor": *sacred space, sacred sight, and sacred sound*. These three themes embraced a spectrum of elements that informed the gathering as a whole: visual arts, musical and literary arts, and architectural and media spaces. As an extension of that plenary framework, the current volume traverses a wide range of themes within the rubric of the arts and imagination. Attention has been given to five different envelopes for conceptual content. The first includes the more *traditional visual arts*, including painting and religious architecture. The second investigates *music* as a communal phenomenon within worship, and also as a formator of individual moral life and the theological personality. The third explores *literary arts*, specifically the impact of short stories, novels, and drama. The fourth envelope takes a step back from the active process of creating works of art, in order to investigate *dimensions of aesthetics, philosophical reflection, and pedagogy*. The fifth and final section probes *contemporary media* as artistic participants in the theological arena, including television, film, and public art.

Visual Arts

Thomas M. Lucas, S.J., opened the conference proceedings with his plenary reflections on the restoration of the cathedral windows in Shanghai, a cultural reclamation of sacred space. He emphasized the complexity of religious "acculturation," a hybrid adaptation of traditional and communal icons. The resulting works are true to the history of the region, in its religious and greater cultural traditions. Susie Paulik Babka's exploration of the *Gnadenstuhl* motif investigates the way in which an art form traverses the "terrain that fails language," affirming the perennial human search for meaning in the reality of the cross, a trinitarian moment that is also a deeply incarnational experience of longing to unite heaven with the catastrophes of human suffering. Babka investigates the nuances of the motif from the twelfth-century Cambrai missal to the mid-seventeenth-century work of Jusepe de Ribera. Sandra Bowden provides a map for the contemporary artistic landscape of Christian art. Her plenary introduced a number of the key organizations and museums dedicated to the presentation and proliferation of such work, including CIVA (Christians in the Visual Arts), MOCRA (the Museum of Contemporary Religious Art) in St. Louis, and MOBIA (the Museum of Biblical Art) in New York.

Musical Arts

Don Saliers presented a plenary reflection on the qualities of "sacred sound" as these have been manifested in his own experience in the worlds of liturgical, classical, and jazz forms. He elicited a global musical montage of practices and traditions (including his artistic ventures with his daughter, Emily Saliers, a member of the popular duo the Indigo Girls), highlighting the manner in which music-making elicits a connection with the divine and with the "narrative" of human experience. James F. Caccamo explores the phenomenology of musical moments as contributors to the formation of the moral life. He notes the two primary models most often employed to assess the impact of music in personal and so-cial formation—the informational model of *instruction* and the motivational model of *inspiration*. The first teaches moral lessons; the second draws participants into a place of emotional receptiv-ity to a moral sensibility. He argues instead for an ethnomusicologi-cal approach that appreciates the listener as participant within the musical context and as an agent who shapes the meaning and moral import of any given musical moment. William Collinge chronicles the journey of John Dunne from his early years as an interpreter of Thomistic thought and hermeneutic dialogue between cultures, to narrative reflections on his global travels, and, most recently, to work concerning music as symbolic form and as a state of being (compositions vs. spontaneous/creative musical events). Dunne offers a theological reflection on the qualities of music as it mani-fests connection to the divine, while reaching out to the human articulation of words and dance in creating a communal narrative.

Literary Arts

Colleen Carpenter Cullinan argues that theology, though gen-erally accepted as a form of reasoned discourse, is originally rooted in the narratives of experience—it is grounded in story. She aligns with Metz's notion that Christians are primarily a storytelling com-munity rather than a rational or argumentative one. Such stories contain *dangerous memories*, recollections of experiences that change life and the world. A theology of redemption does not merely link stories to ideas, but rather to actions. Cullinan investigates Barbara Kingsolver's *Animal Dreams* as a fictional model of the impact of dangerous memory, of the ways in which remembered stories can be replaced by other narratives, allowing redemptive choice and transformation. Julie Hanlon Rubio draws our atten-tion to the very human dimensions of faith and moral choice in the novels and stories of Flannery O'Connor. She notes that O'Connor's fiction in no way idolizes the religious identities of her characters, but instead intentionally portrays human potential through the lens of human flaws. Rubio highlights the moral and ethical lessons elicited in O'Connor's work as a creative reservoir for a Catholic theology of the family. Randall S. Rosenberg focuses on von Balthasar's notion of the nature of dramatic time and its contrast to an evolutionary model of endless progress. Linked to Metz's denial of *Zeitlosigkeit* (a modern understanding of inexorable, mechanical time) and his appreciation for the apocalyptic nature of human temporality in the face of suffering, Balthasar looks to dramatic time as a model for expressing the horizontal time frame of human experience, while maintaining a vertical connection to the transcendent and the infinite.

Aesthetics and Education

Kimberly Vrudny provides a focus on the pedagogical dimensions of aesthetics. She analyzes the effectiveness of incorporating service learning into a course entitled "Art, Beauty, and the Revelation of the Divine." While studying classics by Plato, Augustine, and Kant, and more contemporary figures such as Tillich, Balthasar, and Tracy, students are engaged in work with a local organization serving the AIDS community. The pedagogical intention behind the course is to explore ideas of beauty in the midst of human loss and suffering, in order to help students discern an authentic distinction between the beautiful and the merely "pretty." Ki Joo Choi offers an expansive reflection on one of the lesser-analyzed aspects of Rahner's thought—namely beauty and the aesthetics of transcendental experience. Choi links Rahner's transcendental anthropology to his understanding of the mediatory role of artistic objects and poetic language. Poetry holds primacy of place as a "primordial symbol" revealing God's presence to human understanding. Jennifer Elisa Veninga investigates the nature of the imagination from the philosophical perspectives of Marcuse and Kierkegaard. She contends that, although their conclusions vary, both recognize the impact of the imagination in aesthetic experience. While Kierkegaard has little use for the self-indulgent aesthete, he views the imagination as a catalyst for human maturation from the aesthetic to the ethical and then to the religious sphere of life. Marcuse, by contrast, views the role of aesthetic imagination and the arts as a creative impulse to carry societies beyond the mechanical and stultifying realities of capitalist and consumerist life to the formation of a new order.

Contemporary Forms

The convention also hosted a number of presentations that ventured beyond the standard confines of theological reflection on the themes of the arts and imagination. Frances M. Leap probes the dimensions of feminist pneumatology in the film *Chocolat*. She examines the movie as a study in the work of Spirit to transform the *ecclesia* or official assembly of the local church, as well as the *koinonia* or community of loving fellowship. She explores the scriptural symbols of wind, water, and fire, and how their sacramental/social significance is played out in the unfolding of immanent divine presence made manifest through a quest for liberation, and a celebration of the elemental power of relationship. Matthew Minix shifts the media focus from film to television with his investigation of the career of Bishop Fulton Sheen, the prototype of a Catholic televangelist before the role had been defined. Minix inspects Sheen's emergence as a TV personality through the vehicle of such programs as *Life Is Worth Living*. He also provides a framework for inspecting Sheen's role within the emerging "culture industry" in the United States, derived from the critical theory of Adorno, Horkheimer, and de Certeau. Maureen H. O'Connell moves the museum to the streets in her study of several products of the Mural Arts Program in Philadelphia, which has produced over twenty-seven hundred murals in underserved urban neighborhoods. O'Connell highlights the importance of these works as symbolic signposts for a theological critique of urban life from the perspectives of poverty, ethics, and justice. She indicates the significance of various manifestations of the wider mural movement for the formulation of black theology and political theology, especially as these are evoked within the confines of sexism, racism, and economic inequity in contemporary American life.

Acknowledgments

If there is one common denominator in every conference, it is the reality that many hands, hearts, and minds are required for a successful outcome. Given the unique demands of the 2006 Col-

lege Theology Society annual meeting, even more communal cooperation was essential. It would be impractical (and perhaps im-
prudent) to attempt a fully comprehensive statement of thanks,
but a representative effort must be made!

John Kane of Regis University in Denver coordinated a plethora
of details on-site to ensure the quality and convenience of the conference. Within the editorial process, which embraced dozens of
generous individuals, members of both the College Theology Society and the Catholic Theological Society of America displayed
enormous kindness and insight in helping to shape the current
volume. The perennial patron saint of these conference editions,
Susan Perry of Orbis Books, maintained both the schedule and the
attention to accuracy and clarity that are essential to reaching the
finish line successfully. Terry Dempsey, S.J., offered invaluable insights in helping to shape the preliminary infrastructure of the
volume, a complex task given the enormous number and breadth
of submissions. Philip Rossi, S.J., and Terrence Tilley provided
numerous recommendations for potential reviewers. Boundless
gratitude must also be extended to the abundant and abidingly
patient contributors—if only the edition could be twice as long!

An eminently harmonious and helpful "chorus" of reviewers
kept the selection and editing process sane and focused. They in-
cluded: Gary Macy, Robert Masson, Tony Godzieba, Susan Ross,
John Downey, Tom McElligott, Julie Reed, Kim Connor, Dennis
Recio, S.J., Maria Morgan, Terrence Tilley, Tom Lucas, S.J., Jo-
seph Morris, Tom Beaudoin, Valerie Lesniak, Ann Riggs, Dominic
Colonna, Kim Vrudny, J. A. Colombo, Rachel Bundang, Joe
Angilella, S.J., Mike McLaughlin, Mary Gerhart, Robert Christie,
Loretta Devoy, and Richard Viladesau. My blessings and thanks
to all.

Part I

VISUAL ARTS

Three Parables of the Rose, or Shanghai-ed into Acculturation

Thomas M. Lucas

I spent an afternoon in the garden pruning roses a few days ago after returning from Shanghai. That activity suggested a metaphor I have chosen to develop as the focus of this brief essay. I should warn my readers that what follows is not a learned treatise on hermeneutics, cultural anthropology, or iconography. Rather, it is a metaphorical field trip into the original sacred space, the garden.

Eminent theologian Kurt Vonnegut insists that "Peculiar travel suggestions are dancing lessons from God." I invite you to take a turn in the rose garden with me, and promise that we'll end up in Shanghai sooner or later.

The First Parable: The Unnatural History of Roses

Once upon a time, after about thirty-five million years of hanging around, a thorny shrub caught somebody's eye in China. Five thousand years ago, the cultivation and hybridization of roses began. Before long, Confucius's library contained six hundred books on roses, and the plant had jumped on a flying carpet for Turkey, where it evolved into the great-grandparent of European roses. The ancient Romans sometimes used rose water instead of gold in trade, and the decadent boy emperor Heliogabalus was so fond of roses that he smothered his guests—literally smothered them to death—with rose petals.

At once both phallic and feminine, Aphrodite gave the rose its

---

Author's note: The following essay was originally presented as a PowerPoint lecture illustrated with almost one hundred images. Practical and budgetary restraints do not permit reproduction of the images here.

3

name, and Dionysus bestowed its fragrance. That, of course, did not prevent it from becoming the preeminent medieval symbol of the Virgin Mary, or from standing as red and white battle emblems for Yorks and Lancasters in the War of the Roses, or from fusing to become the symbol of united England in the Tudor rose.

Ever-blooming red roses were first imported into Europe from China in the 1790s, and pale white and pink European roses that only bloomed once a year were quickly hybridized into a staggering variety of flower forms. Before long, Puccini has Callas as Cio-Cio San singing the "Flower Duet" in Italian in *Madame Butterfly*. It was all but inevitable that, although she never promised us a rose garden (that was Lynn Anderson), Dolly Parton's name would be affixed to a blowsy, lipstick red-orange hybrid tea rose. Recently, another favorite, the "buttery yellow" Julia Child hybrid tea rose, was named one of 2006's All American Rose Selections.

We can only speculate what future roses will look like, and when we attain to the Celestial Rose, we can only hope that it is even more sublime than Doré's engravings of Dante's vision, utterly beautiful beyond our imaginings.[1]

This short, unnatural natural history of roses points to a fact of life: the creation of hybrids is one of nature's and humanity's most creative and dangerous processes. Almost everything we eat and most of what we grow in our gardens is the result of selection, fusion, or transformation, whether through natural selection or deliberate manipulation. Many consider hybridized food products the promise for a well-fed world; others dub them "frankenfoods." But like it or not, it's how nature and we humans do business.

The history of the use of imagery in the Catholic Christian tradition is a story of successful and unsuccessful hybridizations, of careful and clumsy fusions. The Catholic tradition, for all its failings, is essentially a world-affirming belief structure. It affirms that because humanity was created in "the image and likeness of God" and because Christ became incarnate, there is no absolute divide between sacred and profane.

The early church, of course, was Jewish in its roots and cautious, wary of making idols. Still, it came of age in the artistically and philosophically sophisticated world of late antiquity. Neoplatonism confidently posited that the visible can move us to the invisible, and the influence of near-Eastern mysticism and mystery religions had already enriched the soil in which Christianity's roots would spread.

From as early as the mid-second century, Christians were adorning their meeting places and cemeteries with frescoes that served to inspire and instruct viewers. With the adoption of Christianity as the imperial state religion in the fourth century, inevitable shifts in imagery occurred: Christ assumed the attributes of Apollo and the *Sol Invictus*, the invincible Sun, whose winter solstice celebration Christ's followers baptized as a celebration of Christ's birth. The Virgin Mary's depiction eventually came to mix imperial, domestic, and even pagan Egyptian elements. She became the Mystical Rose.

The move away from the anti-iconic traditions of Judaism required theological justification. The orthodox Christian response came from a number of directions. As the Christological crises eventually worked themselves out, a coherent theology of the incarnation emerged, in which Christ's visible humanity became the warrant for making images of the Word made flesh. Theologians like Basil the Great and Athanasius justified the veneration of images by making a crucial distinction between the sign and what it signifies, while affirming the analogical unity between them. They held that because of that linkage, honor moves naturally from image to prototype.

> Just as no one who looks at the imperial image in the marketplace and acknowledges the emperor would deduce the existence of two emperors, first the image and then the real emperor, that is the situation here, too. If the image and the emperor can be one (for an image does not cause a multiplication of the emperor) the same holds true of the divine *logos* and God.[2]

This essentially Neoplatonic system was severely challenged during the iconoclastic crisis of the eighth and ninth centuries. The causes and history of the crisis are far too complicated to detail here. They entail, among other factors, centralizing geopolitical and economic factors in a Monophysite-friendly imperial court, as well as a general questioning, provoked by Islam's rapid and relentless spread, of the protective and wonder-working powers of images. In response to the iconoclastic challenge, St. John Damascene (675-749) framed Christianity's first coherent theology of images.

In the rejection of images, John Damascene saw a rejection of the incarnation of Christ. "I worship Him who clothed himself in the royal purple of my flesh. . . . I do not worship matter; I worship the Creator of matter who took flesh."³ John created a Neoplatonic "great chain of images" linking the comprehensible— read "visible"—revelation of the Trinity to all creation. The Son is the visible image of the Father; humanity is created in the image and likeness of God; the visible world is an imaging-forth of the power of God; and the figures and types of the Old Testament are prefigurations of the revelation of the New Covenant.

> Finally the sixth class comprised the material remembrances of past events, be they the words of scripture, icons, or objects such as Aaron's rod or the jar of manna. In all these categories of images, the divine power was in some measure revealed, and, if the Holy Spirit dwelt within the saints, so also he stayed close to their images and tombs. Thus it was not only Christ's images that were to be venerated, but also the likenesses of his mother, the saints, and the angels.⁴

Inherent in this system is an epistemology that grounds the reality of image in the archetype, the seen in the unseen. The image is thus understood as a vessel that contains and participates in the divine reality, rather than standing as a mere re-presentation of it. That vessel provides the individual believer and the community free and unmediated access to what it contains.

In the ruder West, Gregory the Great taught that images serve practically as the "bible of the poor." In popular devotional life, sacramentals, icons, relics, and later sculptural images and stained glass windows became commonplace, literally common places where the unsophisticated and unlettered could encounter the transcendent. In such a world where the line between miraculous and mundane had yet to be drawn, the medieval iconographic synthesis of Celtic, Visigoth, Byzantine, and Islamic elements engendered rich, colorful hybrids.

The moral of our first parable? Things change.

The Second Parable: The Lady amid the Roses

The discovery of the New World at the end of the fifteenth century coincided with a last great yet ambiguous flowering of the medieval tradition in Spain. The religious devotion of Ferdinand,

Isabella, and the Spanish Hapsburg dynasty they founded was largely untouched by the winds of theological and philosophical change blowing over northern Europe. It was this devotional tradition that the Spanish conquistadors brought with them to Mexico in 1521, along with less salubrious items, including firearms, smallpox, and measles.

Meanwhile, halfway around the world from Europe, on a hemisphere with twenty-five native roses of its own, legends say that a Dark Lady appeared amid the out-of-season roses in December to an indigenous catechumen named Juan Diego. It is the hybridization story *par excellence*.[5]

To grossly oversimplify a very complicated discourse, there are three paradigmatic approaches that attempt to describe and explain the religious colonization of the "New World": what we might call the "white" legend, the "black" legend, and the "gray" legend. The traditionalist Euro-Catholic "white" legend sees the importation of Catholicism and European values and systems as the salvation of a benighted, primitive, even demonic Western hemisphere. Rooted in Enlightenment skepticism and espoused uncritically by many contemporary cultural historians, the "black" legend focuses almost entirely on the destruction of indigenous culture, religion, and hegemony at the hands of corrupt invaders who used religion as a cynical tool for enslavement and exploitation. What I dub the "gray legend," the dialectic of inculturation or "acculturation," is a much more complicated, nuanced, and difficult position to maintain, because it attempts to understand and interpret how old world and new world religious worldviews mutually shaped one another and ultimately influenced and transformed Christianity, even as Christianity reshaped already flexible indigenous beliefs and structures. It occurred more at the popular level than among hierarchies, and narrative, images, symbol, ritual, performance, and rich sensual experience played immensely important roles.[6]

No single image better demonstrates the thesis and ambiguities of the "gray legend" than Guadalupe. In her, the gray legend bursts into vivid, living color. What can be told with historical-critical certainty can be summed up briefly. As early as 1550, a shrine of the Virgin Mary had replaced a sanctuary of Tonantzin, the Aztec mother goddess-force, just north of Mexico City. Franciscan missionaries railed against the shrine at Tepeyac because of the danger of syncretism and idolatry they saw implicit in it. They claimed that the image had been created "yesterday" by an Indio named Marcos. Despite opposition, it became a local pilgrimage destination for Spaniards, *Criollos*, *mestizos*, and indigenous people alike.

In the late 1640s, two books were published, one in Spanish and the other in Nahuatl, laying out detailed narrative accounts that grounded the devotion in Marian apparitions to Juan Diego in 1531, more than a century before. A representative passage from the Nahuatl *Nican Mopohua* gives a hint of the text's sensual richness:

> And the Queen of Heaven ordered him then to go to the top of the little hill, where he had seen her before:
> She said to him: "Go up, my dearest son, to the top of the hill, to where you saw me and I told you what to do. There you will see that there are different kinds of flowers: cut them, gather them, put them all together, then come down here. Bring them here into my presence."
> Juan Diego climbed to the top of the hill right away and when he reached the top, he was astonished by all of them, blooming, open, flowers of every kind, lovely and beautiful, when it still was not their season: because really that was the season in which the frost was very harsh. They were giving off an extremely soft fragrance; like precious pearls, as if filled with the dew of the night. Then he began to cut them, he gathered them all, he put them in the hollow of his tilma.
> The top of the little hill was certainly not a place in which any flowers grew; there are only plenty of rocks, thorns, spines, prickly pears and mesquite trees. And even though some little herbs or grasses might grow, it was then the month of December, in which the frost eats everything up and destroys it.
> And immediately he came back down, he came to bring the Heavenly Maiden the different kinds of flowers, which he had gone up to cut. And when she saw them, she took them with her precious hands. Then she put them all together into the hollow of his ayate again and said: "My youngest and dearest son, these different kinds of flowers are the proof, the sign that you will take to the bishop. You will tell him from me that he is to see in them my desire, and that therefore he is to carry out my wish, my will.[7]

Redolent and harmonious in the *flor y canto* tradition of Nahuatl literature, it suggests something entirely new occurring in a violent and brutal world.

Dismissed by the proponents of the "black" legend as one more imperialist manipulation, and defended by supporters of the "white" legend as a literal miracle, the image is full of enigmas. Some art historians who have closely studied this Inmaculada-type image suggest that the image itself underwent significant changes early on.

The floral arabesques on the gown, the angel and silvered moon under her feet, the constellated stars on her mantle, and most especially the golden solar rays she stands before seem to have been applied to, or enhanced on, the original image, although no documentary evidence has been found to date or justify the additions. It is intriguing to speculate that the inclusion of flowers, sun, moon, and stars was perhaps an attempt, explicit or implied, to further indigenize the dark lady and bring her more into the realm of native iconography that often featured these same floral and cosmic elements.[8]

In both Central and South America, the Jesuits generally took on the mantle of intercultural dialogue after their arrival in the Viceroyalties of New Spain (1572) and of Peru (1568). They came late to the colonies, but their internationalist perspective and world-affirming spirituality and humanism made them more confident partners in cultural dialogue than the mendicant orders of medieval origin.

The intellectual climate of late seventeenth- and eighteenth-century Mexico in the Jesuit colleges was a heady one. Recent research convincingly demonstrates great interest in the Greek Fathers of the church, including Basil the Great and John Damascene. Jesuits became the foremost Guadalupan apologists, led by Florida-born Francisco de Florencia. His apologetic work *La Estrella del Norte de Mexico* (The Polestar of Mexico) included a résumé of historical research and theories surrounding the image and the devotion up to his time. Much influenced by fifteenth-century Franciscan mystic Blessed Amadeus of Portugal, Florencia improvised several "riffs" on Amadeus's revelation that Mary would be present in her images.

Florencia and a generation of Jesuit preachers after him posited a kind of quasi-sacramental presence, a parallel to eucharistic transubstantiation, which takes place in certain powerful images.

"Know you my children," said the Lady, "that through the
grace of my Lord Jesus Christ I shall also be with you bodily
until the end of the world: not in the Sacrament of the Altar,
as is my Son, since that is neither convenient nor decent, but
in my Images, of brush (as is that of Guadalupe of Mexico) or
of sculpture, and then you shall know that I am in them . . .
when you see that some miracles are made through them."

This image . . . is not to be considered simply as Image, but as
Mary, not only as the image of Mary, but as Mary herself,
Virgin and mother of God.[9]

While undergirding his argument with patristic proof-texts,
Florencia's daring affirmation of enduring, quasi-sacramental presence is a decided step beyond the traditional European understanding of images, relying more on the exuberance of indigenous *flor y
canto* traditions than on biblical proof-texts.

As the cult matured, the image underwent what we might call
"progressive indigenization" in its decoration, use, and appeal to
every rung of society. *Criollos*, *mestizos*, and *indios* saw this dark-
skinned American Madonna as guarantor of their legitimacy and
as the icon of a new world order growing out of the new world's
soil. As time went on, she was embroidered on the peasants' flag
of rebellion against Spanish rule in 1810; worn as a cockade on
the hats of Pancho Villa's insurgents and by Cristero martyrs in
the 1920s; and in the 1960s she marched with the United Farm
Workers through California's Central Valley.

Like all great symbols, she is capable of every kind of transformation, from J. Michael Walker's "Pensando planchando," to con-
victs' tattoos, to Yolanda Lopez's sneaker-wearing modern jogger,
and to Alma Lopez's rose-bikini reinterpretation that riled the faithful and attracted large crowds recently in New Mexico.

The moral of the second parable? Things change people.

The Third Parable: The Roses of Zi-ka-wei

The Jesuit mission to East Asia began when Francisco Javier
arrived in Japan in 1549. Convinced by hard experience that dialogue with culture was more useful than merely waving a crucifix,
he and those who followed him, most notably mission superior
Alessandro Valignano (†1606) and the bona fide polymath Matteo

Ricci (†1610), sought to adapt themselves and, where possible, Christianity to local customs, languages, and cultures.

Their companions built great churches in Kyoto, Macau, and on the palace grounds in Beijing. They built European equipment—clocks, cannons, and celestial spheres—and manned the imperial observatory in Beijing, They developed a beautiful material culture of religious artifacts and even trade ware that carried the Jesuit "IHS" logo.

Ricci requested good quality religious images be sent from Rome, and had copies of important images like the "Madonna of St. Luke" from Santa Maria Maggiore sent to the imperial court. The Dowager Empress burned incense in front of a copy of the Roman Madonna. The dowager's appropriation of the image points to its resonant power: the Roman Madonna echoed the popular Chinese Buddhist devotion to the bodhisattva of mercy, the Songzi Guanyin, "the sender of sons," who is portrayed as a woman with a male child on her lap. After initial hesitation, Ricci and his companions built on this resonance as a catechetical tool, much as the Jesuits in Japan used the parallel *kannon* form as an iconographic tool.[10]

At the beginning of the seventeenth century, they produced remarkable books of wood block engravings of the gospel stories that copied Flemish exemplars, but demonstrated sensitivity for local styles. Wu Li (†1718), a Chinese convert who became a Jesuit, produced magisterial works in classical Chinese style; Lang Shi Ning, Giuseppe Castiglione by birth (†1766), amused a bored court with inculturated genre paintings, European pleasure gardens, and portraits of the emperor, the emperor's first wife, and the concubines.

The Chinese Rites controversy that uprooted the Jesuits' efforts in the eighteenth century is far too complicated to deal with here, except to note that cultural intransigency in the main offices on both sides, in Rome and at the Imperial Palace in Beijing, caused the loss of great potential advantage. The suppression of the Jesuits in 1773 and recurring waves of Chinese xenophobia weakened the church even more.

The Jesuits returned to China in the early 1840s, and in 1847 they had a piece of good fortune: they acquired the Zi-Ka-Wei estate of Paul Xu Guang Xi, Ricci's most influential convert. There, next to Xu Guang Xi's tomb and on the edge of the French Concession, they built a mile-and-a-half square complex, sometimes referred to as the "Chinese Vatican," complete with seminaries, a trade school, an observatory, convents, a huge library, and a grand red brick, neo-Gothic church of St. Ignatius, dedicated in 1910.

The boys of Zi-Ka-Wei's Tou'se'wei trade school fabricated 3,500 square feet of glass for St. Ignatius under the supervision of Spanish Jesuit brothers. The cathedral was badly damaged during the Cultural Revolution in 1966, and all its stained glass windows were destroyed. For almost fifteen years, it was used as a warehouse.

Times change. In 1979, the church was reopened, and its burned spires were rebuilt in 1982. It is now a municipally protected cultural landmark.[11] Cleaned and repaired, its luminous interior nevertheless lacks the vibrant color of former days, and the catechetically useful windows that once graced it.

Several years ago, Jesuit Bishop Aloysius Jin, now ninety years old and himself a prisoner of the regime for twenty-seven years, invited me to work with a lay artist, Teresa Wo Ye, to come up with an iconographic and technical program to restore the windows. I made polite noises of demurral, but Jin is not easily dissuaded. I finally relented, and went to Shanghai in 2001 to explore the project with Wo Ye. She had talent and drive, and the bishop was willing to commit both financial as well as human resources in the form of religious women from the local Presentation community to work in a studio.

The crucial question emerged early on: in the new windows, should we attempt to copy the old days, or explore trying something entirely new? None of the old panels had survived, nor was any photographic documentation to be found. What was clear from the living memory of a few older people (including the bishop, who was raised in the neighborhood and educated there at the Jesuit schools and seminary) is that the old windows were emphatically Western, neo-Gothic French in style. Should the guiding principle be restoration or renovation? Western or inculturated? Could we put "Chinese flesh on French bones?"

I discussed the options with Wo Ye, who was trained both in classic Chinese and Western traditions. She concurred with the idea of Chinese-style glass for the cathedral. Much to my amazement, when we proposed the options to the old bishop, he thought for a minute and then said: "I'm going to die soon; I love the old things, but we have to work for the future. Chinese windows!" Wrong answer for me perhaps, as I was still trying to find a way out, but the right one for Shanghai and its growing community of 150,000 Catholics.

Phoenix detail from new Chinese-style stained glass windows in Shanghai's St. Ignatius Cathedral. Design by Teresa Wo Ye.

Work on the new windows began in 2003, in a studio at St. Teresa's Church, Da Tian Lu, in central Shanghai. Three young nuns, none of whom had ever cut a piece of glass before, generously took to the craft and became world-class craftswomen. Their task is daunting: fabricating more than one thousand panels according to Wo Ye's designs. To date, about two hundred panels have been completed and installed. Classic European techniques are used to build each panel, but, with Bishop Jin's encouragement, the design for the new glass is emphatically Chinese in style. What we are trying to do is express the gospel, the Christian narrative, and the Catholic tradition in Chinese as well as Western idioms, symbols, and colors.

The first forty-four large windows show scenes from the life of Christ, done in the style of Chinese folk art paper cutouts. Each window has an explanatory text in the form of a Chinese chop stamp, and a Chinese symbolic element that illustrates the gospel scene. Backgrounds are done in the style of Chinese garden pavilion windows.

The chalice of the Agony in the Garden becomes a *jue*, a traditional Chinese wine cup; the animals above the manger are a ram and water buffalo. A mocking bird, harbinger of good news, accompanies the Magi. A Chinese rose for Mary crowns the chapel with the scenes of annunciation, visitation, and nativity.

The work is brilliantly colorful, and getting more so as the project progresses. Some fifty feet off the floor, thirty huge sets of clerestory windows will become a golden garden of bamboo and Chinese flowers, echoing the neo-Gothic stone ribbing that holds up the building like a bamboo scaffold.

Like every church renovation project everywhere in the world, this project has not been without controversy and crisis. A few zealous souls there have expressed fears that use of Chinese imagery as well as Western prototypes might lead to confusion and superstition. Compromise has been necessary. Original plans to surround the great eastern rose window with the twelve animals of the Chinese zodiac ran aground when the dragon reminded people of the beast in Revelation 12. So the window becomes, instead, a more abstract celebration of creation, interwoven with the Easter Vigil prayer "Christ yesterday, the beginning and end."

Nevertheless, the work goes on, week after week, year after year, in a small studio on Da Tian Lu in Shanghai. A studio of Chinese women is reimagining and reimaging a cathedral. Eventually three huge rose windows will emerge as well to crown their work.

The moral of the third parable? Things get changed by people, even as things change them.

Conclusion

These three parables of roses point metaphorically to some of the major issues around the hybridization of religious images. It is complicated, and needs to be a careful process. While risks range from simple misunderstandings to overly facile syncretistic moves, experience has taught me, at least, that the risks are worth taking. My work as an artist and historian leads me to affirm, simply, that things change, and must change, and that sometimes, at least, they can change for the better. Moreover, things change us; religious art helps us to see the invisible mystery, to connect ourselves with it, and to be transformed in surprising, simple, and profound ways. If we are humble enough to let them, images can still be vessels that contain and transmit the color and fragrance of the sacred to us in our own time and place and cultures. There is a huge task yet to be done, in Shanghai, in our research, and in our classrooms.

Poet T.S. Eliot speaks to the final moral at the end of his *Four Quartets*:

> We shall not cease from exploration
> And the end of all our exploring
> Will be to arrive where we started
> And know the place for the first time. . . .
>
> When the tongues of flames are in-folded
> Into the crowned knot of fire
> And the fire and the rose are one.

Notes

[1] For a brief history of roses, see Eric V. Allen, "The Great History of Roses," at www.dundeemessenger.co.uk/garden/roses/rose_history.htm.

[2] Basil the Great, *De Spiritu Sanctu,* 17.44; cf. Athanasius, *Oratio III Contra Arianos*, 3.5 and 5; "In the image, the features of the emperor have been preserved unchanged, so that anyone who looks at it recognizes him in the image. . . . Thus the image would say 'I and the emperor are one.' . . . He who honors the imperial icon therefore, honors in it the emperor himself,'" both cited in Hans Belting, *Likeness and Presence: A History of the Image before the Era of Art*, trans. Edmund Jephcott (Chicago: University of Chicago Press, 1994), 153. Also see D. A. Brading, *Mexican Phoenix, Our Lady of Guadalupe: Image and Tradition across Five Centuries* (Cambridge, England: Cambridge University Press, 2001), 14.

[3] St. John Damascene, *On the Divine Images*, trans. David Anderson (Crestwood, NY: St. Vladimir's Seminary Press, 1980), 16-17, 52-53.

[4] St. John Damascene, *On the Divine Images*, 73-73; see also Jaroslav Pelikan, *Imago Dei: The Byzantine Apologia for Icons* (Princeton: Princeton University Press, 1990), 159-76.

[5] For a more detailed analysis of the Guadalupe phenomenon and bibliography on it, see Thomas Lucas, "Virtual Vessels, Mystical Signs: Contemplating Mary's Images in the Jesuit Tradition," *Studies in the Spirituality of Jesuits* 35, no. 5 (November 2003): 27-36. Parts of this paper first appeared there in slightly different forms.

[6] For a useful discussion on the language of "inculturation" and "accul-

turation," see Gauvin A. Bailey, *Art on the Jesuit Missions in Asia and Latin America, 1542-1773* (Toronto: University of Toronto Press, 1999), chap. 1, esp. 22-31.

[7]*Nican Mopohua*, paragraphs 124-38. The complete text of the *Nican Mopohua* in English can be found at the Basilica of Our Lady of Guadalupe website at http://www.virgendeguadalupe.org.mx/apariciones/Nican%20 Mopohua/Nican%20Mopohua%20ingles.htm.

[8]Philip Serna Callahan, *The Tilma under Infra-red Radiation*, C.A.R.A. Studies on Popular Devotion 2, Guadalupan Studies 3 (Washington, DC, 1981), 6-21; and Stafford Poole, *Our Lady of Guadalupe: The Origins and Sources of a Mexican National Symbol, 1531-1797* (Tucson: University of Arizona Press, 1997), 279, n. 53.

[9]Francisco de Florencia, *Origen de los dos célebres santuarios de la Nueva Galacia: Obispado de Guadalajara en la América Septentrional*, 3rd ed. (Mexico City, n.p., 1766), 150 and 49, cited in Brading, *Mexican Phoenix: Our Lady of Guadalupe*, 113.

[10]Pascuale D'Elia, "La Prima diffusione nel mondo dell'imagine di Maria 'Salus Populi Romani,'" *Fede e Arte* (October 1954): 5-6; on *guanyin* and *kannon* images, see Bailey, *Art on the Jesuit Missions in Asia and Latin America*, 89.

[11]For the history of the Zi-ka-wei complex, see Anonymous, *A Guide to Catholic Shanghai* (Shanghai: T'ou Se We Press, 1937), and Zhou Xiufen, ed., *Zikawei in History*, trans. Gu Jianguang (Shanghai: Shanghai Sanhua, 2005). The cathedral is the largest Catholic church in China: it is 79 meters long, and 44 meters wide at the transept.

The Trinity in the *Gnadenstuhl* Motif

Illustrating the Cross as an Event of the Triune God

Susie Paulik Babka

Since the Enlightenment, art has been an undervalued resource for theological reflection.[1] The neglect in theology of one of humanity's most important forms of knowledge has been crippling; theology can be so tied to the validity of a proposition that when it attempts to argue for the necessity of an apophatic approach, it risks doing the opposite, turning *apophasis* into a trend, thereby *naming* the ineffable. To paraphrase Augustine, "anything deemed ineffable is not ineffable."

If we wish to recover art as a fundamental and legitimate source of theology's attempt to articulate faith, it is because art assists in the navigation of a terrain that fails language, particularly the terrain of reconciling God's existence with catastrophic suffering.[2] Theodor Adorno has written extensively on the failure of rational thought after the *Shoah* and cautiously recommends "the idea that art may be the only remaining medium of truth in an age of incomprehensible terror and suffering."[3] This is because "Reason can subsume suffering under concepts; it can furnish means to alleviate suffering; but it can never express suffering in the medium of experience, for to do so would be irrational by reason's own standards. Therefore, even when it is understood, suffering becomes mute and inconsequential—a truth, incidentally, that everybody can verify for himself by taking a look at Germany after Hitler."[4]

If Christian theology is to express the relationship of God to catastrophic suffering, it has to reach beyond proposition and logic. Otherwise, it risks classifying something such as extreme poverty—which, by global statistics, claims the life of a child every three seconds—as included in the divine intention for creation, even necessary for its fulfillment. For Jürgen Moltmann, who appropriates the negative dialectic of the Frankfurt School in his theology, if Christianity does not measure itself against the criterion of the crucified God in the cross of Christ, it "loses its identity and becomes confused with the surrounding world; it becomes the religious fulfillment of the prevailing social interests, or of the interests of those who dominate society."[5]

In this sense, the cross is not a symbol of our salvation if it represents the machinations of a God who wishes a blood sacrifice to reconcile Godself to sinful humanity. Nor is the cross a triumphal moment that, as Adorno put it, "shows us humanity blossoming in so-called extreme situations . . . this becomes a dreary metaphysics that affirms the horror . . . by virtue of the notion that the authenticity of the human being is manifested there."[6] The justification of catastrophic suffering due to the manifestation of human virtue in the midst of it is a "dreary metaphysics," indeed, giving indirect sanction to the torturer and leaving ambiguous God's will for humanity.

Alternatively, the cross is the place where God becomes the victim of human hegemony. God addresses the persistence of catastrophic suffering in the world by identifying Godself with the powerless, abandoned, and oppressed so that they may be exalted in the resurrection. Moltmann writes, "A theology after Auschwitz would be impossible, were not the *sch'ma* Israel and the Lord's Prayer prayed in Auschwitz itself, were not God himself in Auschwitz, suffering with the martyred and the murdered. Every other answer would be blasphemy."[7] But it is not enough to say that God is the "fellow-sufferer," as Alfred North Whitehead so famously claimed. If God is merely sympathetic to catastrophic suffering but does not somehow contradict the "officially optimistic" society that led to it, if God is "the idol of mankind's history of success,"[8] then catastrophic suffering will continue to be defensible as an unfortunate side-effect of the progression of the divine plan. The cross as an event of the triune God must be the symbol for what it means to abandon both our expectations of God as the source of hegemonic power and the comfort we feel within those expectations, as though it would be better to be slaves than to die in the wilderness (Ex 14:11-12).

The *Gnadenstuhl* (Mercy Seat) motif in art, and its endurance across Europe and through the centuries, is an affirmation that the cross is an event of the triune God and, as such, merges the human longing for the beauty and peace of heaven with the reality of catastrophic suffering. I will trace the notion that the passion of the Son of God is a trinitarian event through the motif in art, generally termed *Gnadenstuhl*, which derives, as legend has it, from Martin Luther's 1534 translation of the Bible, specifically Hebrews 4:16.[9] Although little has been written about the *Gnadenstuhl* motif, regarding both its significance in the history of art,[10] as well as its potential significance in theological reflection, its compelling emotional presentation and fascinating combination of scriptural, doctrinal, and liturgical allusions deserve consideration in both regards.

In this motif, God the Father is usually seated, in some cases on a throne, and supports the dying or dead Christ, in some cases on the beams of a cross, in others without the cross in a pietà-like composition. The Holy Spirit, usually represented by a dove, is between the Father and Son or among the figures elsewhere in the composition. Whether or not the actual cross is present, the unifying thread of all the works of art that utilize the *Gnadenstuhl* motif is the theme of a unity between heaven and earth in the passion of Christ, such that the experience of catastrophic suffering affects all three divine persons. Just as heaven and earth join to praise God in the liturgy, emphasized in the Jewish mystical traditions that led to the insertion of the *Sanctus* in the eucharistic anaphora, heaven and earth join to mourn the death of the Son of God in solidarity with all those who suffer catastrophically. The shared passion of heaven and earth in the *Gnadenstuhl* motif is thus supported by a complex set of symbols that derive from Jewish Throne-Chariot or *Merkabah* mysticism and the visions of Ezekiel, Isaiah, Daniel, and the author of Revelation.

While the earliest known appearance is in a missal from Cambrai in the twelfth century, the *Gnadenstuhl* soon becomes part of the Gothic renovation of Saint-Denis in Paris and moves into the Netherlands and Germany. It was first employed in Italy by Luca di Tommè in Tuscany, c. 1355, and later in Florence, in the phenomenal Masaccio *Trinity* at Santa Maria Novella, c. 1427.[11] As noted above, the motif's history begins with worship: in the missal, inserted between the *Sanctus* and *Te Igitur* (the cross of the motif often forming the "T"), it later frequents altarpieces, frescoes, and *andachtsbilder*, or devotional works. The motif's usage in manuscript illuminations is consistently associated both with the praise of God and the acknowledgment of the passion of God. The present discussion moves between a description of different works featuring the *Gnadenstuhl* and a theological interpretation of their symbolic allusions and contemporary significance. We begin by visiting a mature example of the motif. Next, we consider the motif's early history, and finally highlight a few representative examples to draw out their theological implications. Although the motif's place in the history of art is certainly a factor in this study, the primary intention here is an exercise in using this motif as a theological resource to explore the relationship between the triune God and suffering.

El Greco's *Holy Trinity* (1577)

One might object at the outset that the motif itself has little to say to contemporary sensibilities. The motif predominately uses "two men and a bird" to represent the three divine persons, sometimes even cloaking the Father in papal attire, and El Greco's *Holy Trinity* is no exception. For present purposes, we shall table these idiosyncrasies, evident in most medieval art in the West, to evaluate the greater message evoked by the motif: that God's response to a world beset by catastrophic suffering is to enter the reality of the suffering, while remaining the God of our eschatological hope.

Trevor Hart asks, "Is there any sense in which art itself, through its capacity to transform our vision of and response to the world, shares in or corresponds to that redemptive activity of God?"[12] If we as Christians take seriously the cross of Christ, then we have to assert with Moltmann and Karl Rahner that the death of Jesus is a statement about God himself.[13] How can the death of Jesus be a statement about God? Do we understand the cross as an event of the triune God, in particular of the eternal Son of God, and not just something that happens to Jesus of Nazareth?

In El Greco's *Holy Trinity*, painted from 1577 to 1579 to be placed above *The Assumption*[14] in the uppermost component of the High Altarpiece of Santo Domingo el Antiguo in Toledo, the death of the Son is reflected in the intense grief on the Father's face and a palpable tension between the belonging of the Son to earth and to heaven. This was Domenikos Theotokopoulos's first commission upon arrival in Toledo, after initially training in Venice (which from 1204 to 1669 had controlled his native Crete) and Rome.[15] The Trinity appears in his work several times, which could

El Greco, *The Holy Trinity*. 1577. Oil on canvas; 300 x 179 cm. Museo del Prado, Madrid. Courtesy Art Resources, Inc.

be due to the influence of the post-Byzantine style to which he was exposed when schooled as an icon painter in his youth.[16] In this work, El Greco depicts the material reality of Christ's body, which would seem to plummet toward us were not the Father holding him back; the conflict between the weight of his body and the celestial scene speaks of the intersection of the human and the divine. The colors further emphasize this conflict: Christ's gray skin is magnified against the vivid hues of the heavenly figures. One figure in particular, clothed in grass green, the sole of a foot gently turned in a step, seems to have recently entered the celestial realm from the terrestrial. The brilliance of the light surrounding the Spirit is reflected in the top of the Father's cloak, but the Father's garments near the dead Christ are dark, as is the composition of the middle of the work. The shadows on the Son's face are shared with the darkness across the Father's face. The Spirit hovers above them, maintaining the celestial glory while heaven mourns. This work follows the *Gnadenstuhl* motif because it shows that all three divine persons are affected in a particular way by the moment of the death of the Son. El Greco's genius is to interpret the motif in both pain and hope.

Jürgen Moltmann points to this paradox: "The cross is not and cannot be loved. Yet only the crucified Christ can bring the freedom which changes the world."[17] The cross is at the center of Christian identity for Moltmann because it is the locus of the work of the triune God for the deliverance of the world from the relentlessness of catastrophic suffering. The doctrine of the incarnation points to the mystery that the being of God is invested in the cross of Jesus Christ. To put it bluntly, if Jesus on the cross is not also the eternal Son of God on the cross, then we Christians are left in the barrenness of a Samuel Beckett play, waiting for the elusive stranger who never comes, who leaves us paralyzed in our own absurdity, before a tree.

Early History of the *Gnadenstuhl* Motif

By the late sixteenth century, El Greco's treatment represents a maturation of the *Gnadenstuhl* motif, and perhaps a bit of a tribute to the Pietà of one of his mentors, Michelangelo, who had died in 1564. Michelangelo's *Rondanini Pietà*, his last, is of a standing Madonna holding the dead Christ, whose body is in a position similar to El Greco's Christ in *Holy Trinity*. But El Greco in Toledo combines influences toward a unique style. He had likely seen the *Gnadenstuhl* employed while in Italy, and was inspired, as was Tintoretto's *Lamentation*, by Albrecht Dürer's 1511 woodcut of the Trinity, which features a *Gnadenstuhl* composition similar to El Greco's.[18]

To understand the complex symbolism behind the *Gnadenstuhl* motif, we must go back about four hundred years before the beginnings of the Renaissance. Going back further still, the crucifixion of Christ is seldom depicted before the Carolingian period. The little Christian art that survives before the Edict of Milan, such as in the catacombs, depicts Christ as the "Good Shepherd" or in other symbols.[19] The earliest depiction of Christ on the cross, a carved ivory relief juxtaposing Christ's death with Judas's suicide, dates from the early fifth century.[20] It is likely that the abolishment of the practice of crucifixion by Constantine made the artistic exploration of Christ on the cross more feasible.[21] Later, in the Carolingian period, the cross is typically adorned in jewels and gold, and if Christ is present on the cross, he does not seem to suffer.[22] But the Gothic period sees a new interest in depicting the reality of Christ's suffering, by contorting his body as it would have hung on the cross, and showing anguish on his face. As interest in portraying the passion increases, so also does an interest in reflecting Christ's pain on the countenance of heavenly figures. Related, perhaps, to the concern with a unity of heaven and earth in the *Gnadenstuhl* motif is a wider interest to show a unity of heaven and earth in other events in salvation history, especially before the Renaissance.[23]

Accepting Erwin Panofsky's famous contention that the rise of Scholasticism and the rise of the Gothic style are bound together, art takes on the task of laboring where language leaves off, as well as serving as language for the illiterate. Christian art of the Middle Ages does not understand itself to create the new, notes Umberto Eco, or to go beyond the boundaries of doctrine, but seeks to edify the world, to represent natural forms because these are inextricably tied to divine revelation, in order to draw near the divine.[24] Although in service of doctrine, we may consider art in this period as reason's attempt to knowingly use the imagination, combined with the beauty of the material world, to enter the immaterial world: such is the Pseudo-Dionysian aesthetic.[25] Ellen Ross argues that for medieval Christians this is especially true of the suffering Christ, made present as much by visual images as by written texts: "The illuminations and paintings were an integral part of the temporal and spatial world believers inhabited, inviting them to become participants in the universe projected therein and to risk identifying with the God-human Jesus who suffered on their behalf."[26]

Such a world is intricately bound to the liturgical environment that witnessed the initial appearances of the *Gnadenstuhl* motif. The earliest known example, a French missal manuscript illumination c. 1120 from Cambrai,[27] is found at the *Te igitur*, beginning the canon of the mass, immediately after the *Sanctus*. "*Te igitur clementissime Pater*" is written across the bottom of this illumination: "You, therefore, most merciful Father," turning to the Father through Christ in the Spirit to ask God to receive our sacrifice. In a similar twelfth-century *Gnadenstuhl* from Cambrai,[28] the cross forms the "T" of *Te igitur*.

The *Sanctus* is derived from Isaiah 6:1-3, in which the prophet sees God "on a high and lofty throne," the train of his garment filling the temple, surrounded by six-winged seraphim.[29] This vision, notes Bryan Spinks, is the basis for the "angelic sanctification" or *Qedussah*, "an extremely ancient part of the Temple liturgy," and occurs three times in the Synagogue Liturgy: before the *Shema*, before the third of the eighteen benedictions, and at the end of the service.[30] Through the *Qedussah*, the faithful prepare themselves for the presence of God. The connection between the *Qedussah* and the *Sanctus* is possibly the hymns of the *Yorde Merkabah*, which are based on the vision in Ezekiel 1.[31] In scripture, the only other visions of God's throne and the surrounding cherubim and creatures occur in Ezekiel 10, Isaiah 6, Daniel 7 and in the Book of Revelation, especially chapter 4. The *Sanctus* also appears in Revelation 4, when the author, upon seeing God enthroned, surrounded by brilliant color, lightning, and thunder, combines the creatures from Ezekiel's vision and the six-winged seraphim from Isaiah's vision, who "without ceasing" sing "Holy Holy Holy, the Lord God the Almighty, who was and is and is to come" (Rv 4:8).

Another feature of this and several other early versions of the *Gnadenstuhl* is the enclosure of the Father, Son, and Spirit within a mandorla, an ancient symbol that appears frequently throughout the history of Christian art. The common area in two overlapping circles forms the shape, which gets its name from the Italian word for "almond"; in Latin it is referred to as the *vesica piscis*.[32] Rendering the mandorla refers to the union of opposites, such as earth and heaven, matter and spirit, time and eternity, immanence and transcendence, image and concealment. Ancient pagan applications of the shape are meant to represent the womb, the doorway into another world; Christians borrowed the symbol to depict Christ's birth into glory.[33]

Furthering the feminine symbolism, the location of the cross in the 1120 Cambrai illumination suggests a birthing stool, a way of depicting the idea that the Son is begotten of the Father, who dominates the composition, as happens in several of the early *Gnadenstuhl* manifestations. Although here the bearded Father figure is clearly male, we may recall that the early church Fathers enjoyed the paradox of bending language used to describe the Father. The Eleventh Council of Toledo in 675 asserts, "We must believe that the Son is begotten or born, not from nothing nor from any other substance, but from the womb of the Father (*de Patris utero*), that is, from his substance."[34] Imagery in art, poetry, or gesture that bends our conceptual categories contributes to being in the presence of the Holy One, and not merely in the presence of our own expectations.

The composition is further enhanced by the placement of the Holy Spirit as a "Holy Kiss," connecting the lips of the Father to those of the Son, and so maintaining their connection even in the Son's death. Moltmann cites Heribert Mühlen's claim that "in the cross, the Father and Son are most deeply separated in forsakenness and at the same time are most inwardly one in their surrender"; the Spirit, Moltmann adds, then opens up the future and creates life for the dead.[35] The Spirit in this *Gnadenstuhl* is a vital part of the composition, as the posture of the dove echoes the shape of the cross, underscoring that the Spirit dwells with Christ throughout his incarnate life, becoming, as Moltmann describes it, Christ's "companion in suffering"; "The Spirit is the transcendent side of Jesus' immanent way of suffering."[36] The Spirit sustains Jesus in his suffering; and because the Spirit is sent out into creation, as the fire of divine presence, the Spirit sustains all those who suffer as well.

The symbolism pertaining to *Merkabah* mysticism in relation to the *Gnadenstuhl* is also apparent in what Erwin Panofsky termed the "Anagogical Window" of the Benedictine Abbey Church of St.-Denis, near Paris.[37] Because of the reform directed by Abbot Suger (1081-1151; abbot from 1122 to 1151), trinitarian symbolism infuses many aspects of St.-Denis: in the central of the three portals of the West façade, the tympanum contains a relief of God the Father cradling a lamb above an enthroned Christ, surrounded by angels carrying the instruments of Christ's torture. The Spirit, as a dove, hovers directly over the Father. It can be argued that the iconography of this tympanum echoes the *Gnadenstuhl* motif captured by the Anagogical Window.[38]

As in the 1120 Cambrai appearances of the *Gnadenstuhl*, the four creatures, which Christians came to associate with the four evangelists, adorn the corners of the Anagogical Window in Ezekiel's vision of the new temple in chapters 40 and 41.[39] The prophet in Ezekiel 1 had experienced God's presence in the "whirlwind," or "stormy wind," from two Hebrew words, *ruach*, "spirit" or "wind," and *ce'arah*, meaning "storm." Next the prophet sees a throne on wheels *('ôphannîm)*, a throne-chariot, or *merkabah*, that is able to travel, roaming the earth and bearing the glory of God. The "spirit of the living creatures was in the wheels" (Ez 1:20 and 21) of the throne-chariot, as the force of its mobility. Ezekiel 1:22-28 describes a platform over the wheels; God's throne and Yahweh in human likeness are above the platform.[40]

The throne-chariot experienced by Ezekiel is connected to symbolism of the Ark of the Covenant as the locus of divine presence. 1 Chronicles 28:18 refers to the Ark of the Covenant as a chariot; Ezekiel, chapter 10, connects the ark with the throne of God. Abbot Suger furnishes an inscription on the window, "On the Ark of the Covenant is established the altar with the Cross of Christ; Here Life wishes to die under a greater covenant."[41] With this, the complex imagery of God enthroned, the mystical chariot, and the Ark of the Covenant come together in the original usage of the term "Mercy Seat." Throne or "seat" imagery first appeared in descriptions of the building of the Ark of the Covenant (Ex 25:21-22).

Although it can be translated as simply "cover" or "lid," the Hebrew *kapporeth* is used exclusively in the Hebrew scriptures to refer to the "Mercy Seat" on the Ark of the Covenant. As a verb, it means "to pardon," or "to atone for," as in "to cover a debt"; hence, "Yom Kippur," the day in which sin is "covered," or expiated. Requesting that God be the one to "offer *kapparah*," an opportunity to start anew, fasting and abstinence are practiced to prepare for encountering God.[42] Kabbalists compared this to Moses's removing his shoes before the burning bush, because he had approached holy ground. To come before the Mercy Seat is to meet God, and so Yom Kippur is the most joyous of the Jewish feast days, the day in which the high priest is permitted to say the name of God, to participate in God's nearness, and to enter into the divine identity.[43]

The tent of the Tabernacle is visible in the Anagogical Window behind the *Gnadenstuhl* and appears in several later versions of the motif, especially in manuscript illuminations. Of the window's iconography, Emile Mâle writes, "The Ark, the tables of the Law, and Aaron's rod, which marked the first covenant of man with God, are only symbols of another covenant that was definitive. The ark appears as a pedestal for the cross."[44] In Revelation 11:19, with the coming of the Messiah, the Ark is restored to its place within the heavenly temple. Louis Grodecki believes that the window's iconography is meant to reflect Hebrews 9, which asserts that Christ is both the high priest who offers, and the sacrifice itself, whose blood replaces that of goats and calves, sprinkled on the Mercy Seat.[45] As in the Letter to the Hebrews, the prevalence of imagery from the Hebrew Bible in the stained glass of the choir of St.-Denis points to Suger's interest in interpreting Christ as both bringer and fulfillment of the Law: "What Moses veils, the doctrine of Christ unveils."[46]

In Suffering, the Question about God

" 'Whence,' he says, 'I will speak to you.' He who strives with eagerness for a divine showing endeavors to obtain these things. The propitiatory is worthily called the mercy-seat for the divine response was given from there. The Lord speaks above the propitiatory when He inspires spiritual things that go beyond our conceptions of Him."[47] Richard of St. Victor (d. 1173) writes this in *The Mystical Ark* in 1153, about a decade after the Anagogical Window was installed in St.-Denis. Richard's work could not have been the inspiration for the window's iconography, but it is possible that the window inspired him. Writing on the Ark's import for the contemplative life, Richard reminds us that it was to be built of only two materials: acacia or "Setim" wood and gold, which represent the coming together of created and divine.[48] Such is not only a metaphor for the two natures in Christ, but is also, in Richard's evaluation, a metaphor for the interaction between God and the soul, between God and God's beloved creation. The holiest of things are in creation, as it is here God places God's Mercy Seat: "Think how great and what sort of a thing it is to consider

God at any hour when there may be a need and in any sort of
necessity to seek and receive divine counsel when it may be necessary. . . . 'Whence I speak to you.' "[49]

That we may call upon God among us in creation, yet enrobed
in transcendent glory, is what both Jewish and Christian mystics
have understood as the significance of the Mercy Seat. The
Gnadenstuhl motif borrows this significance and affixes it to the
cross. According to Ellen Ross, the trinitarian framing of the crucifixion scene reminds us that the one who suffers is divine.[50] That
the cross, in its horror, be associated with the locus of divine presence, demands that we abandon our presumptions, what we consider to be rational or comforting without reference to what has
been revealed by God as God's will: a world in which children are
not born for war (Is 65:23).

In the *Gnadenstuhl* of an Unknown German Master in Cologne,[51] the locus of divine presence is placed in our space, in our
time, as the Father supports the Son while seeming to stand on
earth. As often appears both in works implementing the
Gnadenstuhl and in depictions of the crucifixion, angels surrounding the divine presence hold the instruments of Christ's torture:
the scourge, flagellation column, stick with the sponge, and lance.
This work captures the closeness and agony of both Father and
Son; they are nearer in age than is typically portrayed. The black
gash in the Son's side is emphasized by the smooth flesh of his
torso, bleeding into the deep gray that cloaks the Father, envelop-
ing Father and Son in nearly a mandorla, against the gold atmosphere. The Spirit is in the position of uniting them in their grief,
as in the earlier versions of the *Gnadenstuhl* motif. The tenderness
of the relationship between the Father and Son, underscored in the
delicacy of fingers and features, is somehow reassuring, even while
it reminds us of the suffering of the tortured.

Moltmann often asserts, "It is in suffering that the whole human question about God arises; for incomprehensible suffering
calls the God of men and women into question."[52] In a way similar to Karl Barth's sober appropriation of Ludwig Feuerbach's critique of Christianity, Moltmann appropriates the critique of protest atheism, which Moltmann calls "the only serious atheism, the
atheism of Camus and Horkheimer,"[53] as the matrix from which
his theology is done. Protest atheism is the rejection of God's existence or concern for creation as evinced by the horror of war, the
humiliation of poverty, and the persistence of oppression.

The challenge is inescapable: why is God the architect of a world in which both moral evil and natural disaster work chaos upon the innocent? Is this God worthy of our worship? To this, there is "no explanation," asserts Moltmann; if we did not long for the God of love, mercy, justice, and peace, we would not ask the question, *Si Deus justus—unde malum?* The question about God and the question about suffering "belong together," and only together can these questions be approached, because no answer will ever be satisfactory in this life. The best we can do is to find a way to live with this open question, and continue to seek "the future in which the desire for God will be fulfilled, suffering will be overcome, and what has been lost will be restored."[54] This is why Moltmann calls the theodicy question "the all embracing eschatological question."[55] Walter Kasper observes, "Metaphysical atheism, too, takes the world as a mirror of the deity. But in the broken mirror of an unjust and absurd world of triumphant evil and suffering without reason and without end it does not see a countenance of a God, but only the grimace of absurdity and nothingness."[56]

We may contrast such a grimace with the Father's countenance in Jusepe de Ribera's 1635 *Holy Trinity*.[57] Ribera's is a study in quiet strength, the Father's eyes in sad inquiry. Ribera skillfully provides in the Father's grief a mirror of our own failure to champion the vulnerable. The Father, seated, holds the Son in the *Gnadenstuhl* position, similar to the birthing stool; Christ's arms are outstretched as if still on the cross (unusual for compositions in which the actual cross is missing), while the Father's hand is caught in mid-caress of the Son's hair. Where El Greco indicates a bright heavenly resolution to Christ's suffering, Ribera wishes us to concentrate on the darkness of the moment and maintains the meeting of heaven and earth characteristic of *Gnadenstuhl*: the stark, flat burial garment is contrasted with the rich red of the Father's cloak.

Kenosis and the Cross

David Tracy believes that a kenotic christology of the cross helps to deepen our understanding "of the mysterious character of the divine self-manifestation as self-sacrificing love—affecting all and affected by all."[58] This type of reflection on the cross, notes Tracy, is a "Trinitarian dialectic of the dynamic self-manifesting God (now reconceived as the totally loving kenotic God)."[59] According to

Karl Rahner, the giving of the Father to the Son in the "immanent self-expression of God in its eternal fullness is the condition which makes possible God's expression outwards and outside himself."[60] In other words, the *kenosis* of the Logos of God in the incarnation is possible because the Father eternally empties the Father's "self" into the Son. The Father's eternal begetting of the Son is therefore related to the Father's creation of the world through the Son.[61]

We use the language of *kenosis* in an often awkward attempt to articulate that the Son's divine nature experiences human life; *kenosis* as a term fails to capture the mystery of what occurs when God becomes human, but by naming the activity as "self-empty-ing," we are trying to maintain that God really experiences human life, suffering and death, while remaining God. *Kenosis* expresses that God has suffered catastrophically in the incarnate Son, but has not ultimately succumbed to the suffering: the suffering has not obliterated the distinction between divine and created. Because of the self-emptying of the Son, we may say with Jürgen Moltmann that creation somehow touches the Father in the self-limiting that takes place in the creation of what is not-God. While from a tradi-tional or Thomistic metaphysics it is difficult to articulate that the Father suffers with the Son, art provides an arena to consider how the death of Jesus is a statement about God. From a pastoral per-spective, that the Father suffers the loss of the Son at the moment of their most intense separation, the moment of the Son's death, can be profoundly edifying for a family dealing with their daughter's terminal cancer.

From a practical perspective, such images provide the opportu-nity to renew the eschatological vision that will overcome accep-tance of the present state of the world, in which genocide and the AIDS epidemic are so overwhelming that we are catatonic, frozen in our inability to conceptualize the radically new, as in Beckett's *Waiting for Godot*. From the opening line, "Nothing to be done," to the final scene, when Vladimir asks Estragon: "*Alors? On y va?*" ("Well? Shall we go?"), Estragon answers: "*Allons-y*" ("Yes, let's go.") But the stage directions read: *They do not move*, and the play ends.[62]

Just as the enemy of love is indifference, the enemy of beauty is stagnation. If we find our senses numbed by indifference when faced with the profound suffering of the world, our best hope is a shift in perspective. Art does this, or at least it should, when con-fronted with Sartre's question, "Does living have any meaning when men exist who beat you until your bones break?"[63] The "meaning" in the *Gnadenstuhl* motif is related precisely to the meaninglessness of the cross. A vision by which we may *become* compassion, become empathy, that leads from horror to action, answers the challenge of protest atheism. Good doctrine awakens the mind much the way good art heightens the senses and turns our complacency upside down. What is beautiful or truthful about art and iconography is that these are not ends in themselves, but rather open us to participate in God's imagination, which Jesus communicates to us in person and act in the gospels, threatening our complacency and indifference. In Jean Malouel's *Lamentation of the Trinity*,[64] we see that God has met our failed imagination with vulnerability, giving Godself over to the suffering of the innocent. God has not remained remote and isolated from the godforsaken. Art provides an amended language in which to express the imagination's apprehension of revelation: this language, because it appeals to our senses, both articulates and makes present the experience of divine revelation.

Conclusion

The nascent impulse of doctrine is doxological; perhaps this is also true of the imaginative faculty's participation in the cycle that leads to the articulation of belief. The sculptor Henry Moore once remarked, "I think it is through art that we artists can come to understand your theology."[65] Especially in the memory of catastrophic suffering, artistic expression may be better suited toward recovering the fullness of the faith experience and the entry into the unknown than rational linguistic expression; the poverty of language when approaching the divine has more aptly been assuaged by mystics and the discipline of *apophasis*. As Theodor Adorno notes in his *Aesthetic Theory*, "the true language of art is speechless."[66]

In the early appearances of the *Gnadenstuhl* motif, the cross of Christ is associated with the throne beheld by the prophets and the ark that contains our longing for God's presence. The motif explores the search for an intimacy with the God whose chariot is mobile and accessible, as well as lofty and obscured by clouds; it encourages an understanding of divine identity as the one who would become incarnate, who empties loftiness into godforsakenness, who becomes the other for the sake of the other in desire for

union with the creature. Through the chaos, in the whirlwind, the
Shoah, God has answered our cry, the cry of Moses and Job, and
the cry of the poor, by becoming himself Job, by becoming himself
poor, by becoming himself the leader who would lead us to the
Promised Land, out of the slavery we have created for ourselves,
the bondage with which we are satisfied. The God who would become incarnate is the God who continues to enter creation in the
most intimate of ways, who suffers in those crying for God, who
suffers in those who mourn for the victims, and still remains, God.

Notes

[1]Dorothy Sayers even asserts that "we have no Christian aesthetic—no
Christian philosophy of the Arts. The Church as a body has never made up her
mind about the Arts, and it is hardly too much to say that she has never tried,"
"Towards a Christian Aesthetic" in Nicholas Wolsterstorff, *Art in Action*
(Grand Rapids: Eerdmans, 1980), ix. Happily, this is changing, thanks to the
efforts of Jeremy Begbie, *Voicing Creation's Praise: Towards a Theology of
the Arts* (Edinburgh: T & T Clark, 1991); Richard Viladesau, *Theological
Aesthetics: God in Imagination, Beauty and Art* (Oxford: Oxford University
Press, 1999); and *Theology and the Arts: Encountering God through Music,
Art, and Rhetoric* (Mahwah, NY: Paulist Press, 2000); Alejandro Garcia-
Rivera, *The Community of the Beautiful: A Theological Aesthetics* (Collegeville,
MN: Liturgical Press, 1999), and David Bentley Hart, *The Beauty of the
Infinite: the Aesthetics of Christian Truth* (Grand Rapids: Eerdmans, 2003),
who follow the line of inquiry begun by such greats as Hans Urs von Balthasar
and Paul Tillich. I am also indebted to Anthony Godzieba, for helpful critique
of this paper as well as his own contribution to the genre, "Caravaggio,
Theologian: Baroque Piety and Poiesis in a Forgotten Chapter of the History
of Catholic Theology," in *Theology and Lived Christianity*, ed. David M.
Hammond (Mystic, CT: Twenty-Third Publications, 2000).

[2]J. Matthew Ashley writes in *Interruptions: Mysticism, Politics and
Theology in the Work of Johann Baptist Metz* (Notre Dame: University of
Notre Dame Press, 1998) that it is the *Leidensfrage*, the "question of
catastrophic, massive and systemic suffering," that provides the context for
Metz's later work (see vii-x). I am using the term "catastrophic suffering" in
this sense, in order to make the case that it is suffering without discernible
purpose or educative goal that creates a problem for belief in a loving God.

[3]Theodor Adorno, *Aesthetic Theory*, ed. Gretel Adorno and Rolf
Tiedemann, trans. C. Lenhardt (London: Routledge & Kegan Paul, 1984), 27.

[4]Ibid.

[5]Jürgen Moltmann, *The Crucified God*, trans. R. A. Wilson and John
Bowden (Minneapolis: Fortress Press, 1993), 38.

[6]Theodor Adorno, "Commitment," in *Can One Live After Auschwitz? A*

Philosophical Reader, ed. Rolf Tiedemann, trans. Rodney Livingstone et al. (Stanford: Stanford University Press, 2003), 253.

[7]Jürgen Moltmann, *The Experiment Hope*, trans. M. Douglas Meeks (Philadelphia: Fortress Press, 1975), 73.

[8]Ibid., 70-71.

[9]According to Wolfgang Braunfels, Franz Xavier Kraus identified this connection between Martin Luther and the term; see *Die Heilige Dreifaltigkeit*, Lukas-Bücherei zur Christlichen Ikonographie, Band 6 (Düsseldorf: L. Schwann, 1954), 35-37. In 1534, Martin Luther used *Gnadenstuhl* in Exodus 25:21-22 and translated Hebrews 4:16, "Darum laßt uns hinzutreten mit Freudigkeit zu dem Gnadenstuhl, auf daß wir Barmherzigkeit empfangen und Gnade finden auf die Zeit, wenn uns Hilfe not sein wird." Luther uses *Gnadenstuhl* in Romans 3:25 as well, translated in the NRSV as "sacrifice" or "place" "of atonement" (see *The Luther Bible of 1534*, ed. Stephan Fussel, available on the web at www.ccel.org/ccel/bible/delut.all.html#i).

[10]François Bœspflug, *La Trinité dans l'Art d'Occident (1400-1460)* (Strasbourg: Presses Universitaires de Strasbourg, 2000), includes some of the motif's history. This work continues the project begun in *Dieu dans l'Art* (Paris: Les Éditions du Cerf, 1984).

[11]Luca di Tommè, *Crucifixion and Trinity*, c. 1355. Tempera on panel; Timken Art Gallery, San Diego. Masaccio, *Trinity*, c. 1427. Fresco, Santa Maria Novella, Florence. With this work, completed in the year before Masaccio's death at 28, John T. Spike writes, "Masaccio himself became a theologian." Here, Masaccio breaks from traditional depictions of the Trinity in significant ways by placing the *Gnadenstuhl* in an earthly space designed by human beings, rather than against the golds or blues of heaven; Mary turns to the viewer rather than remain separated in her grief (see Spike, *Masaccio* [New York: Abbeville Press, 1996], 61-68). Rather than depict heaven or the fulfillment of creation in terms of traditional colors and clouds, heaven here is represented by a divine desire for order, reflected in the Brunelleschi-inspired vault that surrounds the scene.

[12]Trevor Hart, "Through the Arts: Hearing, Seeing, and Touching the Truth," in *Beholding the Glory: Incarnation Through the Arts*, ed. Jeremy Begbie (London: Dartman, Longman & Todd, 2000), 21.

[13]See Karl Rahner, *Foundations of the Christian Faith*, trans. William V. Dych (New York: Crossroad, 1990), 305.

[14]Domenikos Theotokopoulos (1541-1614), or "El Greco," *The Holy Trinity*. Oil on canvas; 300 x 179 cm. Museo del Prado, Madrid. Compare the weight of Christ's body pulling him into our world with Robert Campin, Master of Flémalle's *Holy Trinity*, c. 1410. (Oil on wood, 148.7 x 61 cm. Städelsches Kunstinstitut, Frankfurt). Hugo van der Goes' *Trinity Altarpiece*, from 1479 (National Galleries of Scotland, Edinburgh) and Lucas Cranach the Elder's 1518 *Trinity* (Museum der Bildenden Künste, Leipzig) also adopt this theme.

[15]See Jonathan Brown, *El Greco of Toledo* (Boston: Little, Brown & Co., 1982), 15-16, for more on his travels and influences.

[16]Jonathan Brown details El Greco's Cretan training in *El Greco of Toledo*, 75-76.

[17]Jürgen Moltmann, *The Crucified God*, 1.

[18]See Francis Russell, *The World of Dürer* (New York: Time Incorporated, 1967), 162-63.

[19]Early Christians were mocked for their reverence of a Savior who was crucified a criminal. This is evident in a first-century graffito from Rome in which a crucified man with an ass's head is worshipped by a man with his arm outstretched; the Greek text scrawled beneath reads, "Alexamenos worships God." See http://faculty.bbc.edu/rdecker/alex_graffito.htm for the image and a description by Rodney Decker. Richard Viladesau explores how the cross went from a symbol of disgrace to the primary symbol of Christian faith in *The Beauty of the Cross* (Oxford: Oxford University Press, 2006), 20-55.

[20]*Christ's Victory on the Cross*, c. 420-430, carved ivory panel, British Museum. See Richard Harries, *The Passion in Art* (Aldershot, England: Ashgate, 2004), 10-11.

[21]See ibid., 12.

[22]There are exceptions to the triumphalism that permeates the age, such as the wooden Crucifix of Archbishop Gero at the Cathedral in Cologne, c. 970. For more on such exceptions, see Celia Chazelle, *The Crucified God in the Carolingian Era* (Cambridge: Cambridge University Press, 2001).

[23]In the thirteenth and fourteenth centuries, this is observed, for instance, in depictions of the Nativity, the Annunciation, the Ascension, and the theme of the Augustinian *City of God*. Giotto's frescoes on the interior of the Capella degli Scrovegni in Padua, c. 1305, are a good example, especially the *Crucifixion*, in which the dying Christ is surrounded by angels above and mourners below.

[24]See Umberto Eco, *Art and Beauty in the Middle Ages*, trans. Hugh Bredin (New Haven: Yale University Press, 1986), 95.

[25]For more on this, see Richard Viladesau, *Theological Aesthetics*, 113-17.

[26]Ellen M. Ross, *The Grief of God: Images of Suffering in Late Medieval England* (New York: Oxford University Press, 1997), 66.

[27]Manuscript illumination, Bibliothèque-Médiathèque Municipale de Cambrai; see Fides Buchheim, *Der Gnadenstuhl: Darstellung der Dreifaltigkeit* (Würzburg: Echter, 1984), 22.

[28]Manuscript illumination, Bibliothèque-Médiathèque Municipale de Cambrai, 12th century. See ibid., 18.

[29]The question of when and where the Sanctus entered the Eucharistic anaphora is a matter of some dispute among historians of the liturgy, but there is little question as to its Jewish origins. See Bryan Spinks, "The Jewish Sources for the Sanctus," *Heythrop Journal* XXI, no. 2 (April 1980): 168-79.

[30]Ibid., 171.

[31]See ibid. and Edward Hardy, "Kedushah and Sanctus," *Studia Liturgica* 6, no. 4 (1969): 183: "In a number of Jewish forms the *Kedushah* of Isaiah 6 is combined with the elements from the mystic vision of the divine chariot (*merkabah* as later called) in Ezekiel 1. The *merkabah*-mystics loved to dwell

on the adoration of the divine majesty by myriads of angels, as expressed in the *Chayoth* (living creatures) and *Ophanim* (wheels) of Ezekiel 1 (with further suggestions from such passages as Daniel 7)." Elements of Jewish Merkabah mysticism appear as early as Qumran community texts from the first century B.C.E., as well as the Ethiopic Book of Enoch and the Fourth Book of Ezra. 1 Clement, composed around 95 and reflecting Jewish influence, writes about the use of the *Sanctus* in early Christian worship (*The Apostolic Fathers*, 2nd ed., ed. and trans. J. B. Lightfoot and J. R. Harmer [Grand Rapids: Baker Book House, 1992], 67). Lucas Cranach, who uses the *Gnadenstuhl* motif at least three times in his work, explicitly connects the Sanctus with the *Gnadenstuhl* in *The Dying, Heinrich Schmitburg's epitaph for his father,* Leipzig, 1518.

[32]Aurelie A. Hagstrom points out that this combination of terms, *vescia*, meaning "vulva," and *piscis*, meaning "fish," "demonstrates that a *vescia piscis* is not only a symbol of the vulva of female genitalia, but also is a symbol of a fish seen vertically," "The Symbol of the Mandorla in Christian Art: Recovery of a Feminine Archetype," *Arts* 10, no. 2 (1998): 25.

[33]Ibid., 26.

[34]"The *Symbol of Faith of the Eleventh Council of Toledo,*" in *The Christian Faith in the Doctrinal Documents of the Catholic Church*, ed. J. Neuner and J. Dupuis (New York: Alba House, 1982), 102-106. Available at http://www.fordham.edu/halsall/source/toledo.txt.

[35]Heribert Mühlen, *Die Veränderlichkeit Gottes als Horizont einer zukunftigen Christologie* (1969), 32, cited by Moltmann, *The Crucified God*, 244.

[36]Jürgen Moltmann, *The Spirit of Life: A Universal Affirmation*, trans. Margaret Kohl (Minneapolis: Fortress Press, 1992), 62.

[37]The "Anagogical Window," or "The Quadriga of Aminadab," from the Chapel of St. Peregrinus, Abbey of St.-Denis, c. 1140-1144. Available at http://vrcoll.fa.pitt.edu/medart/ image/France/sdenis/windows/Anagogical/ Sdenwind-Anagog.html. Erwin Panofsky calls this the "Anagogical Window" because of Abbot Suger's interest in following pseudo-Dionysius's "anagogical approach," or "upward-leading method." See Panofsky, *Abbot Suger on the Abbey Church of St.-Denis and Its Art Treasures*, ed., trans., and annot. Erwin Panofsky, 2nd ed. by Gerda Panofsky-Soergel (Princeton: Princeton University Press, 1979), 20.

[38]Although she does not connect the Trinitarian imagery of the "Anagogical Window" to the tympanum of the west façade, Paula Lieber Gerson notes the importance of the Trinity to Suger. See Gerson, "Suger as Iconographer: The Central Portal of the West Façade of Saint-Denis," in *Abbot Suger and Saint-Denis: A Symposium*, ed. Paula Lieber Gerson (New York: Metropolitan Museum of Art, 1986), 192-94.

[39]This relatively common device in manuscript illumination occurs in several works featuring the *Gnadenstuhl*, as well as in works depicting Christ enthroned. John is associated with the eagle; the lion with Mark; the ox with Luke; the angel or man with Matthew. These symbols refer to Ezekiel's vision

in 1:4-14. Irenaeus, in *Against Heresies* 3.11.8, is perhaps the earliest to assign the creatures of the throne visions to symbols of the evangelists.

[40]This platform is visible in many manuscript illuminations of the *Gnadenstuhl*, even when the wheels and creatures are not present. It seems to be associated with the throne, as it does not appear where the throne is missing. Early association between the throne and platform can be seen in the German *Altarpiece with Gnadenstuhl*, c. 1260, Staatliche Museen, Berlin.

[41]Abbot Suger, *De Administratione* 34, trans. Panofsky, *Abbot Suger on the Abbey Church of St.-Denis*, 75.

[42]See Michael Strassfeld, *The Jewish Holidays: A Guide and Commentary* (New York: Harper and Row, 1985), 111.

[43]See Franz Rosenzweig, *The Star of Redemption*, trans. William W. Hallo (Notre Dame: University of Notre Dame Press, 1985), 324.

[44]Emile Mâle, *Religious Art in France: The Thirteenth Century*, trans. Marthiel Matthews (Princeton: Princeton University Press, 1984), 180.

[45]Louis Grodecki, "Les vitraux allégoriques de Saint-Denis," *Art de France* 1 (1961): 26-30. Cf. Mâle, *Religious Art in France: the Thirteenth Century*, 452. Mâle stresses that the chariot is that from the Song of Songs 6:12, from where the inscription under the ark, "Quadrige Aminadab," is taken: "Honorius of Autun, a contemporary of Suger, explained that Aminadab, standing in the chariot, is the crucified Christ, and the four horses of the quadriga are the four evangelists," ibid.

[46]Abbot Suger, *De Administratione* 34, trans. Panofsky, in *Abbot Suger on the Abbey Church of Saint-Denis*, 75. For more on the iconography of the stained glass, see Louis Grodecki, *Les Vitraux de Saint-Denis, etude sur le vitrail au XIIe siècle* (Corpus Vitrearum Medii Aevi) *France "Études"* (Paris, 1976), vol. 1.

[47]Richard of St. Victor, *Some Allegories of the Tabernacle of the Covenant*, trans. Grover A. Zinn, in *The Classics of Western Spirituality: Richard of St. Victor*, trans. and ed. Grover A. Zinn (New York: Paulist Press, 1979), 362.

[48]See Richard of St. Victor, *The Mystical Ark*, Book II.1 in ibid., 174.

[49]Ibid., Book IV.21, 300.

[50]Ross, *The Grief of God*, 48.

[51]Unknown Master, German. *Trinity*. Active 1415-30 in Cologne. Oil on oak panel. 23.2 x 15.9 cm. Wallraf-Richartz Museum, Cologne. On the web at www.wga.hu/framex-e.html?file=html/m/master/zunk_ge/zunk_ge1/061pieta.html&find=trinity.

[52]Jürgen Moltmann, *The Trinity and the Kingdom*, trans. Margaret Kohl (Minneapolis: Fortress Press, 1993), 47. Moltmann often calls himself an "a-theist," "Only a Christian can be a good atheist," reversing Ernst Bloch's statement, "Only an atheist can be a good Christian." Moltmann admires Bloch's assertion that "consistent atheism liberates one from the gods and idols of this world" (*History and the Triune God*, trans. John Bowden [New York: Crossroad, 1992], 145). In this sense, Moltmann views atheism as a liberation from all patriarchy and authority constituted on the fear of the father. See *The Crucified God*, 195, and *The Trinity and the Kingdom*, 163.

[53]Moltmann, *The Crucified God*, 252.

[54]Moltmann, *The Trinity and the Kingdom*, 48-49.

[55]Ibid., 49.

[56]Walter Kasper, *Jesus the Christ*, trans. V. Green (Mahwah, NJ: Paulist Press, 1985), 82.

[57]Jusepe de Ribera, *Holy Trinity*, c. 1635. Oil on canvas, 226 x 181 cm. Museo del Prado, Madrid. On the web at www.wga.hu/framex-e.html?file=html/m/master/zunk_ge/zunk_ge1/061pieta.html&find=trinity.

[58]David Tracy, "*Kenosis, Sunyata* and Trinity," in *The Emptying God: A Buddhist-Jewish-Christian Conversation*, ed. John B. Cobb, Jr., and Christopher Ives (Maryknoll, NY: Orbis Books, 1990), 153.

[59]Ibid., 154.

[60]Rahner, *Foundations of the Christian Faith*, 223.

[61]Rahner writes, "The possibility that there be men is grounded in the greater, more comprehensive and more radical possibility of God to express himself in the Logos which becomes a creature" (ibid., 223).

[62]Samuel Beckett, *Waiting for Godot*, in *The Complete Dramatic Works of Samuel Beckett* (London: Faber & Faber, 1986), 11, 88. Of this, Theodor Adorno notes wryly, "It does more than just abstractly negate meaning, though. What it does is carry the empirical process of the disappearance of meaning into the traditional categories of art, negating them concretely and extrapolating new categories from nothingness. Theology heaves a sigh of relief every time its cause is put on the agenda, no matter how it is judged in the end. That is why for theologians Beckett comes in handy" (*Aesthetic Theory*, 220).

[63]Quoted by Theodor Adorno, "Commitment," 252.

[64]Jean Malouel, *Lamentation of the Holy Trinity*, c. 1390-1410, Musée du Louvre, Paris. On the web at www.wga.hu/index1.html. Although considered by the Louvre as simply a pietà, this work follows the *Gnadenstuhl* theme of the Father seated, bearing the body of Christ in his arms. Mary tries in vain to meet the eyes of her dead Son, cradling his arm as she did when she held him as an infant. Through the transparency of the veil and intricacy of the fingers, Malouel provides a fragility that accentuates both helplessness and compassion.

[65]Quoted by Jeremy Begbie in *Beholding the Glory*, xiii.

[66]Theodor Adorno, *Aesthetic Theory*, 164. In "Commitment," he writes: "The abundance of real suffering permits no forgetting. . . . But that suffering—what Hegel called the awareness of affliction—also demands the continued existence of the very art it forbids; hardly anywhere else does suffering still find its own voice, a consolation that does not immediately betray it. The most significant artists of the period have followed this course. The uncompromising radicalism of their works, the very moments denounced as formalist, endows them with a frightening power that impotent poems about the victims lack" (252).

A Quiet Renaissance

Artists of Faith for a New Century

Sandra Bowden

While I was watching the evening news, the CNN headline caught my attention—"Jesus Saves Hollywood." Listening further, I realized that the report was about *The Da Vinci Code* being released that weekend. The broadcaster went on to say that movies about Jesus, including last year's *The Passion of the Christ* and, more recently, *The Da Vinci Code* were attracting the public's attention and filling theaters. It seems that movies about Jesus were piquing a curiosity and interest that was not expected, at least by the critical community that had all but written off Christianity as irrelevant and out of date. Somehow those who critique culture had missed the fact that faith is still very important to the American people.

I was reminded that at the turn of the millennium there were two international art exhibitions that focused on the life of Jesus: *Seeing Salvation* at the National Gallery in London, and *Anno Domini: Jesus through the Centuries* at the Provincial Museum in Edmonton, Alberta. After much resistance from their museum boards both exhibitions were mounted—only because two individuals insisted that the shows must go forward.

Neil MacGregor, Director of the National Gallery in London, realized that visitors to the museum, most of whom were not believers, were nevertheless gripped by the imagery of Christianity. Their interest in the work was not in the formal elements, those qualities of interest to modern critics, but rather in the stories behind the images. MacGregor found that many of the visitors did not know the biblical narrative, even the story of Christ's baptism, and therefore struggled to understand its meaning. Since about one-third of the works in the National Gallery represent Christian subjects, MacGregor wanted an exhibition that would emphasize the narrative aspects of these works. Initially, he met strong resistance to mounting a show of this nature. However, *Seeing Salvation* proved to be a blockbuster, with the National Gallery extending its hours and the number of days to accommodate the vast crowds. I believe this expresses the culture's hunger for more than just "the spiritual" in art, but rather a substantive source of meaning such as Christianity offers. It also demonstrates how important the visual arts are in communicating and continuing the rich legacy of the Bible and faith.

Visual Culture

We live in an image-saturated culture, awash in a sea of images that bombard us from every angle. I believe that we stand at a new point in the history of the church, where art is going to be central in sharing the gospel in such a culture. Some have said that we are living in a post-literate time, where a vast amount of information intake is visual, including television, computers, video, film, and DVDs. Many church leaders are now suggesting that if the church is going to remain relevant and reach out to contemporary culture, it will have to embrace the arts in vital ways. We have, in a way, returned to a medieval style, where the image is of primary importance in communication.

Art is a powerful means of communication because it heightens perception, takes things out of the ordinary, and places them in an often unexpected context, so they can be appreciated afresh from a new perspective. To be ready to meet emerging challenges and opportunities, we must embrace the gift of art as we live out our lives as Christians and artists, both in the church and in wider cultural and social venues.

For centuries, the visual arts were central and vital to the life of the church. What has happened to the church's conviction that art can inspire, teach, and lead to faith? I am not an art historian and I can make no claim to fully answer this question, but there are certainly some influences that contributed to the decline of art in the church. The Renaissance was the beginning of a shift in faith's central importance in the life of individuals and society. The human being became the measure of all things (symbolized in

DaVinci's well known *Vitruvian Man*). The Reformation, with its focus on the importance of the word, set the stage for the removal of art as a needed element in worship. As the Reformation progressed, zealous Protestants stripped many Catholic churches of statues, paintings, and objects of beauty that enhanced the worship setting.

The Enlightenment, an age of science and rationalism, further undermined the centrality of faith, and, as a result, there was a diminishing need to express the spiritual and eternal realities of that faith in visual form. With the church having little or no interest in art, artists were forced to find other venues for their work. Rembrandt's *Christ Healing the Sick* (Hundred Gilder print) is an excellent example of the plight of an artist in this environment. In the Protestant Netherlands at the time of Rembrandt, the church concluded it no longer needed art to express liturgical beliefs. No commissions came from these churches, as the worship setting wanted no distraction from the word. Thus, Rembrandt's small etchings were created for the home, not the church. His biblical paintings were done for his own benefit, out of a need to struggle personally with the rich stories of the scriptures, translating them into his own visual language of intimate human understanding. To a great extent, artists who have continued to work with biblical themes have had to pursue this journey devoid of support from the church, either Protestant or Catholic.

In 1950, Father Marie-Alain Couturier, a Dominican monk and founder of the periodical *L'Arte Sacré*, embarked upon an ambitious project of placing contemporary art in Notre-Dame-de-Toute-Grâce, at Plateau d'Assy in France. He hoped to raise the standards for, and the relevance of, religous art in the twentieth century, by inviting artists of the highest quality to create works for the church connected to the sanatorium in that town—artists such as Georges Rouault, Jacques Lipchitz, and Marc Chagall. *The Crucifix* by Germaine Richier caused a major controversy that spread throughout Catholic circles, setting in motion a debate about modern art and the church. In the end, Richier's *Crucifix* was removed because it looked "more like a bombed victim than the typical glorified crucified Christ." The church had lost its vision that the visual arts could provide renewed insight into the life of faith. It no longer embraced its role as a major voice in culture, creating art that would define the way we see and interpret the world.

When the church relinquished its role as patron of the arts, secular society picked up that responsibility. We are witnessing the tragic results of a total role reversal. When the San Francisco Museum of Modern Art opened in 1995, I remember seeing a clip on CNN proclaiming it was "the new temple," and that people were flocking to museums "to find meaning and ponder the mysteries of life." It is interesting to note that at this point in history, while we are not building many cathedrals, we find that major museums, even in difficult financial times, are launching building programs to expand their "temples."

For too long the church has retreated from being the leader of culture. William Rubin, founding director at the Museum of Modern Art in New York, in his book on Notre-Dame-de-Toute-Grâce, essentially claimed that Christianity had lost its ability to inspire great art. This was a tragic commentary on the church, and I think Rubin was misguided. There has been a quiet renaissance movement among artists of faith. Art of incredible beauty and quality is being created by a growing number of artists all over North America. These artists are Catholics, Episcopalians, Evangelicals—representing the most diverse and ecumenical group imaginable. Their work flies just below the radar screen of contemporary art critique; nevertheless, it is being created.

Christians in the Visual Arts (CIVA) is the largest organization devoted solely to the visual arts and Christianity. In the twenty-five years since its foundation, CIVA has been laying the groundwork, helping to prepare and nurture artists to take on the task of creating compelling art, resplendent with beauty and reflective of truth. Not only has CIVA helped artists mature and become more free to create works relating to their deepest spiritual yearnings, it has also had a tremendous influence in promoting church-related and commercial galleries, such as the Visions Gallery in the Catholic Diocese of Albany, New York. In addition, two national museums now present exhibitions devoted to religion and art.

MOCRA

Saint Louis University's Museum of Contemporary Religious Art (MOCRA), the world's first museum of interfaith contemporary art, opened in February of 1993. This museum is dedicated to the dialogue between contemporary artists and the faith traditions of the world. Occupying a spacious chapel used for thirty-five years by Jesuits studying philosophy at St. Louis University, MOCRA provides a meditative environment in which to display both its permanent collection and changing shows. The museum presents a range of contemporary religious artistic expression, including the work of artists of local, national, and international stature.

MOBIA

Another bright spot on the horizon is MOBIA, the Museum of Biblical Art that opened in May of 2005. Located on Broadway near Lincoln Center, in the building of the American Bible Society, this beautiful space has set a new standard of excellence in exhibitions of religious art. Ena Heller, MOBIA's Executive Director, was hired to bring together artwork that illuminates the Bible. The distinguishing feature of this museum is a scholarly approach to elements that are artistic and biblical, and shows are accompanied by catalogs that include substantial research.

In 2005, the year of MOBIA's opening in New York, four books showcasing artists of faith were released. Half of these were catalogs from two national exhibitions celebrating works by artists of faith. The same year, CIVA also celebrated its twenty-fifth anniversary.

The Next Generation: Contemporary Expressions of Faith

Drawn from the inaugural contemporary art triennial at the Museum of Biblical Art, "The Next Generation: Contemporary Expressions of Faith" featured the works of thirty-two artists active in the field of contemporary Judeo-Christian art and demonstrated the variety inherent in the field. Working from the very broad question—"What is contemporary Judeo-Christian art?" MOBIA sought to get a sense of the basic elements surrounding the art's production and broad patronage. Simply stated, MOBIA wanted to understand the nature of Judeo-Christian art, who creates it, who sees it, who supports it, and who displays it. In short, MOBIA sought to understand the context for this genre—a topic that scholars and artists alike have been addressing in various ways with increasing frequency over the last ten years. A few selections from this collection may help to highlight the quality and diversity of the artistic vision(s) shaping the form of contemporary Christian art.

Lynn Aldrich, Baptistry, *gold leaf paint on passes from pool*

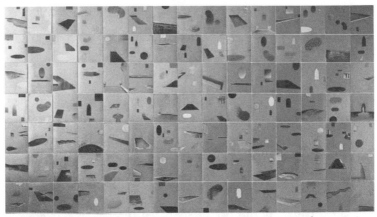

Lynn Aldrich, *Baptistry*. 2003. Gold leaf paint on passes from pool design books, 78 x 140 inches. Courtesy Lynn Aldrich.

design books, 78" x 140", 2003. Lynn Aldrich, a Los Angeles-based artist, works exclusively with objects that are not "art." She transforms these items, hoping to give them what she calls their "incarnational possibilities." Her explanation reads, "For *Baptistry*, I collected pages of pool design images from glossy coffee-table books. Then with gold leaf paint, I obscured each page except for the architectural shapes of pools or windows. Thus, I have attempted to represent a 'text' describing, among other tendencies, an architecture for the sacrament of baptism."[1] Wayne Roosa notes, "Aldrich's *Baptistry* in fact comes nicely full circle in the way that the artist has poetically transformed domestic images of people swimming recreationally in their backyards into a shimmering 'icon' of people immersed in the baptismal waters of rebirth. What makes this piece so successful is the way that it causes the eye and mind to shift constantly between what is ordinary and what is spiritual."[2]

Joel Sheesley, Winter Conversation, *Oil on Canvas, 30" x 45", 2003*. Sheesley writes about this piece, "*Winter Conversation* is a view of a print of the Portinari Altarpiece that hangs in the hall of my house. Over time I have watched the print interact with a wide range of family activities and artifacts. In 1999, I began using my house as a context in which to set a variety of subjects for visual/poetic exploration. The presence of Christian subject matter sometimes becomes a feature guiding the interpretation of these paintings."[3]

Winter Conversation presents a complex view of the Pontinari Altarpiece print. As seen from this angle, a window reflection on the glass covering the print fills up the central panel of the altarpiece. Thus, a snowy Mid-western morning invades the print. The silhouette of two women sitting on a couch in front of the reflected window blocks out the sun and allows part of the print to be visible. The figures and shapes in the print now interact with these reflected figures. The world of the Incarnation is seen to be co-existent with this suburban-life reflection. *Winter Conversation* records a simple phenomenon and at the same time invites the viewer to consider the collision of worlds this optical phenomenon suggests.[4]

Roosa explains, "In this brief visual moment, two contemporary women are simply themselves, sitting in a living room. But they become the Annunciate Angel and the Virgin Mary of van der Goes's fifteenth-century altarpiece, which in turn references the first century. What is ancient and what is contemporary merge."[5] We are reminded that faith involves remembering and living. The painting creates a kind of palimpsest, with various layers of time peering through the veils and layers of paint. Sheesley invites us to reflect on the idea that the first-century Holy Family, the interpretations of the Dutch fifteenth-century artist, and the contemporary world have joined in a contemplative "Winter Conversation."

Ellie Murphy, In the Beginning Was the Word. . . *Binary Triptych, Clay, metal, wood, and cement, 1 $\frac{1}{3}$' x 6', 1 $\frac{1}{3}$' x 7', 1 $\frac{1}{3}$' x 8', 2001.* Ellie Murphy's art takes us in a totally different direction. She writes, "This work is from a series I call "Digital Sculpture," in which I was contemplating the idea of creation vis-à-vis individual existence. *Digitus* is the Latin root for both digit, the word meaning finger (implying making by hand and the actual or the physical), and digital, the unseen electronic language of the binary system in which all computers are programmed, the ones indicating that the electronic circuit is on, the zeros that it is off (implying that which is unseen, or the sublime and the spiritual)."

The artist tells us,

By hand, I formed 8-bit binary code out of clay and then strung it on wire to spell out the phrase that is the first verse in the Gospel of John. The three sections literally spell out

John 1:1: "In the beginning was the word" (panel 1), "and the Word was with God" (panel 2), and "and the Word was God" (panel 3). I wanted to show how the most recent technological developments continue to relate to man's search for meaning through our own human experience, to show a commonality between art, science, religion and quite literally show the primacy of language and symbol in forming and passing on our basic principles of what is true, beautiful, and divine.[6]

"A Broken Beauty"

A second national exhibition, accompanied by an exemplary book with worthy essays, opened at the Laguna Art Museum in Laguna Beach, California, in Fall 2005. Richard Chang, art critic for the *Orange County Register*, began his review (a sad commentary on the state of art and Christianity to say the least) of "A Broken Beauty" by saying,

We expect to encounter Jesus Christ at church. He's in the sermons. He's in the Bible. He's in the crucifixes hanging on the wall. But we don't expect to encounter Jesus in the contemporary art museum. Though he's been a favorite, and dominant, topic of artists for centuries, he's not as popular in art made since the turn of the 20th century. As aesthetic tastes have evolved, a separation of church and the artistic state seems to have occurred, and Christian art sometimes isn't taken as seriously as secular creations in the modern art space.[7]

"A Broken Beauty: Figuration, Narrative and the Transcendent in North American Art" features the work of fifteen contemporary North American artists who use a range of figurative and narrative approaches in painting, sculpture, and mixed media. As artists who work in the postmodern milieu of the late twentieth and early twenty-first centuries, they consider the meaning of the human body by portraying states of physical, mental, and spiritual brokenness. The title of the exhibition, "A Broken Beauty," was conceived from the writing of Simone Weil (1909-1943), the French metaphysical philosopher who saw a symbiotic relationship between beauty and brokenness that she felt was necessary to understand the complexities of the human condition in the modern world. The exhibit invites viewers to consider the body, with its capacity for beauty, even with its brokenness. The twenty-seven works in the exhibition challenge us to be present to the struggle and grace emerging from deeply personal stories, historical and sacred narratives, and the terrors of modern history—the horrific events of the past and present century that overshadow and seep into our present, and threaten to shape our future.[8] We might briefly explore two items from this exhibition.

Bruce Herman, Annunciation *(from the series* Elegy for Witness*), diptych, oil and alkyd resin on wood panels with silver leaf, 76" x 96", 2001.* Using the theme of the annunciation, Bruce Herman's diptych altarpiece celebrates the incarnation. Two panels are juxtaposed to each other, with the left side conceived in abstract forms and the right more figuratively. Wayne Roosa writes of this piece, "Herman prefers the notion of what he calls 'broken beauty.' Hence, his Virgin is painted in a fashion that partly references the classical tradition. That is, she is a nude whose powerful dignity comes from her three-dimensional presence. And yet, she is also a fragment, with one arm broken off, suggesting that the classical, rational conception of beauty does not redeem."[9] Even though the left panel is essentially abstract, there are hints of architectural elements that reference Christian tradition. The diptych allows the artist to suggest the meeting of two worlds, heaven and earth, as well as spirit and flesh.

Patty Wickman, Overshadowed, *oil on canvas, 78" x 104" x 2", 2001.* Another very different interpretation of the annunciation is offered by Patty Wickman, an art professor at the University of California in Los Angeles. Her piece is reminiscent of Henry Ossawa Tanner's *Annunciation* at the Philadelphia Museum of Art. Tanner's late nineteenth-century painting depicts a young girl from the biblical narrative, shrinking from the intense presence of light that floods her room. Wickman's *Overshadowed* places the virgin in a contemporary twenty-first-century teenager's bedroom, fully equipped with all the trappings of a young adolescent. Subtle details point to the ominous moment: she kneels before a bare lamp, suggesting the presence of the Holy Spirit; a hand-held telephone strewn on the floor is a symbol of the angel who delivers the message from God; and her crossed arms in front form a winged shape that appears on her chest.

Sandra Bowden, Artist

As part of this presentation, I was asked to give a short over-view of my own artwork. For the last forty years, I have explored the relationship between word and image, both of central impor-tance within the Christian tradition. My work celebrates the won-derful gift of language that allows us to communicate across time and place. Reading and seeing, image and text, have provided a rich well of material from which I have drawn my inspirations. Being an artist is really a journey, one in which the work deter-mines the direction. Each piece raises questions, leading me to the next step in the development of my vision. The few images that I shall present trace that journey in part.

In the Beginning Was the Word, *collagraph and embossing, 30" x 18", 1982*. This work portrays an exchange between the Old and New Testaments. The Hebrew text, "In the beginning God created," begins the first chapter of Genesis and is the central fo-cus of this print. A Greek embossing surrounds the Hebrew with "In the beginning was the Word . . . the Word became flesh and dwelt among us" (Jn 1:1, 14).

It Is Finished, *oil, 48" x 36", 1976*. The crucifixion event has compelled artists for centuries to contemplate its meaning. The inscription above Christ's head reads "Jesus of Nazareth, King of the Jews," written in Hebrew, Greek and Latin. Layers of fabric and other materials provide the surface texture. The crown of thorns has been constructed using old floor nails. The abstracted form speaks to the brokenness Christ endured as a means to re-store humanity to wholeness. Contained within the torso is a large arrow shape, thrusting itself into a flat broad area of red.

A Reading, *collage mixed media, 26" x 20", 2000*. Buried be-neath the layers of oriental papers and a handwritten passage of the Law are pages from a Hebrew Bible containing the story of Ezra reading the Law to the Israelites after their return to Jerusa-lem from captivity in Babylon. Attached to the surface of the col-lage is a Jewish coin with the Lion of Judah, and a leather cover from an old book with a Star of David scratched into its surface. The central panel of gilded Hebrew text is a portion of the Decalogue. These elements bring together a conversation that dem-onstrates the centrality of the Law to the Jewish people.

Sandra Bowden, *It Is Finished*. 1976. Oil, 48 x 36 inches. Courtesy Sandra Bowden.

Visual Record

This brief exploration has indicated that there are artists of faith, artists of great talent, insight, and ability, who have struggled with important topics of our time. Now we have to ask, where are the collectors? Where are the patrons of the arts? Where are the commissions from churches and universities that will bring about new works of integrity and meaning for this generation? So many have traveled to view the powerful works of art that fill the churches and museums of Europe. Past centuries have given us a vast treasury, some of the world's most important creations, recording the story of faith and leaving a rich legacy for coming generations. Will our generation leave a visual record that faith was alive and well in our time?

Notes

[1] Patricia C. Pongrancz and Wayne Roosa, *The Next Generation: Contemporary Expressions of Faith* (Grand Rapids: Eerdman's and Museum of Biblical Art, New York City, 2005), 168.

[2] Ibid., 70.

[3] Ibid., 86.

[4] Ibid.

[5] Ibid., 15.

[6] Ibid., 102.

[7] Richard Chang, *Orange County Review*, November 27, 2005.

[8] This information and much more can be found at www.abrokenbeauty.com.

[9] Pongrancz and Roosa, *The Next Generation*, 65.

Part II

MUSICAL ARTS

Sacred Sound

Don Saliers

As a liturgical musician, I am constantly working within the repertoires of the "sacred music" tradition and my own background in jazz and the classics. As a singer/songwriter deeply engaged in justice work, Emily is keenly aware of where music has taken her, from Native American rights, to children's education, environmental causes, and Habitat for Humanity. As someone who has a profound lover's quarrel with much of the church, she also has a deep prophetic strand inherited from Christian scripture and tradition.

In Gerard Manley Hopkins's poem "God's Grandeur," the Hopkinsian "sound" and characteristic *in-scaping* and *in-stressing* speak of the tensive contrasts between the world "charged with the grandeur of God," flaming out, shining, and the world that is "seared, bleared, smeared with toil," wearing the human "smudge and sharing the human smell." Although his aim is to sharpen the contrast between the God-given natural world and our human despoilage of nature, I propose that we can extend those powerful synaesthetic images to bear directly on the theme of sacred sound: "There lives the dearest freshness deep down things;/And though the last lights off the black West went/Oh, morning, at the brown brink eastward, springs—Because the Holy Ghost over the bent/World broods with warm breast and with ah! bright wings."

This is where theology must always learn to live: between the IS

My presentation included a video-taped performance that my daughter and I gave to a conference of eight thousand United Methodist women. Emily is one-half of the singer/songwriter duo known as the Indigo Girls. Last year we published a book together, *A Song to Sing, A Life to Live: Reflections on Music as Spiritual Practice* (Jossey-Bass, 2005), in which we explored music as a spiritual practice. At the heart of our explorations is how the music of Saturday night and Sunday morning may have more in common than we first think.

and the OUGHT of this created order; between the extremities of
the beauty of what we proclaim and receive in word and sacrament, and the inexorable, seemingly unlimited pain and suffering
and ugliness of a damaged, down-trodden world. Music can, I
think, hold a clue to how we may live, and pray, and bring our
best intellect to voice on this set of paradoxes. When we speak of
"sacred sound," we certainly have in mind the way in which particular religious traditions have employed music to awaken a deep
awareness of the world. At the same time, the "sacrality" of ordered sound cannot be confined to ritual or to officially sanctioned
ecclesial uses.

Traditions of communal spiritual practice have always employed
a variety of sounds to awaken, elicit, and to sustain particular
states of consciousness. Consider the bell in Hindu temples, in
Buddhism, and in Shamanism, as well as ringing from church spires.
Drums and cymbals, the shofar and the trumpet sound and signify
a range of religious sensibility in Jewish tradition, as is well at-
tested in the Hebrew psalms. At the heart of so many traditions of
"sacred sound" is, of course, the human voice. Thus chant and
song mark a central practice among religious ceremonies. Communal singing is itself a powerful force for identity and social co-
hesion. Sacred texts are carried more deeply into the human body
and the human psyche when they are chanted and sung than when
they are only "read" or spoken. This, of course, opens up the fascinating question of "heightened speech" and when the implicit
music of oral language becomes the explicit music of shared song.

Speaking within the Christian tradition, I think of St. Augustine's
references to the beautiful melodies of the psalm settings he heard
in Ambrose's Milan. He reports that he wept with joy at the "de-
lights of the ear" in praying the psalms. Yet he wishes at other
times to banish the sound of the melodies because of their sensual-
ity. This feature of music was too powerful—as Plato observed
well before. Augustine desired also a "pure" hearing of God's word
(cf. Book X, 33 of the *Confessions*). Christian tradition inherited
this ambivalence toward the aesthetic aspects of religious singing
of sacred words. I contend that his tears of recognition at the Word
were indeed part of his hearing. So "sacred sound" may also bring
with it certain tensions within particular religious traditions. This
ambivalence was to break out again vigorously during the Reformation, especially with Ulrich Zwingli, who banned music from

the churches even while he nurtured music outside the church in the city. He was an accomplished musician himself.

However the history of this peculiar Christian ambivalence goes, I think we can offer a first reflection. *Music is the language of the soul made audible, conferring upon human speech addressed to the divine its origin and mystery—particularly as music becomes a performative mode of a community's life.* This implies that ordered sound has the power to elicit deep emotions—both as "feeling states" and as long-term emotional dispositions. Hence, music enters into the manner by which a community expresses and discovers joy and sorrow, praise and lament, grief and consolation. Ordered sound can thus confer a certain "sacrality" on the whole of human life.

Every religious tradition and every human culture inherits a set of acoustical images and convictions that define what makes music "sacred." Within Judaism and Christianity this is a complex history. Thus, when Pius X's *motu proprio* (1903) declared Gregorian chant to be the supremely sacred music for the liturgy, with Renaissance polyphony a close second, he was reflecting the ideals of the nineteenth-century European Roman Catholic sensibility. It was during the nineteenth century that a vigorous recovery of chant (the Benedictines) and polyphonic music (the Caecelian Movement) was taking place. Within Judaism and the Enlightenment in Germany and Austria, a new music entered the synagogue, heavily influenced by Western music theory and composition.

In our own time, we are familiar with the clashes of sensibility in the contemporary churches, so much so that many despair of having any norms at all to govern music suitable to prayer and the enactment of the mysteries. As one wag quipped right after the Second Vatican Council, "Suppress the Latin and you get *glossolalia!*" Beneath our often well-defined concepts of what is "sacred" and what is "secular" is a history of changing cultural assessments. Unfortunately, this may lead us to demythologize the very idea of "sacred sound" into little more than an arbitrary social construction.

While liturgical music is but a sub-set of the larger notion of "sacred music" and "religious music," it still may hold a key to the issues we face. As we consider what our own musical experience has been, we may ask when we have been moved to a sense of wonder, of sheer beauty, or transcendence, or of such sheer vitality

and energy that we perceived it as the breath of the Spirit, enliven-
ing our sense of life. Recently, I heard the "Passion According to
Mark" by Golijov. This extraordinary, layered convergence of Jewish, Christian, and Latin-American texts and music overwhelmed
me with the vitality and energy of the Spirit.

Indeed, with the crossing-over of cultures and musical traditions, we now bring a new set of listening ears—a new attentiveness—to the intrinsic qualities of music. This new global awareness in our hearing shows the ambiguity of drawing the *sacred/
secular* distinction too sharply. We cannot do away with such contrasts, for we still recognize a difference between what moves us
most deeply in contrast to what merely entertains us. The "sacral"
qualities of music have both contemplative and prophetic powers,
and characteristically lead to visionary and synaesthetic "senses"
of life and world, or, as T. S. Eliot has observed, "Music heard so
deeply that you are the music while the music lasts." And, of course,
we should not be surprised at the cross-over artists: Benny
Goodman playing Mozart and *Stompin' at the Savoy*; Yo Yo Ma
playing an unaccompanied Bach cello sonata and the tango; Renee
Fleming singing Puccini arias and the blues.

Some music still astonishes us, and we keep returning to it: Bach's
B Minor Mass, Mahler's *Resurrection Symphony*, a late Beethoven
string quartet, Messiaen's *Quartet for the End of Time*. To these
we may add Duke Ellington's "Come Sunday," Dave Brubeck's
Light in the Wilderness, or Art Tatum's "Somewhere Over the
Rainbow." Other music carries sacrality because it takes words so
deeply into us and our world that we and the world are changed:
"We Shall Overcome," "Siyahamba" (a South African anti-apart-
heid song), and even "Strange Fruit."

Some music is of such beauty we cannot be without it. Some
music and song in times of great anguish and disorientation suddenly empower and illuminate the truth. I want to include a broader
notion of "sacred sound." This, of course, takes us well beyond
"church music" or the bounded traditions of the "sacred music"
canon. In my own experience of my daughter's music, I find this to
be true. Here we enter a dialogue between generations, and between a singer-songwriter with a passion for justice and a liturgical musician. Following are the lyrics of a song Emily performed
in a recent "dialogue" we had. The song was sung at Ground Zero,
New York, not long after people began to make pilgrimages there.

Emily and Amy were stunned at the extraordinary response of applause, following a long silence.

Our Deliverance

Now we can say that nothing's lost, only time brings round
     the prophecy
Where now it's melting, the solid frost was once a veil on
     greener landscapes we would see
Beneath my surface the water's heating
And steam comes up and out the tears you see me shine
For every strange and bitter moment, there was never
     a better time
For every pleasure exacts its pain
How you hurt me how you were good to me
Beneath my window a mournful train
That makes me smile at my bad poetry

Beneath my surface a song is rising
It may be simple while it hides its true intent
We may be looking for our deliverance
But it has already been sent.

Conclusion

I think that we must also include the qualities of the performance of music in the domain of "sacred sound," especially when it comes to the sounding of justice, or of any elemental human desire for a transformed world. I would offer four proposals that may guide us in our further explorations of "sacrality" in music and what is meant by "sacred sound." We attribute to music and song the sense of the sacred when:

1. Music confers upon human words addressed to the divine its originating deep silence and mystery.

2. Music is intimately related to the narrative quality of our experience of life at full stretch. That is when we "hear" in the music our own temporality and mortality, our hopes and our fears, our joys and deepest loves. The sound of the human voice is thus primordial.

3. Music approaches the inexpressible, and awakens what is

most valuable and most intensely real—opening the soul and what is most real simultaneously.

4. Music awakens our "hearing" of what is other to us, especially to accents of transcendence.

Finally, the history of "sacred" music is remarkably like the history of "sacred" texts, "sacred" space, and "sacred" images in art. There is nothing static or fixed. There is immense diversity, yet there is also an "open canon" of characteristics such as have been proposed here.

Epilogue

Occasionally, we discern when the songs of earth and heaven meet. There are times and places when music and song together reveal more than a beautiful sound. One such occasion occurred for me in 1985 during an ecumenical gathering outside of Geneva, Switzerland, and the Orthodox Center, Chambezy. There were people participating in the Orthodox Holy Week liturgies from countries then behind the iron curtain—from the Soviet Union, East Germany, Czechoslovakia, and Romania. Others were from Ethiopia and several English-speaking countries. All were invited to attend the Easter Vigil in one of several churches grouped together. Those of us in the seminar moved to and from the French-speaking Greek Orthodox and the Russian Orthodox liturgies. I chose to spend most of the night with a small, expatriate Romanian assembly. I did not understand the language, but the sound of the chant and the folk-based hymns carried me through the lengthy liturgy. Then, after midnight, as each community concluded, all of us poured out of the buildings into the chill, starry night, singing in several languages, "Christ is risen! He is risen indeed!" Bells sounded in the Easter-morning air. It was as though we stood—from so many different cultures, languages, and Christian traditions—at the very center of the cosmos, singing and receiving the song in which heaven and earth embraced.

The Listener as Musician

The Importance of Audience
in the Moral Power of Music

James F. Caccamo

Over the course of the past two thousand years, theologians have struggled to understand the power of music on the moral life. Saint Augustine, Martin Luther, and John Calvin, among many others, were concerned about the effect of the musical arts on the lives and the beliefs of Christians.[1] Given the tremendous increase in the availability and presence of music in people's lives over the past century, understanding its power and influence has become all the more important.

One may wonder, however, whether we have any deeper understanding of music than Calvin, Luther, or even Augustine. Despite the wide variety of analytical tools at the disposal of contemporary scholars, we seem to have little better grasp of the ways in which music influences human action. We alternately praise and denounce various styles of music for what we believe to be their good or bad influences on society, yet we are at a loss to see the precise connections between such music and particular actions. Some, for instance, believe that Goth metal leads people to commit violent acts. Yet, if this is so, why are incidents like the shootings at Colombine High School, which the popular music style is supposed to have spawned, not more common? Some believe that the music of Bono and his band U2 inspires a sense of justice and compassion in their listeners. If this is so, why have peace and justice organizations not been overwhelmed by massive increases in charitable donations and volunteers as their millions of fans convert their inspiration to action? In truth, we have yet to move very far beyond identifying the correspondence of music and action to understanding the complex web of relations that might begin to reveal some aspect of causality.

One of the central reasons we still have so far to go in understanding the relationship between music and the moral life is that we frequently fail to consider the full range of what is actually happening in a musical event. From the very beginning, the absence of a full account of the phenomenon of music itself undermines any attempt to understand its role in the moral life. The present discussion will draw upon literature from ethnomusicology, a field that takes the study of music as its primary focus, with the goal of identifying ways in which theologians can expand their vision of the relationship between music and the moral life. Such an examination may help develop our thinking about music and enable us to more fruitfully explore its relation to the moral life.

Theological Investigations of Music's Moral Power[2]

When scholars in theological disciplines think about the moral impact of the musical arts in human life, they often approach effectiveness in terms of two notions: instruction and inspiration.

Instruction

Music is understood by some to affect the moral life by the way it instructs people about moral values and disvalues. Like an auditory counterpart to the *Biblia pauperum,* music teaches Christians about the principles and norms that undergird the Christian life without resorting to theoretical or technical knowledge. Music— especially when joined with words in song—provides a means for expressing meaningful ideas about human life and for communicating one's place in, and relationship to, the world.[3] Insofar as these meanings positively impact a listener's understanding of the human person, the good, or a just society, music is seen to provide positive moral instruction.

Literature on music and morality within the theological disciplines often makes use of the instructional approach. This approach is employed, for instance, in the numerous case studies that focus on critical analyses of lyrics as the sole method for determining the moral voice of a musical work.[4] It also operates in those far less numerous studies that go beyond the analysis of lyrics to consider the musical aspects of a given work.[5] When they do occur, studies of the instructional power of the music itself tend to focus on the impact of musical styles, such as hip-hop or jazz, or musical structures (for example, how the different forms of liturgical music create various social relations).[6] In these cases, the moral content tends to be articulated in terms of "tones" and overarching "sensibilities" rather than in detailed moral ideas noted in lyrical studies.[7]

Inspiration

In contrast to a focus on instruction, some theologians understand the moral power of music by the way music inspires people to do good. In this case, music does not communicate concepts, but rather creates emotions that can motivate people to live up to moral principles and norms. The moral effects of music in terms of inspiration can operate at several levels. The first level is that of emotion. Pope John Paul II suggested that the ability to sway the emotions, inspiring love of God and acts of charity, was music's greatest power.[8] Throughout history, however, Christians have been wary of this power that can also lead people to do evil things. One of the primary arguments against the use of instruments in the liturgy was the suspicion that they would cause unseemly emotions in worshippers, just as instruments sometimes did in the theater, the military, and in the worship practices of other religious groups.[9]

Other theologians understand the inspirational power of music to operate at the level of the moral affections, which include a deeply rooted connection with, and attention to, God that "lie at the heart of a person's way of being."[10] In this view, moral acts are understood as externalizations or incarnations of a person's deep-seated desires and commitments. Don Saliers, one of the primary proponents of this approach, believes that song is a uniquely powerful means of forming such affections.[11] Thus, music inspires moral action by evoking those things that people most deeply love and desire.[12]

Finally, at perhaps the deepest level, some theologians suggest that music can inspire moral action by being a sacramental or quasi-sacramental event that transforms a person through a direct experience of God. Scholars use a variety of terms to refer to the phenomena involved, including "sacrament," "conversion," "theophany," and "anamnesis."[13] But in each case, they operate under the belief that music is a means through which God enters profoundly into one's life, directly transforming the fundamental character of one's actions.

Broadly speaking, the notions of instruction and inspiration have served as the foundation for current Christian theological work on the moral power of music.[14] These two approaches have taught us a great deal about the dynamic role of music, and have advanced our understanding of the contributions of various songs, composers, and musical traditions to the Christian moral life.

The Lost Listener

The instructional and inspirational approaches have proven fruitful in helping us understand the role of music in the moral life. However, despite their differences, they share the key underlying assumption that the morally relevant aspect of any musical event is the musical composition itself. Whether it comes through teaching moral ideas or evoking laudable emotions, the moral effect of a song results from the characteristics of the composition. Indeed, many works on music and the moral life seem to operate under the assumption that a given piece of music will have a single moral effect. Case studies seldom, if ever, suggest a variety of interpretations of the piece of music or song text under consideration. Rather they tend to suggest that there is a single authentic interpretation or experience of each musical composition and that the interpretation or experience results from the features of the composition. This approach is standard, despite the commonplace experience that pieces of music can be interpreted in many ways.

This focus on the composition leaves out something essential—the listener. Listeners are conspicuously absent in studies of the ethics of music. In work on music and the moral life, we find few significant descriptions of listeners or their listening practices. Paul Westermeyer's *Let Justice Sing: Hymnody and Justice* is typical of efforts in this area.[15] In his treatment of the moral aspects of hymnody, Westermeyer gives no description of the listener. He offers five pages on the liturgical context for hymn-listening practice, but does not suggest ways in which differences in congregations, liturgical traditions, or denominations might change the meaning of hymns.[16] The reader is left to imagine that "The Church's One Foundation" will mean the same thing to Roman Catholic, mainline Protestant, and evangelical Christians. On occasion, scholars do indicate the kinds of ideal listeners they have in mind or different contexts in which people might listen to the music under consideration, as Westermeyer does.[17] These factors, however, are not always taken into account when the author begins to analyze the music. Finally, several scholars, primarily in the area of theological aesthetics, have argued for consideration of the audience in understanding the theological import of the arts, or attempted to work out theories of reception.[18] Unfortunately, their efforts have had little impact on those who study the moral power of music. For the most part, the story of the contemporary analysis of the ethics of music within theology is the story of the lost listener.[19]

In many ways, this absence of the listener is not unexpected. Generally speaking, we tend to operate under the assumption that listeners contribute very little to the music-making process. As members of a society that bases its economic viability on the division of labor and productive specialization, we have come to expect that a particular set of individuals will take responsibility for producing the music that society requires.[20] People purchase recordings by composers or performers regarded as "professionals" precisely to enjoy the products that those composers and performers have labored to create. Indeed, we tend to reserve the description "musical" for those people who perform music.[21] Of course, the corollary to this notion is that those who receive the musical product are receivers because they do not possess the skills necessary to generate music. More precisely, the hearer is seen as a passive, non-artistic receiver of an object that has been produced by someone properly regarded as a musician or composer.[22] Just as the use of soap requires no knowledge of soap-making, listening to music requires no musical ability. If listening is the proper activity of the unmusical, then we should expect listeners to be absent from our accounts of music.

It must be noted, however, that this model of music as a specialized task reserved for a few professionals lies in stark contrast to what influential ethnomusicologist and social anthropologist John Blacking found in his ethnographic fieldwork outside of the industrialized West.[23] Among the Venda people of the Transvaal region in southern Africa, Blacking found that music was not understood as the product of a technical elite for the benefit of others. Rather, musical performance was a social practice participated in by all members of a community. No sharp lines were drawn between the musical abilities of composers, musicians, and audience members. This is not to say that distinctions between participants in musical events were entirely absent. Participants were, for instance, distinguished by their roles in the music-making process (such as drummers, song leaders, and singers). Likewise, high levels of musical ability were noted and appreciated. But Blacking did not see the kind of differentiation in acclaim and reward that is made between musicians and audiences in contemporary American society, be it in our churches or concert venues. Among the Venda, everyone participated in a musical performance and all had roles to play. All were musicians.[24]

An Ethnomusicological Account of Music

Given the pervasiveness of the Western production model of music, it is not surprising that theologians tend to focus on the musical composition when examining the moral power of music. Yet Blacking's observations might offer important insights that can enrich current thinking on music and the moral life. Within the field of ethnomusicology, the exclusive focus on the musical composition has come under close scrutiny over the past few decades and has been, ultimately, rejected. Grounding itself in anthropological methods, ethnomusicology has effected a "turn to the listener," as it were, within the study of music. Through the use of fieldwork and participant observation, ethnomusicologists study not only the music that is produced, but also the people who are involved in the music, the means through which it is made, the events in which it is used, and what music-making accomplishes in a society. I would suggest that including the listener and listening practices as primary factors in the musical event can ultimately increase the depth and accuracy of our understanding of music's effects on the moral life.

Listening as Musical Action

The first step toward reassessing one's understanding of music involves stepping back from the composition to think about the nature of the music itself. Often, when people discuss music, they speak as if it were an object that simply exists. The fact that musical performances are often immobilized by composers and musicians in plastic (recordings) and paper (sheet music) like bugs in amber enables this way of thinking. For ethnomusicologists, however, music is not an object at all; rather, it is an intentional human act.[25] Whether for enjoyment, social bonding, praise of a deity, diversion, or communication, music is always the result of someone structuring sounds in order to achieve a particular purpose.[26]

In all music, at least three levels of organization are evident. At the most fundamental level, music is made up of individual tones.[27] Tones might best be described as sonic events that are structured by human beings to have specific characteristics.[28] By manipulating the frequency, amplitude, duration, and wave forms of sound waves—what we refer to as pitch, volume, duration, and timbre—humans create the rudiments of music. These tones are then arranged into organized groups or musical units, the most basic of which is the melody: a progression of tones, organized in time.[29] Each line in a song is a melody, as is every line played by an instrument. Once organized, these melodies are arranged into discrete musical works. Composers arrange melodies in alternating and repeating patterns over time, add and remove melodies to create harmonic shifts, and alter melodies to suggest development and change.

Not every grouping of tones or musical units qualifies as a melody or a musical work. A progression of tones and melodies must "make sense" to listeners.[30] In order to be identified as a melody, this progression must display a "sonic order" that allows a listener native to the musical culture to identify it as a melody, rather than a cacophony.[31] Likewise, in order to be perceived as a piece of music, a collection of melodies must demonstrate discernible characteristics of sonic order that are appropriate to the particular culture in which the piece is composed and played (even if those characteristics are not discernible to members of another musical culture).[32]

Thus, in order for music to occur, three roles must be fulfilled: envisioning the sonic order, instantiating the sonic order, and apprehending that sonic order *as* sonic order.[33] Composition is the act of envisioning a plan for the progression of sounds into the world. Playing or singing a piece of music is the act of instantiating that progression in the physical world. Listening to music is the act of receiving that progression of sound and apprehending it as "sonic order" in ways that render it meaningful, significant, or affecting. Hence, listening is in no way passive; it is a properly musical activity that also requires musical competence. Without such competence, listeners would not be able to distinguish sonic order from sonic chaos, or the planned from the haphazard. While people rarely have an ability to perceive universally the sonic order of musical cultures, all people have the ability to perceive the sonic order native to their own culture. All people are musical.[34] John Blacking finds the contribution made by the listener to the musical process so important that he views it as a part of musical creation, noting that "the composition of music has always required its re-composition by . . . audiences."[35] For musicologist Victor Zuckerkandl, listening is the fundamental musical activity; composition and performance are secondary, existing merely to serve the human ear.[36]

Given this focus on the listener rather than on the composition, the account of music offered by ethnomusicology could scarcely be more different from the one that undergirds theological reflection on the role of music in the moral life. Were theologians to approach the listener as an active part of the music-making process, it would certainly influence our understanding of both the instructional and inspirational power of music. In instructional terms, scholars could consider a broad range of ways in which listeners *actually* interpret the formal elements of a musical work. Scholarly studies of the ethics of music tend to assume the normativity of the point of view of the interpreter. Yet, we know that people interpret music in different ways. Even iconic songs like "We Shall Overcome," which we expect to have a single interpretation, are subject to this reality. I recall some young people of my parish in Chicago, who felt utterly uninspired by the song. For them, it was a musically boring historical artifact: alternately a quaint song from a time when Americans actually thought that we could change people's minds with protests and legislation, or an endless complaint about a problem we took care of in the 1960s. While such interpretations might seem strange, they are *real*, and they certainly affect the ability of the song to function as a moral instructor. Recognition of the multifaceted character of musical interpretation might even lead scholars to do something that is essentially unheard of: to present multiple interpretations of a musical work as part of an analysis of its moral content. Because moral instruction is grounded in interpretation, investigation of the range of plausible interpretations of a given work may be the only way to identify the breadth of its moral character.

Were theologians to approach the listener as an active part of the music-making process, it would also lead them to consider the ways in which listeners are actually affected or inspired by the expressive aspects of musical works. Literary theorist M. H. Abrams notes that critical work on expression in poetry tends to assume the normativity of the artist's emotional response.[37] The same sort of phenomenon can be seen in studies of the moral power of music. Insofar as the musical artist has composed a song in a way that captures a particular mood or feeling for him or her, we expect that listeners will respond in a comparable manner. It would be considered quite strange, or even offensive, if someone were to respond to "On Eagles Wings" or "Be Not Afraid" with laughter. One would argue that the composers certainly did not intend these songs to be amusing. But for someone who is exasperated by the narrowness of his or her parish's repertoire over the past thirty years, such a response may certainly be understandable. Despite the fact that we know people experience a given song differently, we rarely investigate variations in the inspirational power of music within a group of listeners, or over time. Because inspiration is grounded in experience, investigating the range of plausible responses to a given musical work may be the only way to identify the actual depth of its moral power.

Listening as Human Practice

As we have seen, far from being passive, non-artistic receivers of an object created by the musical few, listeners are people who actively contribute to the meaning and expression of a musical work. The resources of ethnomusicology enable us to expand our vision of the moral power of music beyond the composition to include the listener as a primary factor in the musical event.

While this expansion is good, it takes us only so far. While we are now including the listener, we have continued to limit ourselves to evaluating the *musical* components of the musical event: the creation, instantiation, and apprehension of sonic order. Ethnomusicologists would challenge this limitation, suggesting that musical events involve more than just music. Listening is more than a cognitive operation: it is a set of related tasks that people carry out in regularized ways to achieve particular goals. What we do to comprehend sound is profoundly material and necessarily involves disposing and manipulating the body in intentional ways. We sit, we stand, we drive a car, we drink a beer, we clap, we yell, we dance, we clean the house, we fall asleep, and we cook dinner. Indeed, it is extraordinarily rare for us to sit down and devote all of our attention to the sole activity of listening.[38] Given the complexity and standardization involved in listening, it is probably more accurate to describe the act as a practice.[39] Like all regularized activities, listening practices form through habituation.[40] This notion is likely to be familiar to theologians generally, and certainly to moral theologians in particular, being the core of the virtue-ethical approach to the moral life in the accounts of the formation of moral habits of Aristotle and Aquinas. Repeated actions lead to the formation of consistent, reliable, and long-lasting habits, not through inspiration or information but through the repetition of bodily acts. As Aquinas observed when discussing acquired moral virtues, "like acts cause like habits."[41]

The ethnomusicological study of music-making practices suggests that music is only one of many things that musical events accomplish. Most important, ways of being are enacted in musical events by means of the listening practices themselves. Some of these practices have little to do with the music we are listening to, being the result of forces external to the musical event, such as the use of a Walkman or iPod to listen to classical music. However, many of our listening practices are grounded in the nature of the music itself. Steven Feld suggests that music demands a particular type of responsive engagement, or "feelingful participation."[42] Experience of the musical relationships within a song (e.g., rhythm, melody, and form) creates a set of "implicative relationships" between the song and the listener.[43] As listeners are "drawn in," the implicative relationships generate expectations about the appropriate ways to respond "feelingfully" to the music (e.g., singing, dancing, silent appreciation). Through rehearsal and repetition, our responses and practices become embodied habits in individuals and groups. Hence they can form a key aspect of the moral power of music.

Ethnomusicologists suggest that listening practices accomplish a number of different non-musical tasks. First and foremost, music is used to achieve social purposes, especially those things that are difficult to do by other means.[44] While the particular social functions that ethnomusicologists identify are extraordinarily varied and often specific to the particular groups under study, several social purposes seem central. An important example is the consolidation of relationships among those who are involved in the music event.[45] Through shared song activity in liturgy, a concert, or singing with children, for example, a "solidarity" can be created that carries beyond the ritual event to form networks of relationships.[46] Another purpose is the creation and enforcement of particular social structures and organization schemes.[47] The ways in which people listen to music influence power structures (as manifested in the distinct roles of cantor and congregation created by the responsory form), economic structures (such as digital sound and the challenge to the current purchase/ownership models of music), and relational structures (including the professional/non-professional duality in music). Finally, listening practices also regulate behavior without needing to explicitly articulate social rules.[48] Each listening practice engages and reinforces particular behaviors that are appropriate to the setting in which the practice occurs. The way we listen to music at a bar, with its noise, chaos, and alcoholic beverages, is generally quite different from the way we listen in church. Our listening practices both introduce and reinforce broader systems of social norms and expectations.

Listening practices also have a formative effect on individuals. Charles Keil envisions music-making and music-apprehending as having two primary personal roles. First, participation in music "capacitates" people: it imparts a set of particular skills, creating in individuals a body of knowledge that is both physical and intellectual.[49] It also brings to many a new sense of their broader power and presence in the world, transforming the way they view themselves and the way they interact with the world. For some, this takes on the character of a conversion experience.[50] John Blacking discusses the changes that occurred amongst the Venda people of the Transvaal region of South Africa in the 1970s. Listening for the first time to recordings created by other black South Africans shaped their awareness of what they had in common with the members of other tribes. These listening practices created a consciousness that transcended tribal divisions and helped black Africans envision a South Africa free of apartheid.[51]

Second, participation in music-making can ease the destructive effects of social ills on individuals. Keil, who has worked primarily in industrialized nations, sees musical grooves as "participatory healings [for individuals] of those alienations from body, labor, society and nature that permeate late capitalism."[52] Listening can be a powerfully formative performance for ordering, not merely tones, but one's person and life.

By moving beyond the musical aspects of the music event, the ethnomusicological account identifies critical ways in which listening affects human life, both socially and personally. Were theologians to approach listening as a practice, the primary effect would be to expand the range of factors that would be considered relevant to the moral influence of music. Scholars would no longer be able to assess music's moral aspects without attending to the variety of listening practices relevant to the work and to the ways in which those practices form the listeners. We might reflect, perhaps, on a listening practice that I frequently observed in my Chicago neighborhood: young parents pushing their wakeful babies and toddlers along in a stroller while they (the parents) listened to music through headphones. As a parent, I recognize that being the primary caretaker for a young child is a tiring endeavor. Parents must frequently take the opportunity for downtime wherever and whenever they can. However, like a good evening walk with a friend, stroller-time can offer a great moment for interaction, as parent and child have fewer distractions that interrupt their connection. When a parent engages in a headphone-based listening practice, the possibility of such a connection is removed. While some listening practices can positively affect social groups by consolidating them, the use of headphones in this situation interrupts the ability to create solidarity. While theologians might be inclined to focus on the instructional and inspirational power of the composition being heard through the headphones, including the listening practice as part of the assessment of the musical event certainly provides a fuller account of its moral impact. No matter how inspiring the lyrics and chords of that liturgical song might be, they may prove less formative than the alienation habituated through the listening practice. Moving beyond the composition to include such practices will ultimately increase the depth and accuracy of our understanding of music's effect on the moral life.

Conclusion: Taking Account of Listeners and Their Practices

In order to identify some of the limitations presented by scholars who investigate the moral power of music within the theological disciplines, I have drawn upon ethnomusicology to suggest that music is both an action and a practice. As active participants in the musical event, listeners affect both the moral instruction and the moral inspiration that occur in music. As complex, standardized, and regularized activities, listening practices form listeners and social groups independently of (or in spite of) the instructional and inspirational aspects of music. These points suggest that understanding listeners and their practices is a necessary part of understanding the moral meaning and power of music.

The notion that listeners and their listening practices have a central role in the moral effects of music may seem eminently reasonable, if not downright obvious. When dealing with texts, we operate in an intellectual environment that understands the audience—the reader—to be a critical part of the meaning-making process. Whether from formal study or general knowledge, we know that the criteria for evaluating the merit and meaning of an artistic work have shifted over time, moving from the work of literature and its faithfulness to nature, to the author and his or her intended meaning, and ultimately landing on the audience and its ability to draw meaning from a text.[53] If we do not know this shift from scholarly reading, we know it from the classroom, where our students enact the most extreme versions of reader/response criticism on a daily basis. While we work to stop the grossest forms of individualistic and solipsistic interpretation, we recognize that interpretation is a dance that requires readers, not just authors, texts, and reality. Thus, it may finally be no surprise that listeners matter.

Rather, the real surprise may be that we fail to treat the musical audience with the same consideration with which we treat the textual audience in our investigations. While we assume that readers come with some capacity to understand and interpret texts, we tend to approach listeners as passive, non-artistic receivers of an object that they cannot really apprehend. We seek out the reader's understanding of texts, yet we tend to look to the musical composition for interpretation of music. If we who examine the connection between music and the moral life ever hope to work as fruitfully with music as we do with texts, we certainly need to begin to attend more fully to listeners and their listening practices.

Admittedly, attending to listeners and their practices is a challenge. As dealing with the composition alone is a complex task, we might wonder what additional questions we must ask in order to achieve the depth of investigation that I am suggesting. Of that, I must confess, I am less certain. At the very least, we need to take seriously the idea that listeners may be informed and inspired by music in ways that differ greatly from what composers might like them to be or what scholars might expect them to be. In explicative work, we must begin by recognizing the range of interpretive variations that are possible for the material under study and account for the ways in which these variations will affect the moral aspects of the music. Additionally, given the high level of cross-musical-cultural engagement that people currently have, we must consider the connection of the listener to the order-making culture that gave birth to the musical work. Is there a shared musical culture between composition and listener, what we could call a consonance with musical sense-making structure? Is there a shared symbolic culture, both in terms of texts and musical symbols, between composition and listener: a consonance with meaning-making structure? Is there a shared emotional culture between composition and listener: a consonance with structures of expression? Differences between composer and audience in matters of musical sense-making will change the way forms and expressions are perceived by audiences, and hence change the subsequent moral information and inspiration.

In addition to investigating the musical cultures of listeners, scholars also need to attend to the connections between actual listeners and the listening practices of the culture that gave birth to the musical work. Every piece of music has a use for which it was originally intended and has implicative relationships built into it. Is there a consonance between intended listening practice and actual listening practice? When this consonance exists, some of the "natural" aspects of musical practice will still hold sway. But, when there are differences, then significant work needs to be done to discern the way in which these practices both form behavior and alter the nature of the music itself.

What if scholars were to include listeners and their practices in work on the moral power of music? How would it change? Would we come to conclusions that differ from those we come to when focusing only on composition? That remains to be seen. But doing so can only lead us to a fuller and potentially more accurate understanding of the way in which music affects the moral life. And as the media expand their role as arbiters of moral wisdom in our society, we may find that understanding the power of music in moral life will be crucial to the task of creating a peaceful and more just world in the twenty-first century.

Notes

[1]For excerpted texts from a variety of theologians and church leaders throughout the history of Christianity on the subject of theology, ethics, and music (of the generally sacred variety), see David W. Music, *Hymnology: A Collection of Source Readings*, Studies in Liturgical Musicology, vol. 4 (Lanham, MD: Scarecrow Press, 1996).

[2]For the purposes of both simplicity and consistency with general usage, the term "music" in this essay refers to both music alone and music wedded to text, which people often refer to as "song."

[3]Some examples of this approach to the moral effectiveness of music include Linda Clark, "Toward a New Working Philosophy of Music in Worship," *Reformed Liturgy and Music* 17 (Summer 1983): 110, who draws heavily on the concept of presentational symbolic forms of Susanne K. Langer, *Philosophy in a New Key: Study in the Symbolism of Reason, Rite, and Art*, 3rd ed. (Cambridge: Harvard University Press, 1942); Max L. Stackhouse, "Ethical Vision and Musical Imagination," *Theological Education* 31, no. 1 (1994): 157-58; Jon Michael Spencer, "A Petition for a Visionary Black Hymnody," in *Sacred Sound and Social Change: Liturgical Music in Jewish and Christian Experience*, ed. Lawrence A. Hoffman and Janet R. Walton, Two Liturgical Traditions, vol. 2 (Notre Dame: University of Notre Dame Press, 1992), 307, 311; E. Byron Anderson, " 'O for a Heart to Praise My God': Hymning the Self before God," in *Liturgy and the Moral Self*, ed. E. Byron Anderson and Bruce T. Morrill (Collegeville, MN: Liturgical Press, 1998), 117, 124; and Ray Repp, "A Modest Proposal to Composers of Liturgical Music," *Spirituality Today* 40 (Fall 1988): 266; even going as far back as John Newton, *The Natural, Moral, and Divine Influences of Musick* (London: E. Cave, 1748).

[4]Given the popularity of such studies in classrooms, conferences, and the literature, we shall prescind from the question of whether or not analysis of lyrics alone would really qualify as the study of "music." Examples of lyric-focused studies of the instructional power of music include Andrew Greeley, "The Catholic Imagination of Bruce Springsteen," *America*, February 6, 1988, 110-15, and "Like a Catholic: Madonna's Challenge to Her Church," *America*, May 13, 1989, 447-49; the music sections of David Dark, *Everyday Apocalypse: The Sacred Revealed in Radiohead, The Simpsons, and Other Pop Culture Icons* (Grand Rapids: Brazos Press, 2002), 63-113; Jay R. Howard, "Contemporary Christian Music: Where Rock Meets Religion," *Journal of Popular Culture* 26, no. 1 (Summer 1992): 123-30; Cheryl Renée Gooch, "Rappin' for the Lord: The Uses of Gospel Rap and Contemporary Black Religious Communities," in *Religion and Mass Media,* ed. Daniel A. Stout and Judith M. Buddenbaum (Thousand Oaks, CA: Sage Publications, 1996), 228-44; Arthur C. Jones, *Wade in the Water: The Wisdom of the*

Spirituals (Maryknoll, NY: Orbis Books, 1993), who includes several performative tableaus, but never really engages in musical analysis; Jon Michael Spencer, *Blues and Evil* (Knoxville: University of Tennessee Press, 1993); as well as a host of articles published in the journal Spencer edited, *Black Sacred Music*, including Earlston E. DeSilva, "The Theology of Black Power and Black Song: James Brown," *Black Sacred Music* 3, no. 2 (Fall 1989): 57-67; Harold Dean Trulear, "The Prophetic Character of Black Secular Music: Stevie Wonder," *Black Sacred Music* 3, no. 2 (Fall 1989): 75-84; Thomas Poole, "Tracy Chapman: *Jedermann,* Prophet, or Cultural Narrator?," *Black Sacred Music* 6, no. 1 (Spring 1992): 253-64; and Mark D. Hulsether, "Jesus and Madonna: North American Liberation Theologies and Secular Popular Music," *Black Sacred Music* 8, no. 1 (Spring 1994): 239-53.

⁵For example, Stephen King and Richard J. Jensen, "Bob Marley's 'Redemption Song': The Rhetoric of Reggae and Rastafari," *Journal of Popular Culture* 29 (Winter 1995): 17-36; and Jon Michael Spencer, *Protest and Praise: Sacred Music of Black Religion* (Minneapolis: Fortress Press, 1990), both of which include music, but rely largely on lyrical analysis.

⁶On the import of style, see, for instance, Michael Eric Dyson, "Rap, Race, and Reality: Run-D.M.C." *Black Sacred Music* 3, no. 2 (Fall 1989): 142-45, and "Rap Culture, the Church and American Society," *Black Sacred Music* 6, no. 1 (Spring 1992): 268-73. On the relation of the musical form of the chorale (hymn) form to social structure, see Frank C. Quinn, "Liturgical Music as Corporate Song 2: Problems of Hymnody in Catholic Worship," in *Liturgy and Music: Lifetime Learning,* ed. Robin A. Leaver and Joyce Ann Zimmerman (Collegeville, MN: Liturgical Press, 1998), 318-20; and Edward Foley, "Musical Forms, Referential Meaning, and Belief," in *Ritual Music: Studies in Liturgical Musicology* (Beltsville, MD: Pastoral Press, 1995), 165f. On the relation of the musical responsory (call and response) form to social structure, see Joseph Gelineau, *Voices and Instruments in Christian Worship: Principles, Laws, Applications,* trans. Clifford Howell (Collegeville, MN: Liturgical Press, 1964), 94; and Jon Michael Spencer, *Protest and Praise,* 233-35.

⁷For instance, the notion "transformative taste" in Frank Burch Brown, *Good Taste, Bad Taste, and Christian Taste* (Oxford: Oxford University Press, 2000) or the observations on the relationship of time to divinity and human action throughout Jeremy Begbie, *Music, Theology, and Time,* Cambridge Studies in Christian Doctrine (Cambridge: Cambridge University Press, 2000).

⁸Pope John Paul II, "Address to the International Youth Orchestra," *Osservatore Romano* 37 (1989), 7; cited in Basil Cole, *Music and Morals: A Theological Appraisal of the Moral and Psychological Effects of Music* (New York: Alba House, 1993), 98. This approach was particularly prevalent in work on music and morals in the late nineteenth and early twentieth centuries, when the Romantic faith in the limitless power of art to evoke emotions had not yet been countered by the cynicism of modernism. See, for instance, H. R. Haweis, *Music and Morals* (New York: Longmans, Green and Co., 1881, 1900), 11-14; William Wingfield Longford, *Music and Religion: A Survey,*

The Waverly Music Lovers' Library, ed. A. Eaglefield Hull (London: K. Paul, Trench, Trubner & Company, 1916), 149-52; and Russell Henry Stafford, "The Meaning of Music," in *Music and Religion*, ed. Stanley Armstrong Hunter (New York: Abingdon Press, 1930; reprint, New York: AMS Press Inc., 1973), 35.

⁹Clement of Alexandria, Tertullian, Basil, John Chrysostom, and Ambrose are among the early church's noteworthy opponents to instruments and instrumental music. See Paul Westermeyer, *Te Deum: The Church and Music* (Minneapolis: Fortress Press, 1998), 66-72, 83, and 119f.

¹⁰Don Saliers, *The Soul in Paraphrase* (New York: Seabury Press, 1980), 7. On the distinction of affections from temporary states (for example, emotions, feelings, and moods), see Don Saliers, "The Integrity of Sung Prayer," *Worship* 55, no. 4 (July 1981): 293.

¹¹Don Saliers, "Sound Spirituality: On the Formative Expressive Power of Music for Christian Spirituality," *Christian Spirituality Bulletin* 8, no. 1 (Spring/Summer 2000): 3. On the particular affections developed through community prayer, see Saliers, *The Soul in Paraphrase*, 11; Saliers's classic article "Liturgy and Ethics: Some New Beginnings," *Journal of Religious Ethics* 7 (1979): 177-79, and Don Saliers, "Liturgy Teaching Us to Pray: Christian Liturgy and Grateful Lives of Prayer," in *Liturgy and Spirituality in Context: Perspectives on Prayer and Culture*, ed. Eleanor Bernstein (Collegeville, MN: Liturgical Press, 1990), 62-82.

¹²Others would include Scott Pilarz, "Music and Mediation: Anamnesis and Catechesis," *The Living Light* 36, no. 2 (Winter 1999): 6-12; and William C. Spohn, *Go and Do Likewise: Jesus and Ethics* (New York: Continuum, 1999), 122f. Spohn draws particular attention to the psalms, referring to the psalter as "a primer of the Christian affections." Notably, Saliers, Pilarz, and Spohn are hesitant to cede complete power over the affections to music, preferring that the affections be normed by other things (such as scripture, the life of Jesus, community, memory, bodily experience). See, for instance, Pilarz, "Music and Mediation," 9-10; Saliers, "Liturgy and Ethics," 187, and "Sound Spirituality," 4; and claims of normative content throughout Spohn, *Go and Do Likewise*.

¹³On sacrament, see Albert L. Blackwell, *The Sacred in Music* (Louisville: Westminster John Knox Press, 1999), and Miriam Therese Winter, "Catholic Prophetic Sound after Vatican II," 169-71. On transformation, see Mary E. McGann, "Interpreting the Ritual Role of Music in Christian Liturgical Practice" (Ph.D. Dissertation, Graduate Theological Union, 1996). On conversion, see Tom Conry, "Calling the Question: Toward a Revisionist Theology of Liturgical Music and Text," *Pastoral Music* 15 (April/May 1981): 28. On theophany, see Anne Margaret Murphy, "Music, Meaning and Mystery: Towards a Theophany of Music," in *Religion and Culture in Dialogue*, ed. Dermot A. Lane (Blackrock: Columba, 1993). On anamnesis, see Robin A. Leaver, "Liturgical Music as Anamnesis," in *Liturgy and Music: Lifetime Learning*, ed. Robin A. Leaver and Joyce Ann Zimmerman (Collegeville, MN: Liturgical Press, 1998), 395-410.

[14]While most scholars lean heavily toward either the instructional or inspirational approach, several scholars combine these approaches. Most notable among these are Judith Marie Kubicki, "The Formative Power of Hymns, Psalms, and Liturgical Songs," *The Living Light* 36, no. 2 (Winter 1999): 36-43; *Liturgical Music as Ritual Symbol*, Liturgia Condenda, vol. 9 (Leuven: Peeters, 1999); "The Role of Music as Ritual Symbol in Roman Catholic Liturgy," *Worship* 69 (September 1995): 427-46; "Using J. L. Austin's Performative Language Theory to Interpret Ritual Music Making," *Worship* 73, no. 4 (September 1999): 310-30. Notable, as well, is Paul Westermeyer, *Let Justice Sing: Hymnody and Justice*, American Essays in Liturgy, ed. Edward Foley (Collegeville, MN: Liturgical Press, 1998).

[15]Westermeyer, *Let Justice Sing.*

[16]Ibid., 81-85.

[17]See the brief description of imagined audience in Jones, *Wade in the Water*, 100, or the recognition of the multiplicity of music's purposes in Begbie, *Theology, Music, and Time*, 16.

[18]See the excellent work by Richard Viladesau on the role of the person in the creation of knowledge in the artistic experience in *Theological Aesthetics: God in Imagination, Beauty, and Art* (Oxford: Oxford University Press, 1999), 73-102. Like other works, however, this text deals more with the visual and literary arts than music and more with knowledge and truth in general than the moral life in particular.

[19]This situation is not unique to theological study of music. Charles Keil took up an ethnomusicological approach after rejecting the compositional focus in his mentor Leonard Meyer's ground-breaking work in musical aesthetics, *Emotion and Meaning in Music* (Chicago: University of Chicago Press, 1965). See Charles Keil, "Motion and Feeling through Music," *Journal of Aesthetics and Art Criticism* 24, no. 3 (1966): 337-39. Even the recent social-scientific study by Jane Brown et al., entitled "Sexy Media Matter: Exposure to Sexual Content in Music, Movies, Television, and Magazines Predicts Black and White Adolescents' Sexual Behavior," *Pediatrics* 117, no. 4 (April 2006), 1018, leaves out the issue of differences in listeners and listening practices. The authors suggest that "exposure to sexual content in music, movies, television, and magazines accelerates white adolescents' sexual activity," but not that of black teens. White teens, they found, are formed by the messages they receive from music, while black teens are formed by the messages from their parents and peers. While their research methods are different, their focus is the same: the symbolic content of the works of art. The way in which adolescents' listening practices might factor into the observed differences was a question left unconsidered, and hence unanswered.

[20]On the effects of social structures on musical practices and attitudes, and the idea of the role of division of labor in particular, see John Blacking, *How Musical Is Man?* (Seattle: University of Washington Press, 1973), 100-103, 54-88.

[21]John Blacking, "Towards a Theory of Musical Competence," in *Man:*

Anthropological Essays Presented to O. F. Raum (Cape Town: C. Struik, 1971), 22.

[22]This belief that listening is not a musical activity can be heard in the common remark, "I'm not musical. I just play the radio."

[23]See, for instance, John Blacking, *Venda Children's Songs* (Johannesburg: Witwatersrand University Press, 1967), 191, and throughout Blacking, *How Musical Is Man?*

[24]Blacking, "Towards a Theory of Musical Competence," 25.

[25]John Blacking, "The Body as the Source of Cosmological Exploration and Personal Experimentation in Venda Tradition," in *Concepts of the Body/Self in Africa*, ed. Joan Maw and John Picton, World Anthropology (Vienna: Afro-Pub, 1992), 3.

[26]On music as organized sound, see Blacking, *How Musical Is Man?*, 3-31; and Victor Zuckerkandl, *Sound and Symbol*, vol. 2, *Man the Musician*, trans. Norbert Guterman (Princeton: Princeton University Press, 1973), 31. Readers might very well notice the inclusion of enjoyment as simply one of many valid uses of music. This approach contrasts the view that aesthetic pleasure is the sole valid purpose of music. After holding sway for centuries, the aesthetic view seems now to be on the decline. Nicholas Wolterstorff's groundbreaking work to establish that, despite the dominance of the Romantic assertion of art for art's sake, aesthetic contemplation is one of the many possible uses of the visual arts influenced a similar recognition within music. See Nicholas Wolterstorff, "Philosophy of Art after Analysis and Romanticism," in *Analytic Aesthetics*, ed. Richard Shusterman (Oxford: Blackwell, 1989), 32-56; and his application of this theory to music in "The Work of Making a Work of Music," in *What Is Music? An Introduction to the Philosophy of Music*, ed. P. J. Alperson (University Park: Pennsylvania State University Press, 1987), 103-29.

[27]Zuckerkandl, *Man the Musician*, 89.

[28]The categories used here are based on those of Zuckerkandl, *Man the Musician*, 97-216, and enhanced and expanded by the categories of Blacking, "Towards a Theory of Musical Competence," 19-34; and Charles Keil, "Motion and Feeling through Music," *Journal of Aesthetics and Art Criticism* 24, no. 3 (1966): 337f. Those who are familiar with Western music theory or notation might wonder why the term "tone" is used instead of "note." The idea of "note" as a useful term to refer to sound events derives from the Western use of visual notation called "notes" to represent pitch and duration information in a written musical score. But unlike tone, the concept "note" allows only for the characteristics of pitch and duration. While loudness and timbre are experienced as part of the sound of the note played, they are properly understood as characteristics not of the note but of the score of the broader musical composition. Thus, because it unifies the key elements of the sound as it is heard and experienced, tone is a more helpful term in the present discussion.

[29]Zuckerkandl, *Man the Musician*, 89.

³⁰Victor Zuckerkandl, *Sound and Symbol*, vol. 1, *Music and the External World*, trans. Williard R. Trask (New York: Pantheon Books, 1956), 15.

³¹Blacking, *How Musical Is Man?*, 11. It should be stressed at this point that use of the category of sonic order does not mean a *universal* sonic order. While many have argued over the years that there is a single, universal "right" sonic order (which has often corresponded with the contemporary standards of Western music), ethnomusicologists reject this idea. Sonic order is more a feature of cultural standards and training than the inherent characteristics of sound. See also Blacking, "Towards a Theory of Musical Competence," 20.

³²Blacking, *How Musical Is Man?*, 43.

³³Musicologist Christopher Small goes so far as to suggest that we should subsume the acts of composing, playing, and listening under the larger category of "musicking," which would be used as a top-level category to refer to all human activity relating to music (Christopher Small, *Musicking: The Meanings of Performing and Listening* [Middletown, CT: Wesleyan University Press, 1998]).

³⁴Blacking, "Towards a Theory of Musical Competence," 21. This is not to say that all people have musical ability in equal measure. Blacking is careful to distinguish "musical competence," which is the universal, fundamental set of human capacities for musical understanding and creation, from "musical ability," which is a "qualitative estimation of a person's realized musical competence." Distinct from both musical competence and musical ability is the recognition of these characteristics. See Blacking, *How Musical Is Man?*, 10-11, and John Blacking, "The Study of Man as Music-Maker," in *Music, Culture, and Experience*, ed. Reginald Byron (Chicago: University of Chicago Press, 1995), 3-7.

³⁵Blacking, "The Study of Man as Music-Maker," 5.

³⁶Zuckerkandl, *Man the Musician*, 83.

³⁷M. H. Abrams, *The Mirror and the Lamp* (New York: Oxford University Press, 1953), 25f.

³⁸In contrast, music theorist Malcolm Budd recognizes the role of the listener in the inspirational power of music, but he stipulates the only people who should be considered listeners are those whose attentions are fully occupied with listening. He argues that those who are dancing, for instance, are not really listening to the music, and are thus unable to have an aesthetic experience (Malcolm Budd, *Music and the Emotions: The Philosophical Theories*, International Library of Philosophy, ed. Ted Honderich [London: Routledge & Kegan Paul, 1985], 16).

³⁹On practice, see Alasdair MacIntyre's classic treatment in *After Virtue* (Notre Dame: University of Notre Dame Press, 1981). See also the helpful work by Craig Dykstra and Dorothy C. Bass to transform practice into a more usable model by explicitly placing it within a theological framework and rejecting the totalizing aspects of its self-norming characteristics (Alasdair MacIntyre, "A Theological Understanding of Christian Practices," in *Practicing Theology: Beliefs and Practices in Christian Life*, ed. Miroslav Volf and Dorothy C. Bass [Grand Rapids: Eerdmans, 2002], 21, n. 8).

[40]Charles Keil, "The Theory of Participatory Discrepancies: A Progress Report," *Ethnomusicology* 39, no. 1 (Winter 1995): 3.

[41]Aquinas, *Treatise on the Virtues*, II-I, q. 52, a. 3, who references Aristotle, *Nicomachean Ethics*, 1103b. See also *The Treatise on the Virtues*, II-I, q. 51, a. 2; q. 63, a. 2.

[42]Steven Feld, "Aesthetics as Iconicity of Style (Uptown Title); or, (Downtown Title) 'Lift-Up-Over Sounding': Getting into the Kaluli Groove," in *Music Grooves: Essays and Dialogues*, ed. Charles Keil and Steven Feld (Chicago: University of Chicago Press, 1994), 110-31.

[43]Ibid., 111f. A similar approach to the relationship between song, form, and participation can be seen in theological approaches to musical settings of the eucharistic prayers in Edward Foley and Mary McGann, *Music and the Eucharistic Prayer*, American Essays in Liturgy, ed. Edward Foley (Washington, DC: Pastoral Press, 1988), 31ff; and the psalms in Tom Conry, "Calling the Question: Toward a Revisionist Theology of Liturgical Music and Text," *Pastoral Music* 15 (April/May 1981): 29.

[44]Blacking, "The Study of Man as Music Maker," 11.

[45]Ibid., 3.

[46]Solidarity is not being used here in the technical sense within moral theology. Rather, it is the general idea of interconnectedness grounded in social practices that reinforce and institutionalize those bonds, thus transforming a "social group" into a "community" (John Blacking, *Venda Children's Songs*, 30-33; "The Body as the Source in Venda Tradition," 88; and "Towards an Anthropology of the Body," in *The Anthropology of the Body*, ed. John Blacking [New York: Academic Press, 1977], 8).

[47]See, for instance, the discussion of *domba* in Blacking, "The Body as the Source of Cosmological Exploration and Personal Experimentation in Venda Tradition," 91-3, and *How Musical Is Man?*, 78-89.

[48]See, for instance, the discussion of appropriate behavior in Blacking, *How Musical Is Man?*, 42.

[49]Keil, "The Theory of Participatory Discrepancies," 12. Keil thinks of musical skill in terms of Michael Polanyi's concept of "tacit knowledge" in *Personal Knowledge* (Chicago: University of Chicago Press, 1962). In the theological world, the same kinds of claims are made by Kubicki in "The Formative Power of Hymns," 40f.

[50]Keil, "The Theory of Participatory Discrepancies," 10.

[51]John Blacking, "Political and Musical Freedom in the Music of Some Black South African Churches," in *The Structure of Folk Models*, ed. Ladislav Holy and Milan Stuchlik (London: Academic Press, 1981), 37.

[52]Keil, "The Theory of Participatory Discrepancies," 2.

[53]Abrams, *The Mirror and the Lamp*, 6-29.

John Dunne's Words: "Explore the Realm of Music"

William J. Collinge

In the early 1990s, when he was already more than sixty years old and the author of nine books, theologian John S. Dunne had a dream. In the dream he heard the words, "Explore the realm of music!"[1] At first he took them to mean that he should explore the realm of feeling, as he had already been doing at least since his fourth book, *The Reasons of the Heart*,[2] but later he began to take them literally.[3]

As a child, Dunne had learned to play the piano, first from his mother, then in school. In his teens he began to compose dances and songs on the piano. Also in his teens he learned to play jazz clarinet, becoming proficient enough to perform on a radio station in his home town of Waco.[4] As a college seminarian at Notre Dame, he composed a Mass and studied with the blind piano master Carl Mathes, but at around the age of twenty, he came to a turning point. While struggling with a mathematics course, he "decided fatefully that I had no time for music."[5]

Dunne chose "the way of words," taking a doctorate in theology at the Gregorian University under Bernard Lonergan and embarking on a writing career that by now, in his seventy-seventh year, has yielded sixteen books. Dunne was captivated by the worldview of Thomas Aquinas's *Summa Theologiae*, with its great Neoplatonic picture of all creation going out from God and then returning to God through Christ. He read the *Summa* over and over, but eventually became dissatisfied with its reliance on Aristotelian physics, so he conceived the idea of doing for Aquinas something like what Aquinas had done for Aristotle, that is, to rethink Aquinas's worldview in the context of Einsteinian physics, with its standpoint of the moving observer. I suppose, though I don't recall Dunne ever saying so, that Lonergan's idea that modern thought shifted from a static, classical mentality to a historically conscious mentality played some role in the development of Dunne's thought. He did not stay with physics for long,[6] but the moving standpoint became integral to his work.

The central idea in Dunne's first four books[7] is "passing over and coming back": one takes stock of one's starting point, then passes over in sympathetic understanding to the standpoint of another life or culture or religion, returning to one's own standpoint with new insight. Such a process is a potentially endless intellectual journey, and the journey became his overarching metaphor, as is apparent in the title of his memoir, *A Journey with God in Time*. Tolkien's *The Lord of the Rings*, the great journey epic of the twentieth century, began to replace the *Summa* as Dunne's basic intellectual template.[8] Dunne keeps the great Thomistic scheme of *exitus* and *reditus*, of the human creature going out from God and returning to God, but now he construes the *reditus* as a journey or a quest.

In his next five books, from 1978 to 1991, Dunne's travels, chiefly to the Middle East and South America, not just his journeys in reading, begin to provide the focus. *The Reasons of the Heart* does not speak of Dunne's travels, but two journeys to the Holy Land influence it. *The Church of the Poor Devil*[9] meditates on journeys to Manaus, Brazil; this is the first book to make mention of Tolkien. *The House of Wisdom*[10] speaks especially of Hagia Sophia (in Turkish, *Ayasofya*) in Istanbul, while *The Homing Spirit*[11] is shaped around three journeys to Jerusalem. *The Peace of the Present*[12] begins from reflection on three journeys to Chile and to Machu Picchu in Peru.

There is a sense in which the music never left the books. They have always followed a process that can be likened to musical development. More or less as in sonata form, each book begins with an introductory statement that announces the main themes, continues through chapters that consider the main themes from different points of view or in different combinations, and concludes with a chapter that recapitulates the themes, joining them in a unified narrative. Dunne tends to proceed by way of meditation on favorite quotations, and the quotations recur again and again, like musical motifs, within individual books and from one book to another. More recent works, except for the memoir, tend toward "minimalism," as in minimalist music, which features repetition of a limited number of motifs or other units with a smaller range of variation.

But after his dream, "Music somehow replaced travel in my life,"[13] and the music became explicit in the books. Dunne began to pass over, not to others' thoughts or to other places, but to another side of himself. Each of his seven books since *Love's Mind*[14] concludes in one or more song cycles. Usually only the words are printed, but most of the books also contain a small amount of musical notation, and several include discussions of his process of composition. Dunne's inspiration and model for his song cycles is *The Road Goes Ever On*, which he always describes as Tolkien's song cycle, but which is in fact a series of Tolkien's poems from various occasions, set to music by Donald Swann.[15] Other influences on Dunne's music to which he makes significant reference are Gregorian Chant, Mozart, Olivier Messiaen, and the American minimalist composer, John Adams. Dunne has supervised many performances of his own song cycles, usually with himself at the piano and one or more Notre Dame students singing; often there are student dancers as well, to whom he leaves the choreography. None of these has been recorded commercially.

The following sections focus on *what Dunne says* about music, concentrating on *The Music of Time* and *The Road of the Heart's Desire*. Analysis of Dunne's music as music is beyond the scope of this paper, though I am hoping that some reader with training in music theory will take up the task.

Music as State of Being and as Symbolic Form

Dunne's first two books after the return of the music were *Love's Mind* (1993) and *The Music of Time* (1995). In both he meditates on a distinction he draws from Charles O. Hartman's *Jazz Text* between "music as a state of being" and "music as symbolic form."[16] The distinction reflects Dunne's own experience of improvising in jazz and composing in a more formal, classical manner. Any instance of music can be looked at from either perspective, but some lend themselves more to one than to the other. Hartman's example of music as a state of being is the musical festivals of various African peoples, which go on for hours or days, lacking a clear beginning, middle, and end, with individual musicians entering and leaving as they please. "Music as symbolic form" is a phrase that Hartman takes from Susanne K. Langer.[17] Here one is to think of a musical "piece," *composed* of melodies and harmonies, made up of tones, chords, beats, and similar elements.

As a state of being, music can express all of the attitudes we can take on our journey through life toward death. In *The Music of Time*, Dunne surveys the genres of popular music, arranging jazz, blues, soul, country, rock, and metal on a spectrum.[18] At the rock and metal end of the spectrum, music often expresses what Rimbaud called the "systematic derangement of the senses," in "its ecstasy, its approach to madness, its yearning towards death, its rapture of the senses."[19] In the middle, country music expresses willingness to walk alone on the journey and the hope for companionship, human and divine. In jazz, Dunne finds popular music that comes closest to the other end of the spectrum, which he designates by a phrase from seventeenth-century philosopher Malebranche, "Attention is the natural prayer of the soul,"[20] a "waiting upon God" as God is found in "things happening, . . . signs, . . . the heart speaking, . . . the way opening."[21] Dunne sees jazz as an invitation to join the timeless festival of life.[22] And yet he experiences a reluctance to let go of autonomy, a fear that joining in music as a state of being will result in the disintegration that he finds expressed in a favorite quotation from Stephen Leacock, "Lord Ronald flung himself upon his horse and rode madly off in all directions."[23]

Autonomy has been the great ideal, and to some extent the achievement, of modern culture, and Dunne does not repudiate it.[24] But with modern autonomy comes an intensified feeling of loneliness. "Symbolic form," Dunne says, "as we know it in classical music, was emerging at the same time as the idea of human autonomy. Mozart was celebrating human autonomy in music at about the same time Kant was formulating the autonomy of reason and of conscience in philosophy."[25] But while Kant's ethics seems to leave no room for grace, in Mozart's symbolic form, Dunne says, following Ivan Nagel, mercy exists alongside autonomy.[26] In Kantian autonomy, we choose one path in life. Similarly, in classical composition, one chooses one's way, and "there is a sense of imposing form, like autonomous reason imposing form upon experience."[27] But mercy appears too in the "element of inspiration in the creative process."[28] Composers, at least many of them, feel they are receiving as well as creating, discovering as well as inventing. "The kindling of my heart and the illumining of my mind [in composition] is my experience of grace, my experience of mercy."[29]

We seem to be in the presence of a larger and deeper life than that of the lonely, autonomous self, resolutely living its "Being toward death." Music, Dunne thinks, can express more of that deeper life than words can. Echoing Michael Polanyi's maxim that "We can know more than we can tell," Dunne holds that "Music can express what we can know and cannot tell of the mystery of life and death."[30] In particular—contradicting Wittgenstein's claim that "Death is not lived through"[31]—"we can know death is lived through, I believe, in a way we cannot tell in words alone but only in words and music."[32] "The point of music as symbolic form," Dunne speculates, is "to embody the symbols such as eternal life that answer to the primal questions of our state of being such as loneliness and death."[33]

How can music give expression to a life that lives beyond death? Dunne gives several examples. Mozart's *Requiem* reveals death as a boundless "opening into infinity,"[34] but his *Ave Verum* shows it as "soothing and consoling."[35] "In Mozart's motet," as compared with the earlier *Ave Verum* by William Byrd, "the rich changing harmony becomes more purposive and more melodic and conveys a sense of movement in time, of life's movement toward death, and of the mystery of passage through death to life."[36] Dunne pays special attention to Olivier Messiaen, who wrote about ways to express the eternal in music. These, Dunne says, consist mainly in "rhythms that cannot be reversed without changing back into themselves, modes that cannot be transposed more than a few times without changing back into themselves."[37] The melody, however, moves forward without reversal, giving a sense not of "pure eternity" but of "time full of eternity."[38] The words of such examples cannot themselves convey the undying or even demonstrate that the music can do so; at best they can point out where to listen and what to listen for.

Meeting Himself at the Crossroads

When Delta bluesman Robert Johnson went to the crossroads, he met the Devil. Dunne meets himself there. "Alone" before death "on the way of music as a state of being, all one" because the loneliness of death is resolved in peace; "on the way of music as symbolic form, I meet myself at the crossroads."[39] Dunne uses similar imagery to depict the joining of words and music. Influenced by Carl Jung's idea of individuation, Dunne has long supposed that there is a wholeness in one's life that seeks expression in one's words and deeds.[40] "Everything that belongs to an individual's life," he quotes Jung, "shall enter into it."[41] One must walk a single path, making choices that exclude others. But when, as in the Robert Frost poem that Dunne is fond of quoting, two roads diverge, one must take one of them, even though the fact that one is *"sorry* I could not travel both and be one traveler" indicates that the other road appeals to something in one's deeper life.

But is there any guarantee that one's life will somehow come together as a whole comprising the road not taken as well as the road taken? Couldn't Sartre be right that my life is simply the story of what I have done, that Eva Cassidy's life was not cut short, that the songs she had in her were all and only the ones she sang?[42] Yes, if my life is nothing but my time. No, if there is an "eternal consciousness" in us.[43] Music, as we have seen, gives expression to the eternal in us, as also do love and understanding.[44] "But if we do recognize the eternal in us, showing itself in things like music and love and understanding, then we can say there is a guiding principle in our lives, and everything that belongs to our lives will enter into them, and this is the process of individuation, of becoming whole."[45] Identifying this guiding principle with the God of Jesus Christ, Dunne sees individuation as "a process of becoming who I am in terms of God-with-us. It is a journey with God in time."[46]

If the guiding principle is indeed God, then all the roads are one, the road I take, the road I haven't taken, and also the roads that you have taken or forsaken. Dunne often quotes Tolkien's song "The Road Goes Ever On," seeing the road as the individual life, which "goes ever on and on . . . until it joins some larger way, where many paths and errands meet."[47] Dunne encapsulates the experience of God's presence on this road in four sentences that he draws but does not quote from Tolkien, "Things are meant. There are signs. The heart speaks. There is a way."[48] The signs of God are precisely the breakthroughs of eternity into the time of the journey, the insights into eternity that enable us to recognize time as "a changing image of eternity."[49]

> What is the eternal in music? . . . It is the element of inspiration. What inspiration is, I believe, is insight into the changing image that time is. In some music, for instance Stravinsky's *Rite of Spring*, time is opaque; in some, for instance a

nocturne of Chopin, it is translucent; and in some, for instance Messiaen's *Quartet for the End of Time*, it is transparent to eternity. There can be inspiration, nevertheless, there can be insight into the changing image that time is, whether time is opaque or translucent or transparent. In opaque time eternity is concealed; in translucent or transparent time it is revealed.[50]

Pianist and critic Charles Rosen has spoken of the period from the Middle Ages to the late eighteenth century as characterized by "the gradual emancipation of music from words."[51] Dunne aligns himself with what he sees as a reverse process that began subsequently. If words reach out to music in order to express the eternity that "we know and cannot tell," music also reaches out to words. Dunne sees this occurring in Beethoven, when the last string quartet culminates in the words, "*Muss es sein? Es muss sein! Es muss sein,*" and the last symphony culminates in the "Ode to Joy." "If words are the missing element in music, as Lévi-Strauss says, then music wants to find words, and when it does, it seems, it turns to joy."[52] The process continued in the twentieth century: "At the beginning of the century, with the coming of atonal music, the larger forms of sonata and symphony based on tonal relations became unworkable and there was a return to the simple forms of song and dance."[53] When the music that expresses eternity rejoins words, the result is "mystical songs," revealing time as a changing image of eternity[54] and expressing "the joy of being on an adventure with God in time."[55]

As long as we are still wistfully feeling the pull of the road not taken, we cannot love God with all our heart and soul and might, as the gospel demands (Mk 12:30). But when the road of words has rejoined the road of music, and we walk in joy, such love becomes possible. "Conceiving the love of God as joy at the thought of God, as I am learning from Spinoza, I see heart and soul and might caught up in this joy, for me joy at the thought of being on a journey with God in time."[56]

Adding dance to the words and the music intensifies the sense of wholeness. Thinking of David "dancing before the Lord with all his might," Dunne says, "I imagine dancers interpreting my song as it is being sung by the singers."[57] Dunne has always left the dancing and the choreography to others, but he sees "something essential" in the dance. Dance, in particular, enables the song to express the love of God with all one's might. "To turn the truth of a life into the poetry of prayer is to love 'with all your heart;' to set the words to music is to love 'with all your soul;' and to turn the song into dance is to love 'with all your might.' "[58] The leap of faith, as Kierkegaard first conceived it, is really a dancer's leap; joining the dance, we commit ourselves to the journey, in full willingness to walk alone, even to die, yet in faith that God is with us and in hope of eternal life.[59]

The Cycle of Story and Song

The return of music in Dunne's life both images and is a part of the larger story of humanity, as told in its stories and songs. A version of the story that Dunne thinks is plausible divides human history into four stages. First, there was a primordial time of unity, when humans felt at one with God and with other creatures. Second came the emergence of the human species, its awareness of its distinctness from all other species, its awareness of its mortality, and its desire to overcome that mortality. Third, in modernity came the separation of the individual, conscious of his or her aloneness in the face of death and experiencing a profound loneliness. Finally, there comes a reunion with God and other humans and other species, but one in which the consciousness of the distinctness of humanity and of each human individual is not lost.[60]

In the first stage, according to the eighteenth-century philosopher Giambattista Vico, human language was in song. Dunne imagines it to be like the speech of Tolkien's Tom Bombadil, "an ancient language whose words were mainly those of wonder and delight."[61] Dunne's own writing belongs to the third stage, as he begins from the modern sense of aloneness before death and expresses his own personal loneliness as an instance of that modern loneliness. Some of his music expresses loneliness too. Starting with the words of an African love song, "I walk alone," he composes a song of "spiritual loneliness."[62] "I take it," he says, "that 'spiritual loneliness,' . . . comes of the historic emergence and separation of the individual, something that has not yet appeared in traditional folksong, though it is very much in evidence in modern folk music."[63] But the rejoining of words and music reaches back to the original unity and anticipates the final unity. "Words and music are one, I expect, in [the] wholeness at the end and in the beginning."[64] If we give expression to our loneliness in song, and recognize in it our deepest heart's desire, we not only hark back to the original unity and anticipate the final unity, but find something of the unity along the way:

> What leads from madrigals [secular love songs] to motets [sacred songs] is the theme of loneliness, if we let loneliness take us to God. And if I do consciously and willingly let my loneliness take me to God, it takes me there right away, so that God is not just the end of my journey but my companion on the way.[65]

Understood this way, both the individual's journey and the story of humankind reflect the "great circle of love." This is the form that Dunne came to give to the Thomistic vision of *exitus* and *reditus*—the emergence of the creature from God and the return of the creature to God. He describes it in words which a desert Bedouin once spoke to T. E. Lawrence, "The love is from God and of God and towards God."[66]

> It is the great circle of love . . . , *The love is from God and of God and towards God*, that is embodied and expressed in the great circle of story and song. . . . Love's direction then is towards reunion, for the great circle is from God and towards God, and at the point of greatest distance from God, the point of greatest loneliness, where we are now in time, it turns out that God is with us, that loneliness becomes love, that life is a journey with God in time.[67]

"The Secret of Grace Is Harmony"

In his most recent book, *A Vision Quest* (2006), Dunne draws on another dream in a way that pulls together many of the themes discussed above. This time it is not his own dream, but a dream narrated by the composer John Adams. In the dream, Adams saw Meister Eckhart with a child on his shoulder, and the child was telling Eckhart that "the secret of grace is harmony."[68] Previously, I cited Dunne's observation that it is the harmony in Mozart's *Ave Verum* that especially conveys the sense of the passage through death to eternal life.[69] In *A Vision Quest*, he speaks of harmony as the analogue on the side of music to stories of God on the side of words. "Our memory of God, then, on the musical side of the brain, is harmony and that is the key to our memory on the verbal side in the stories of God, as in Dante's saying, 'His will is our peace.' "[70] Musical harmony, Dunne says, "is an image of the inner harmony or inner peace we find in our soul's center."[71] Like the stories of God, musical harmony carries our memory of the original harmony we enjoyed as individuals and as a species and our hopes of a final harmony to be recovered.[72] It is more than an image, however; insight into this image discloses the peace of living in the presence of God, of being on a journey with God, moving on like the quiet eye of a hurricane. In this ongoing relationship with God, eternal life is already begun.[73]

Notes

[1] John S. Dunne, *A Journey with God in Time: A Spiritual Quest* (Notre Dame: University of Notre Dame Press, 2003), 21.

[2] John S. Dunne, *The Reasons of the Heart: A Journey into Solitude and Back Again into the Human Circle* (New York: Macmillan, 1978).

[3] Dunne, *A Journey with God in Time,* 78.

[4] Ibid., 9.

[5] Ibid., 20.

[6] But see Dunne, *The Mystic Road of Love* (Notre Dame: University of Notre Dame Press, 1999), 137-41, where Dunne proposes and works out the mathematics of a theory of matter as a dimension; the idea is that matter not only *is situated* in the other dimensions of space and time, but *situates*; for instance, the brain situates the mind. He returns to this theme in *A Vision Quest* (Notre Dame: University of Notre Dame Press, 2006), especially 34-35.

[7] *The City of the Gods: A Study in Myth and Mortality* (New York: Macmillan, 1965), *A Search for God in Time and Memory* (New York: Macmillan, 1969), *The Way of All the Earth: Experiments in Truth and Religion* (New York: Macmillan, 1972), *Time and Myth: A Meditation on Storytelling as an Exploration of Life and Death* (New York: Doubleday, 1973).

[8] Dunne, *The Mystic Road of Love,* 29.

[9] *The Church of the Poor Devil: Reflections on a Riverboat Voyage and a Spiritual Journey* (New York: Macmillan, 1982).

[10] *The House of Wisdom: A Pilgrimage* (San Francisco: Harper & Row, 1985).

[11] *The Homing Spirit: A Pilgrimage of the Mind, of the Heart, of the Soul* (New York: Crossroad, 1987).

[12] *The Peace of the Present: An Unviolent Way of Life* (Notre Dame: University of Notre Dame Press, 1991).

[13] *A Journey with God in Time,* 89.

[14] *Love's Mind: An Essay on Contemplative Life* (1993), *The Music of*

Time: Words and Music and Spiritual Friendship (1995), *The Mystic Road of Love* (1999), *Reading the Gospel* (2000), *The Road of the Heart's Desire: An Essay on the Cycles of Story and Song* (2002), *A Journey with God in Time* (2003), *A Vision Quest* (2006). All are published by University of Notre Dame Press.

[15]J. R. R. Tolkien and Donald Swann, *The Road Goes Ever On: A Song Cycle* (Boston: Houghton Mifflin, 1967). Besides the poems, Tolkien contributed illustrations, notes, and supplementary material to the volume.

[16]Charles O. Hartman, *Jazz Text: Voice and Improvisation in Poetry, Jazz, and Song* (Princeton: Princeton University Press, 1991), 9.

[17]Neither Dunne nor Hartman cites Langer directly, but for a theory of musical elements as audible forms, see Langer's *Feeling and Form* (New York: Scribner, 1953), 104-15.

[18]*The Music of Time*, 94-105. In *The Road of the Heart's Desire* (33), Dunne adds rap to the list, without comment.

[19]*The Music of Time*, 95.

[20]Ibid., 95.

[21]Ibid., 65. See below, text at note 49.

[22]*The Music of Time*, 104.

[23]From "Gertrude the Governess," in Stephen Leacock, *Nonsense Novels* (New York: Dodd, Mead, 1943), 60.

[24]See *A Search for God in Time and Memory*, 119-68, and *The Way of All the Earth*, 13-24.

[25]*The Music of Time*, 105.

[26]Dunne cites Ivan Nagel, *Autonomy and Mercy: Reflections on Mozart's Operas*, trans. Mario Faber and Ivan Nagel (Cambridge: Harvard University Press, 1991).

[27]Ibid., 106.

[28]Ibid., 114.

[29]Ibid.

[30]Ibid., 118.

[31]*Tractatus Logico-Philosophicus*, trans. C. K. Ogden (London: Routledge & Kegan Paul, 1992), 6.4311.

[32]*The Music of Time*, 118.

[33]Ibid., 119.

[34]Ibid., 120.

[35]Mozart's own words, quoted, *The Music of Time*, 120.

[36]Ibid.

[37]Ibid., 127.

[38]Ibid.

[39]Ibid., 117.

[40]See *The Way of All the Earth*, 39-40.

[41]The quotation is from *Answer to Job*, trans. R. F. C. Hull (New York: Meridian, 1960), 184.

[42]Jean-Paul Sartre, "Existentialism" ["Existentialism Is a Humanism"],

trans. Bernard Frechtman, in *Existentialism and Human Emotions* (New York: Philosophical Library, 1957), 32-33.

[43]*The Road of the Heart's Desire*, 24, citing Kierkegaard.

[44]Dunne often quotes the Chinese grandmother of one of his students: "Music must be treated as all things that are eternal, such as love and understanding, because it is these things that will carry us through the darkness of our lives and the death of our bodies to the moon of everlasting peace"; see especially *A Vision Quest*, 117.

[45]*The Road of the Heart's Desire*, 24.

[46]Ibid., 27. *A Journey with God in Time* became the title of Dunne's subsequent memoir.

[47]Tolkien and Swann, *The Road Goes Ever On*, 2.

[48]See *The Road of the Heart's Desire*, 23-61.

[49]*The Road of the Heart's Desire*, 33, citing Plato, *Timaeus* 37d. See the entire section "The Signs of a Time," in *The Road of the Heart's Desire*, 33-40.

[50]*The Road of the Heart's Desire*, 77-78.

[51]"From the Troubadours to Frank Sinatra," *The New York Review of Books* (February 23, 2006), 43.

[52]*The Road of the Heart's Desire*, 95.

[53]*The Music of Time*, 115.

[54]*The Road of the Heart's Desire*, 86.

[55]Ibid., 101.

[56]Ibid.

[57]Ibid.

[58]*A Vision Quest*, 22.

[59]*The Road of the Heart's Desire*, 93, 114-15.

[60]Dunne's fullest telling of this story is in "Waymarks," at the beginning of *The Road of the Heart's Desire*, xi-xii.

[61]J. R. R. Tolkien, *The Lord of the Rings*, 1-vol. ed. (London: George Allen & Unwin, 1969), 162, quoted in *The Road of the Heart's Desire*, 18. For a scientific view that has interesting affinities—and also significant contrasts—see Steven Mithen, *The Singing Neanderthals: The Origins of Language, Mind, and Body* (Cambridge: Harvard University Press, 2005).

[62]*The Road of the Heart's Desire*, 96-103.

[63]Ibid., 108.

[64]Ibid., 17.

[65]Ibid., 111.

[66]T. E. Lawrence, *Seven Pillars of Wisdom* (Harmondsworth, England: Penguin and Jonathan Cape, 1971), 364, quoted by Dunne first in *The Reasons of the Heart* (New York: Macmillan, 1978), 1, and frequently throughout his subsequent works.

[67]*The Road of the Heart's Desire*, 117, italics in original.

[68]Adams recounts the dream in an interview by Jonathan Cott, June 1985, which accompanies the compact disc recording of Adams' *Harmonielehre*

(Nonesuch Digital, 1985). Dunne first cites this text in *Reading the Gospel*, 31, but I am following the account in *A Vision Quest*, 39, from which I took the citation.

[69]See the text at note 35.

[70]*A Vision Quest*, 40.

[71]Ibid.

[72]Ibid.

[73]Ibid., 61-65. In the image of the eye of a hurricane, which he uses frequently to symbolize the journey with God, Dunne is drawing on his own experience of being in a hurricane on Houston Bay in 1940. See *A Journey with God in Time*, 11-12.

Part III

LITERARY ARTS

Imagining Redemption

The Novel as a Source of Dangerous Memory

Colleen Carpenter Cullinan

Reason, Johann Metz reminds us, "is not the original form of theological expression."[1] Certainly it is true that much theology *is* reasoned discourse—rational argument—that proceeds through judicious definition of the terms at issue, thoughtful linkages of certain concepts to other concepts, and the human ability to demonstrate truths both inductively and deductively. Theology is a rational enterprise, we theologians insist, and in a scientific and secular age, we perhaps cling too tightly to that fact, attempting to defend ourselves from charges of irrationality and blind belief. However, we cannot and should not forget that the original form of theological expression is not reason but *narrative*: messy, mushy, non-scientific narrative. Narrative is not as clean and bright as philosophical reason; it is subjective and can be interpreted in too many different ways, and yet it is where theology begins. As Metz forcefully reminds us, "theology is, above all, concerned with direct experiences expressed in narrative language."[2]

The fact that theology is rooted in narrative is one we cannot afford to overlook or to downplay. What is at issue here is not simply the stories that make up the great bulk of scripture (powerful as they are, and central as they are to theologizing), but the narrative accounts of the lives and experiences of all of us as Christian believers. Experience, feminist theologians reminded us as they began to incorporate women's experience into theological reflection, is not a new, suspect, and subjective source of theological reflection: instead, "what have been called the objective sources of theology, Scripture and tradition, are themselves codified collective human experience."[3] To pay attention to experience—and we cannot avoid it—we must pay attention to narrative. Metz points out that "Christians do not primarily form an argumentative and reasoning community, but a storytelling community and . . . the exchange of experiences of faith . . . takes a narrative form."[4] Thus "if the category of narrative is lost or outlawed by theology as precritical, then real or original experiences of faith may . . . become silenced, and . . . the experience of faith will become vague."[5] We need narrative accounts of the experience of faith; it is upon this foundation (as solid or shaky as it may be) that our theological house is built.

With this in mind, I have previously examined our theological understanding of redemption through the lens of stories—specifically, stories women tell and have told about suffering, healing, and transformation. Women's experiences of each of these, I believe, are necessary for appropriately nuanced theological reflection on redemption. In my book *Redeeming the Story: Women, Suffering, and Christ*, my goal was threefold: I wanted to hold up the story we tell about our redemption through Jesus's death on the cross next to women's stories and see what I could learn about 1) how the Jesus story affects women; 2) what it teaches them about themselves and their lives; and 3) how it functions to both help and hurt them.[6] The intersection of women's stories—women's imaginations, the way women construct an understanding of the world around them—and classical theological concepts is a rich and exciting place to be. This is not simply because women's experience and women's narratives are a recent addition to theological reflection, but because theology is at home in the realm of the imagination. The imagination, after all, is not limited to the (potentially useless, potentially dangerous) ability "to make things up." Instead—more broadly, and far more important—the imagination is "our constructive capacity to integrate our experience into dynamic and effective wholes which then function as the interpretive grids of further experience."[7]

The imagination, then, is what makes sense of human experience: it integrates experience into something a person can grasp, think about, comprehend—and then use in order to make sense of the *next* thing that happens. One way this happens is through storytelling, which is perhaps the most powerful way human beings have of making sense of experience. To tell a story, we take the facts or events around us and find ways to link them together. We discover meaning, or intent, or cause and effect; we choose which events are important and which can be discarded as peripheral: we create a story out of bare facts or incidents. This creative activity brings order out of chaos; it makes the world manageable.

Some argue that storytelling necessarily falsifies our experience (by leaving things out; by mistakenly choosing one cause over another) and it is certainly true that many of the stories we tell and have told about the world are demonstrably false, but in the end this argument misses the point. We cannot escape the necessity of storytelling, of narrative: the human capacity to selectively interpret events over time is the only thing that makes the category of "experience" at all useful or graspable. We cannot think of everything all at once in an undifferentiated mass: we need the imagination as the faculty through which we construct an understanding of our experience, our history, and our place in the world. The imagination, then, as the governor of our experience, is central to our experience of anything and everything—including our experience of God.[8]

Sandra Schneiders claims that because of the immense role of the imagination in shaping human experience and human understanding, theological problems (such as the devastating impact of patriarchy on Christian theology) cannot be solved by rational theological argument alone, but must be addressed imaginatively as well. In the classic example, it is possible to argue that God is neither male nor female, and prove it through detailed and elegant argument, but hear in response, "You're right. God is neither male nor female. He's a spirit." The careful, rational theological argument hasn't touched the hearer's image of God, nor the experience of the Holy. Schneiders puts it quite forcefully:

> It is not primarily abstract ideas which affect our spirituality, that is, our experience of and with God. Important as correct ideas about God may be, it is the imagination which governs our experience of God because it is the imagination which creates our God-image and our self-image. Consequently, if the demonic influence of patriarchy on the religious imagination is to be exorcised, if the neurotic repression of the feminine dimension of divinity is to be overcome, the imagination must be healed.[9]

This healing of the imagination, Schneiders adds, can happen only through symbol, metaphor, gesture, music, and story. *The imagination is necessary in order to heal the imagination.*

This idea has been very important to me as a feminist theologian. In *Redeeming the Story*, I wrote about stories that might help us shake up the patriarchal version of the story of redemption, and rethink how the stories of redemption that we have were co-opted into destructive theological ideas. The relationship between stories and theology is so important, in fact, that I think it has the potential to be understood not only as affecting our *ideas*, but also our *actions*.

In Johann Metz's political theology, a "dangerous memory" is a memory that can shake things up—change people—even become the impetus to make changes in society as a whole.[10] Here, instead of the relationship between a story and an idea—both of which are in some sense theoretical, or at least located mostly in our heads—we have the relationship between a story (the dangerous memory) and *action*. This is something quite different—and potentially more powerful. In order to explore this intriguing notion, I shall first look back at the relationship between theology and story as I see it, focusing on the problem of women and redemption. Next, I shall glance briefly at how this plays out in a particular novel, Barbara Kingsolver's *Animal Dreams*. Third, I shall turn to dangerous memory, setting out what it is and how it might or might not be related to fiction, or the novel. Finally, I shall attempt to make the case that Barbara Kingsolver's *Animal Dreams* can serve as a dangerous memory for those who read it.

I begin with story and theology, and how I see story as central to our understanding of redemption. As soon as women's experience becomes part of the discussion of redemption, long-accepted images and ideas become wildly problematic. Do we really want to glorify suffering, insist on obedience as the key virtue in following God, emphasize sacrifice, imply "divine child abuse," or fall into still other pitfalls pointed out in recent years by feminist and liberation theologians?[11] The answer is clearly no. However, in the end the problem is less with the *theology* associated with these ideas than with the *story* itself. Women's imaginations—and men's too—are often held in thrall by one story we have traditionally told about Jesus: the story of an angry Father God who desires the death of his beloved son in order that sinful humans can be forgiven for their sins and not sent, as they deserve to be, to a fiery hell forever. That story has as its centerpiece the brutal crucifixion, which is presented as not only necessary but desired by God *in his goodness*, a paradox that can only poison our understanding of goodness, love, justice, and mercy. Critiquing the story is not enough; theologizing in a new direction is not enough. To break the hold this story has on the Christian imagination, we need to address the imagination itself, and we can only do this in ways that fully engage the imagination: that is to say, this is a problem that can be solved only with a new story.

Only a story can replace a story: a rational argument and a logical theory may make sense, but they won't transform our hearts and lives. New "images" of God that don't fit into the old stories have no anchor, no hold on our hearts. They exist in the rational corner of our minds—but not in the worshipping center of our existence, the core of our being where we meet God. That core has been shaped by a lifetime of story, song, and symbol, and if rationally we wish to change, then we must seek out new stories, new songs, and new symbols. The story we know of sacrifice, anger, and sin needs to be replaced by other stories—stories of love, forgiveness, and renewal, stories like the ones Jesus told. Unfortunately, while theology can point us to the need for those stories, it cannot write them.

Even more disturbing, we need to face the fact that stories, however powerful, can be rejected—or worse, misinterpreted. After all, Jesus told stories, and we have fairly persistently ignored or reshaped them in order to avoid their challenge. For example, the story of the Prodigal Son envisions a father who is not interested in or concerned with sin, but longs only for joyful reunion with his lost son. As a thought experiment, theologian Robin Collins once retold that story in such a way that, when the younger son begs forgiveness, he does not receive it. Instead, the father tells him that he cannot return to the family until his debt is repaid. Knowing that he will never be able to pay it, the younger son despairs—until his older brother steps in and offers to pay what his brother owes. The older brother goes out to the fields, and works until he drops dead of exhaustion—at which point the father proclaims the debt forgiven, and welcomes the younger son into the house. This is a complete reversal of the story as we know it, and yet, Collins points out, it is a frighteningly accurate account of the story through which many of us understand redemption.[12]

Clearly, then, stories can't stand alone—the theology that accompanies them, or the background assumptions we bring to them, can in fact overwhelm them. In this case, our background assumptions about justice and punishment were so powerful that they essentially shut off our ability to listen to Jesus's parable. In any case, the stories we tell about redemption are inextricably bound up in the theology and anthropology surrounding them. With that in mind, we turn to Kingsolver's novel, which I see as a story that helps us come to grips with one of the most vexing problems involved in making sense of redemption: the problem of time.

Time—both its existence and the way we expect it to behave—is such a basic part of the way we tell stories that we rarely stop to examine our assumptions about it. This, of course, is a problem—because our *assumptions* about time and the *truth* about time are two very different things. Indeed, our common-sense understanding of what time is and how it works leads us into theological difficulties so serious we usually prefer not to think about them at all. For example: time, as we understand it, would not seem to permit redemption to take place at all. We see time as heading only in one direction—from the past, through the present, and on into the future—and so the past is lost to us forever. But if the past is gone, then gone too is any chance of redeeming, in any meaningful way, the suffering that took place in the past. As Christians, we hold the conviction that the redemption of suffering is and must be more than a belated consolation or "pie in the sky by and by," and so we need to figure out how to deal with the troubling fact that we cannot go back in time to right wrongs. Theologian Marjorie Suchocki points out that true justice, like true redemption, would have to mean "the redress of evil and the restoration of well-being to those for whom it has been violated or lost," but laments that such a justice can never be achieved:

> Too often injustice has crushed its victims, making reparation impossible. How is a broken mind repaired, a lost limb returned, a stunted ability to love reshaped, a murder undone? . . . The more one begins to consider the problem of justice, the more impossible and visionary any full justice appears to be. . . . Only if the past can somehow be brought into the present, and only if a sufficient flexibility of vision can allow radical diversities to co-exist in well-being, only then can justice in its fullest dimensions be established. Under the circumstances of our finitude, however, such conditions cannot be secured.[13]

Although Suchocki's concern here is justice, not redemption, the problem remains the same: how are terrible wrongs righted?

How can injustice be undone? How can suffering be not only healed but redeemed (made whole)? She not only identifies the problem in clear, even shocking terms (how *is* a broken mind repaired?) and declares it impossible to solve, she also identifies the key aspect of the problem that makes it unsolvable: time. "Only if the past can somehow be brought into the present," she declares, and then dismisses that as impossible "under the circumstances of our finitude."[14] Given our typical understanding of time, she is absolutely right. However, we also believe that redemption is real, and available to us here and now. How are we to make sense of this contradiction? We are boxed in by the limitations inherent in the story we tell about time and how it works, even as our hope and our experience (of healing, of wholeness, of redeeming love) tell us that redemption is possible.

Kingsolver tackles this problem in her novel *Animal Dreams* in surprising and very effective ways. She deploys several rhetorical strategies to shake up our understanding of time—the use of letters, for example, and the use of annual holidays as marking points in the story.[15] She also explicitly attacks our understanding of memory, since one of the main characters has Alzheimer's, and the other worries constantly that she has forgotten her childhood—the places, the people, everything that happened.

Codi Noline, the heroine of *Animal Dreams*, is a young woman in her thirties who cannot remember her childhood. Returning home to Grace, Arizona, after fourteen years away, Codi is unable to recognize the woman who raised her after her mother's death, and is not entirely certain she can even find her way from the bus stop to her father's home. She is startled by friends' memories of their past together, and denies that she could possibly have done the things they describe. Even when the stories are confirmed by her sister, she persists in her surprise, denial, and unbelief. Her fallible voice reminds the reader of the gap between memory and reality. "Memory is a complicated thing," Codi muses, "a relative to truth but not its twin."[16] Throughout the novel, Codi experiences her memory as untrustworthy, fragmented, and disruptive— but as she and the reader eventually learn, this is because what she "knows" about the past is often wrong. As an adolescent, she settled the conflict between what she remembered and what she knew to be true by deciding that her memories must be wrong, and thus denying/"forgetting" them; when she finally learned that it was her understanding of the past that was in error, her lost memories returned. One significant instance of this was Codi's belief that she had not been present when her mother was airlifted to a hospital shortly after her sister Hallie's birth: Codi had always been convinced that, since she had not truly been there, her fragmented memories of the day were simply wishful thinking, but when she is told that she was in fact there, the fragments resolve into a flood of clear recollection. As a no-nonsense grandmother explained to her at the end of the novel, "No, if you remember something, then it's true. . . . In the long run, that's what you've got."[17]

Kingsolver makes it clear to the reader from the beginning that Codi's voice is fallible when speaking of the past. As narrator, Codi herself confesses to remembering what she has not seen, and failing to remember what she has.[18] However, her openness with us about her memory problems serves as a cover for the memory problems she neither confesses nor knows about. Throughout much of the story, we know that Codi cannot remember a great deal of her childhood, but we accept—as she does—the memories that do exist. When Kingsolver reveals these memories to be false constructions, Codi's understanding of herself undergoes a radical shift—and the reader's understanding of her and of time itself undergoes a corresponding disruption. In the beginning, we assumed with Codi that the past was fixed but often unknowable; in the end, her experience teaches us that *what is known changes what is real*. The most potent example of this comes at Hallie's funeral, when she realizes that the distant townswomen of her childhood were in fact all the mothers she never had:

> Doña Althea clumped forward with her cane and set down a miniature, perfectly made peacock piñata. . . . [I]t was for Hallie. I tried to listen to what she was saying. She said, "I made one like this for both of you girls, for your *cumpleaños* when you were ten."
>
> To my surprise, this was also true. I remembered every toy, every birthday party, each one of these fifty mothers who'd been standing at the edges of my childhood, ready to make whatever contribution was needed at the time.
>
> "*Gracias, Abuelita*," I said softly to Doña Althea as she clumped away.
>
> She didn't look at me, but she heard me say it and she didn't deny that she was my relative. Her small head crowned with its great white braid nodded a little. No hugs or confessions of love. We were all a little stiff, I understood that. Family

constellations are fixed things. They don't change just because you've learned the names of the stars.[19]

The reality of Codi's loneliness and isolation as a child is not denied, but new facts change the picture by making it more complete. Codi was not an outsider rejected by the community, but a semi-acknowledged insider whose relationships to the community were denied by her father, hidden by many relatives, and completely unknown to her. The deadly combination of secrecy, shame, and ignorance made it difficult for family members to acknowledge her, much as they tried. When she learned the truth about her family, her new understanding of the past altered what she remembered about her childhood. She was able to see new things, and remember old things in a new way, once her vision was cleared. This is remarkably similar to being shown the "secret" to a well-known visual illusion: whereas before only an ornate vase is visible, once one's eyes know how and where to look, the silhouette of a face emerges on either side of the vase. Similarly, we see that the past, like our perception of the vase, is not as fixed as we imagined. Codi's pain as a child is still there, but it is newly comforted by the knowledge that she was not, as she imagined (remembered), alone.

Thus in Kingsolver's *Animal Dreams*, we have a novel that constructs the reader's experience of time and memory in such a way that we realize what we think we understand about both is questionable at best. We think that the past and present are separate—yet somehow they intertwine; they do indeed affect each other. We think that the past is fixed and unchangeable—yet adding a few hitherto unknown facts to the mix can radically change what things *meant*, or "what was really going on." With Kingsolver, we begin to understand that our own past might be more reachable than we had imagined—perhaps old wrongs can be righted, perhaps forgiveness can reach back through time and change things. Through her novel, we begin to suspect that redemption might indeed be possible.

However, we still have the difficult transition to make from *ideas* to *action*—or from what we *think* to what is *real*. How is it possible for a narrative to move us to action, and, more important, given my focus on Kingsolver, how is it possible for a *fictional* narrative to perform the work of an actual dangerous memory? To answer these questions, we first need to examine the notion of dangerous memory in more depth.

Most memories are not dangerous. Indeed, sharing memories is a common pastime: it can reconnect old friends, give family members a sense of belonging, and is often accompanied by laughter and goodwill. This form of remembering, while common, is not at all what is at issue for Metz. For him, memory has a serious and powerful function that is undermined only when memory is reduced to mere nostalgia. Dangerous memories are not the cheerful, happy, harmless memories that "just do not take the past seriously enough," sugarcoating reality for the sake of present comfort.[20] They are not sentimental; they do not make things easy. Rather, dangerous memories are the ones that "illuminate for a few moments and with a harsh steady light the questionable nature of things we have apparently come to terms with": they are memories that shake us out of our complacency and wake us up to a reality we would prefer to avoid.[21] They are, inevitably, memories of suffering.[22]

Dangerous memories undermine history—or at least, they undermine "the history of what has prevailed . . . the history of the successful and the established."[23] By insisting on memories of suffering, and thus the remembrance of the defeated, the lost, and the dis-remembered,[24] dangerous memories reshape how we understand history—and how we imagine reality. And because they shape our imaginations, they enable us to act in new ways: when our "interpretive grid" shifts (recalling Schneiders's definition of imagination), so too do the possibilities for action open to us.

For Christians, of course, the dangerous memory at the heart of everything is the memory of Jesus: his life, his death, and his resurrection.[25] For us, that memory of suffering and of hope is at the core of how we understand reality—and how we act in the world. Elizabeth Johnson describes how the dangerous memory of Jesus links itself with the dangerous memories of Jesus's followers over the centuries, forming the basis of a "community of memory and hope."[26] This community, she argues, "becomes through its prayer a community that struggles for justice, peace, and the well-being of the earth."[27] Not a community that dreams about these things, but a community that struggles toward them, knowing that the troubles of the present—the seemingly intractable, unshakeable present—are in the end part of a larger story, a story that is still unfinished. Memory's danger, Johnson says, "lies precisely in its ability to detach people from the grip of a given situation, if only for an instant, and by bringing to light new possibilities, to empower hope for a different future."[28]

Interestingly, Metz himself points to fiction as a source of dangerous memory. Great literature, he says, "has always tried . . . to search out the continuity and meaning of history in precisely the suppressed and buried 'traces of suffering,' to inquire after the forgotten and unsuccessful ones of history, and in this way, to write a kind of antihistory."[29] By telling stories of the defeated and forgotten, then, great literature adds to our store of dangerous memories—because the mere act of "remembering the dead, telling their stories . . . strike[s] a blow against oppression."[30] Despite our tendency to want to remember only the victors and their heroic stories, we are called to remember those who suffered, those who were pushed aside by the victors. Is the victory truly just, or is there an implicit cost that we would so much prefer to ignore?

Perhaps the most dramatic theological use of narrative today is to be found in womanist theological reflection. In *Black Womanist Ethics*, Katie Cannon argues forcefully that the black woman's literary tradition not only mirrors the reality of the black community, but records and transforms the oral tradition and folk culture that undergird that community.[31] The stories, novels, and poems act as dangerous memories because they detach us from the relentless and seemingly inevitable present; they are deeply linked to reality, yet serve to transform it as well. The imaginative and historical come together in this literary tradition, offering readers "the sharpest available view of the Black community's soul."[32] Novels by Zora Neale Hurston, Jessie Redmond Fauset, and Nella Larsen, among others, depict not only the horrors of racism but also the "richness and wholeness of Black culture,"[33] thus providing readers with dangerous memories of a suffering past and (perhaps even more dangerous) memories of the hope that flourished in the midst of that suffering.

And so we return to Kingsolver, who is engaged in a much different project than the writers Cannon describes. Kingsolver's novels do not (typically) address racism, nor do they dramatize the suffering it is all too common to endure in America because of race—but they do attack, with careful precision and deadly accuracy, the many stories (white) Americans tell themselves about the greatness, uniqueness, and heroic stature of America. *Animal Dreams* is a wonderful love story about a confused young woman returning home to discover her lost past, lost family, and lost love, and it is also the story of a different young woman, the heroine's sister, who travelled to Nicaragua to work in the cotton fields and use her education in agriculture and agricultural pest management to help struggling peasant farmers. The dangerous memories here do not support a struggling community but instead burst the complacent bubble of the community of the victors. *Animal Dreams* is set in 1985, when war was raging in Nicaragua, and the United States was sending arms to the contras—or, as Ronald Reagan preferred to call them, "freedom fighters." Hallie, the sister who travels to Nicaragua, is kidnapped by the contras and murdered late in the novel: she had up until that point seemed to be a side story to all that was happening to Codi, but suddenly she becomes the center of the novel, the still point around which Codi revolves. Suddenly it becomes clear that the novel is not about Codi's past but about her *fear*—and our own fear—of getting hurt, of losing, of not being the victor. And Hallie's words—even after her death, in letters her sister continues to receive—speak passionately *beyond* that fear, into hope. Hallie's life and death become a dangerous memory for those whose memories of the past had never known danger before; the novel opens up a chasm in our sentimentalized past and complacent present, allowing us as readers to glimpse the questionable nature of things we never should have come to terms with in the first place.

In her last letter to Codi, Hallie describes for her sister what it means to have hope as the *driving force* of her life, even when the main *task* of her life is to spend "one more morning in a muggy cotton field, checking the undersides of leaves to see what's been there, figuring out what to do that won't clear a path for worse problems next week."[34] The problems and work of her daily life are the measure of her hope; as she tells Codi: "Wars and elections are both too big and too small to matter in the long run. The daily work—that goes on, it adds up. It goes into the ground, into crops, into children's bellies and their bright eyes. Good things don't get lost."[35]

This is a description of hope that is rooted in both the present and the future; it is not merely entertaining the idea of a possible forthcoming goodness, but is instead hope in its properly Christian form: an *activity* that works toward a blessed future, confident that the "fragments of well-being becom[ing] embodied in the world [are] real if transitory anticipations of the coming well-being, even here, even now."[36] Hallie attempts to explain to Codi her understanding of hope and her commitment to life as shaped by that hope, but this is something that Codi does not and cannot grasp until after Hallie's death:

Codi, here's what I've decided: the very least you can do in
your life is to figure out what you hope for. And the most you
can do is live inside that hope. Not admire it from a distance
but live right in it, under its roof. What I want is so simple I
almost can't say it: elementary kindness. Enough to eat,
enough to go around. The possibility that kids might one day
grow up to be neither the destroyers nor the destroyed. That's
about it. Right now I'm living in that hope, running down its
hallway and touching the walls on both sides.
     I can't tell you how good it feels. I wish you knew.[37]

Through her death (and the choices she made during her life),
Hallie becomes for Codi a dangerous memory, a memory that makes
demands on her, that changes her life. "Everything we'd been, I was
now," Codi realizes at her sister's funeral.[38] And this is what is truly
significant: Hallie also becomes *for the reader*, for all of us, a dangerous memory. Even though she never actually lived, her story of
suffering and hope is one that shocks and changes the reader. Her
hope is not the hope of American triumphalism; it is smaller than
that, somehow, and oddly haunting because of its different shape.
Hallie's suffering, too, is something that cannot and will not fit into
the frame of American history as taught in American schools, and
so the reader finds herself readjusting the frame, asking new questions, beginning to wonder. Her imagination shifts. The interpretive
grid through which she understands the world is being remade.
     Fiction like Kingsolver's—the telling of stories that shake up
not only our understanding of abstract ideas (like time or memory)
but also our understanding of the actual functioning of the world
around us—is a powerful force. Womanist theologians have long
recognized the power of fiction in shaping a community's memory.
This rich insight can and should be explored with respect to the
storytelling of other communities as well. Not all fiction has the
power of dangerous memory, but some does. Cannon's turn to the
black women's literary tradition opened up a new realm in which
we can see dangerous memories at work. However, we have much
to do to explore how Metz's understanding of dangerous memory
can and does spill over into still other imaginative constructions
of the human self and human reality. Kingsolver's novel, and other
novels[39] and poems[40] with the same power, inhabit an unusual and
often unrecognized place in our lives. They are not history, though
sometimes they have historical elements. They are not journalism,

though sometimes they pull events straight from the headlines. They are not factual in the way our culture craves facts, and the way our often literalist culture so facilely links the factual and the true, but they are nevertheless real and nevertheless true. And that makes them dangerous.

Notes

[1] Johann Baptist Metz, "A Short Apology of Narrative," in *Love's Strategy: The Political Theology of Johann Baptist Metz*, ed. John K. Downey (Harrisburg, PA: Trinity Press, 1999), 103. Original translation by David Smith published in *Concilium* 85 (1973): 84-96.

[2] Ibid., 103.

[3] Rosemary Radford Ruether, *Sexism and God-Talk* (Boston: Beacon Press, 1983), 12.

[4] Metz, "A Short Apology of Narrative," 105.

[5] Ibid., 102-3.

[6] Some of the material in this essay first appeared in Colleen Carpenter Cullinan, *Redeeming the Story: Women, Suffering, and Christ* (New York: Continuum, 2004).

[7] Sandra M. Schneiders, *Women and the Word: The Gender of God in the New Testament and the Spirituality of Women* (New York: Paulist Press, 1986), 16.

[8] Ibid., 70.

[9] Ibid., 70-71.

[10] Johann Baptist Metz, *Faith in History and Society: Toward a Practical Fundamental Theology* (New York: Crossroad, 1980), 109. For a fuller explanation of the term, see 109-15.

[11] For a fuller treatment of the feminist critique(s) of traditional atonement theory, see chapter 1, "Telling the Wrong Story," in Cullinan, *Redeeming the Story*, 5-30.

[12] Robin Collins, "Understanding Atonement: A New and Orthodox Theory," unpublished paper delivered at the American Academy of Religion annual meeting, 1995.

[13] Marjorie Hewitt Suchocki, *God Christ Church: A Practical Guide to Process Theology*, rev. ed. (New York: Crossroad, 1993), 74-75.

[14] Ibid., 75.

[15] A detailed treatment of the many strategies used by Kingsolver to complicate and question our understanding of time (most of which are not mentioned in this essay) can be found in "Time and the Telling of Stories: Redemption in *Animal Dreams*," chapter 4 of Cullinan, *Redeeming the Story*, 88-120.

[16] Barbara Kingsolver, *Animal Dreams* (New York: HarperCollins, 1990), 48.

[17] Ibid., 342.

[18] Ibid., 48.

[19]Ibid., 328.

[20]Metz, *Faith in History and Society*, 109.

[21]Ibid., 109-10.

[22]Elizabeth A. Johnson, *Friends of God and Prophets: A Feminist Theological Reading of the Communion of Saints* (New York: Continuum, 1998), 165. Johnson describes the power of the memory of suffering this way: "Witness the fact that every protest and rebellion is fed by the subversive power of remembered sufferings and freedoms. . . . Memory that dares to connect with the pain, the beauty, the defeat, the victory of love and freedom, and the unfinished agenda of those who went before acts like an incalculable visitation from the past that energizes persons. It interrupts the omnipotence of the present moment with the dream, however fleeting, that something else might indeed be possible. Consequently, instead of keeping attention pinned in the past, this kind of memory turns mind and heart to the future" (165).

[23]Johann Baptist Metz, "The Future in the Memory of Suffering," in *Faith and the Future: Essays on Theology, Solidarity, and Modernity*, ed. Johann Baptist Metz and Jürgen Moltmann (Maryknoll, NY: Orbis, 1995), 9.

[24]See Toni Morrison's *Beloved* (New York: Knopf, 1987) for a story focusing entirely on "the dis-remembered." *Beloved* is dedicated to the "60 million and more" Africans estimated to have died on slave ships; it is the story of one particular dis-remembered girl and the community that cannot, in the end, forget her.

[25]Johnson, *Friends of God and Prophets*, 167-68.

[26]Ibid., 164.

[27]Ibid.

[28]Ibid., 167.

[29]Metz, "The Future in the Memory of Suffering," 12.

[30]Johnson, *Friends of God and Prophets*, 174.

[31]Katie G. Cannon, *Black Womanist Ethics* (Atlanta: Scholars Press, 1988), 90.

[32]Ibid.

[33]Ibid., 82-83.

[34]Kingsolver, *Animal Dreams*, 299.

[35]Ibid.

[36]Johnson, *Friends of God and Prophets*, 217.

[37]Kingsolver, *Animal Dreams*, 299.

[38]Ibid., 328.

[39]Toni Morrison's *Beloved*, Leslie Marmon Silko's *Ceremony*, and Alan Paton's *Cry, the Beloved Country* are a few such novels; clearly there are many, many more.

[40]I would suggest Maya Angelou, Emily Dickinson, and Gerard Manley Hopkins as a few of the poets who are capable of completely upending a reader's understanding of the world.

Flannery O'Connor and Catholic Theology of the Family

Julie Hanlon Rubio

Why Literature?

In Catholic liturgy and popular piety, the dominant image of the family is the holy family. This family is most commonly portrayed as abounding in quiet harmony, with each member attentive to the duties of his or her role—Mary submissive and nurturing, Joseph, quietly protective, a good provider, and Jesus, the holy obedient child.[1] Apart from the holy family, Catholics have frequently upheld images of large families who sacrifice financial gain and luxury in order to cooperate with God in creating life. Before Vatican II, images of families gathered at daily mass or bedtime rosaries were common in popular Catholic literature, and large, pious families were frequently revered as models by the magisterium, theologians, and leaders of lay family movements.[2]

Even today, these powerful images shape responses to Catholics writing on the family. John Paul II, for instance, writes, "the family has a mission to guard, reveal, and communicate love, and this is a living reflection of and a real sharing in God's love for humanity and the love of Christ the Lord for the church, his bride,"[3] speaking of both an ideal and a reality, a gift and a task. When Catholics read this, images of holy families cannot be far from their minds. The pope asks families to "become what you are" or to live up to the mission that is rightfully yours, to your truest identity.[4] His language has the power to be both inspiring and potentially alienating. Faced with an image that is manifestly different from their own lives, many turn away, assuming that theology about families will elicit feelings of guilt or inferiority. Or, knowing the strengths of their structurally imperfect families, they disregard what seems to be sentimental piety without nuance. In short, images of holy families often stand in the way of right hearing and impair right response. Theologians writing about families need different kinds of images if they are to have any hope of reaching ordinary families.

Flannery O'Connor (1925-1964), American Catholic writer of two novels and thirty short stories, was criticized in her time for not publishing stories that would inspire a large audience to strive for greater holiness. Her own mother once asked if she thought she was really using the gifts God gave her, writing stories so few people enjoyed.[5] In fact, her stories were notoriously difficult for many people to understand, let alone enjoy. Filled with strange characters seemingly lacking in faith, they are not an obvious choice as a source for theologians writing about Christian family ethics.

Most who are familiar with O'Connor's letters and essays know that all of her stories concern the inbreaking of grace in the face of darkness and offer the possibility of conversion. However, in O'Connor's stories only rarely does conversion happen within a family setting. They include no positive portrayals of parents praying with their children, teaching them sound moral values, or going to church. There are no heartwarming homecomings, festive meals, and few significant confrontations. Intact nuclear families are a relatively rare subject of O'Connor's writing. The few that do appear are somewhat less than ideal. Frequently, these families' positive view of themselves is revealed to be more distortion than reality. In "A Good Man Is Hard to Find," for instance, a family with parents, two children, and a grandmother set off on vacation in a car trip marked by the grandmother's comments about how few good people are left in the world. O'Connor portrays the grandmother's excessive view of her own goodness by showing her concern with superficial manners that separate "nice people" from everyone else.[6] Only when confronted with a murderer who ought to be the epitome of what she disdains does the grandmother realize the wrongness of her attempts to classify and separate people.[7] Traditional families may first appear in O'Connor stories in picturesque settings, but it is their imperfection rather than their ideal status that is significant. This makes her work an ideal source for a tradition dominated by holy family imagery.

O'Connor's potential contribution to Christian family ethics lies in her portraits of non-ideal families that reveal theological truths theologians struggle to communicate: the ultimate importance of faith, the frailty of human beings, the need for solidarity, and the importance of "local ethics" or the moral life of families and communities.

Seeing: The Importance of Faith

O'Connor's stories bring readers back to the most crucial issue in the lives of religious persons. Behind traditional practices and ethical demands central to most theology on the family lies the question of faith. O'Connor thought of herself as a moralist because her stories concerned evil. However, the crucial moral issue for her was seeing rightly—through the eyes of faith. She sought to enable her audience to see evil where they might otherwise miss it and to encourage in them the sorts of small steps toward better faith her unlikely heroes take. In the terms of moral theology, fundamental option is primary for O'Connor.[8] "What, ultimately, is one's life about?" she forces her readers to ask.

One might argue that O'Connor would have been more effective as a moralist concerned with right seeing if she wrote stories about good rather than evil. However, O'Connor was convinced that stories involving the pious practice of good people would not reveal faith for her secular or lightly Christian audience. Thus she exaggerated to show how people run from faith or only glimpse it. "When you can assume that your audience holds the same beliefs you do, you can relax a little and use more normal means of talking to it; when you have to assume it does not, then you have to make our vision apparent by shock—to the hard of hearing you shout, and for the almost-blind you draw large and startling figures."[9] Using this method, she sought to reveal not "what we ought to be but . . . what we are at a given time and under given circumstances."[10] Though O'Connor acknowledged that a reader rightly turns to literature seeking inspiration, or in her terms, redemption, she maintained that "[h]is sense of evil is diluted or lacking altogether, and so he has forgotten the price of restoration."[11] Thus the hope she offers is costly and it is drawn starkly, plain enough for readers to see.

Her characters, then, are not moral exemplars inspiring us to go and do likewise. By "focusing on characters who, far from representing the faith, are set apart by it,"[12] O'Connor restores an understanding of the difficulties human beings can have when they try to live without God. She gives readers characters claimed by faith against their will or despite their attempts to run, so the need for faith and the meaninglessness of existence without it comes through.[13]

This approach differs from most Catholic theology on the family, in which faith is assumed. Most theologians exhort Christian families to live more actively Christian lives, while mourning the waywardness of the world and its encroachment on "the family."[14] However, given the reality of mixed marriages (40 percent and growing)[15] and the varying degrees of commitment among people of faith, O'Connor's realism is a good corrective. Plurality, doubt, and evil exist not only "out there" in the world, but also "in here"— in the church and in Christian families. Seeing that is the precondition for true concern with the moral dilemmas central to family ethics. O'Connor allows readers to see the depth of the problem and the need for an alternative.

Concern that such an approach will leave out the majority of less than perfect believers would be unwarranted, for O'Connor does not simply speak in black and white terms of accepting or rejecting faith. Rather, she writes about the struggle of keeping faith and taking it seriously. This understanding, though sometimes hard to discern in the midst of casts of grotesque characters, is central. As she put it,

> I don't think you should write something as long as a novel around anything that is not of the gravest concern to you and everybody else, and for me this is always the conflict between an attraction for the Holy and disbelief in it that we breathe with the air of our times. It's hard to believe always but more so in the world we live in now. There are some of us who have to pay for our faith every step of the way and who have to work out dramatically what it would be like without it and if being without it would be ultimately possible or not.[16]

In families, the difficulty of belief and life without faith is perhaps even harder to see than in individuals because families are likelier to engage in traditional faith practices. Yet, often they are so busy that larger questions of what faith really means and how it shapes life from the center out—or does not—remain unasked and unanswered. O'Connor's narratives beg readers to ask those questions.

Hazel Motes, hero of the novel *Wise Blood*, struggles with faith.[17]

Tempted by atheism, he tries to run from the faith of his ancestors. He mocks his grandfather's life as a preacher by going from town to town, standing on top of his big car and preaching the Church Without Christ. Many of O'Connor's readers believed Hazel to be a hero because he rejected and mocked the simplistic faith of Southern fundamentalism. However, O'Connor wrote that in Hazel's character, there are "a number of conflicting wills in one person."[18] His struggle is difficult because as much as he wants to, he simply cannot leave faith alone. This, as O'Connor revealed in the second edition of the novel, is why she admires him.[19]

But O'Connor is not only concerned with fundamental option, for many of her characters are baptized members of the church. She also writes of how hard it is to live up to the ethical implications of one's faith. In "The Displaced Person," Mrs. McKinley, a land owner, tries to be a good Christian woman by inviting the displaced Guizac family to work on her property and by trying to treat all of her workers as well as she can, but she is blind to the real moral evil around her.[20] She cannot see that her black workers deserve more than her tolerance of their supposed moral weakness and lax work ethic, that her view of her own largess depends on a false picture of her independence. She, like the rest of her household, does not want to recognize Mr. Guizac's goodness, and in the end she and the others watch as he is plowed under by a tractor.[21] Yet these people are not so evil that they can be dismissed. Readers sympathize with characters who, so like themselves, stand by in the face of moral atrocity because they cannot see rightly.[22]

Despite O'Connor's pessimism about human nature, she offers hope in her portrayals of people who are searching. Though they might go through most of their daily lives unperturbed by questions of faith, in the end most of her characters reveal themselves to be spiritually hungry.[23] Ordinary people, O'Connor maintains, want to see.

And there is much to see when one's eyes are opened. The contrast between Mrs. McKinley and the priest in "The Displaced Person" makes this clear. The priest alone notices and appreciates the beauty of Mrs. McKinley's peacock, though others think him an idiot for making a fuss over the animal.[24] Mrs. McKinley thinks that the "DP" (as Mr. Guizac is called in the story) is her salvation because he works hard, but the DP, like all the others who work for her, is not real to her.[25] Instead of seeing them as persons like herself, she insists that they are all "the same" or "extra."[26] The priest, however, sees the DP as the Christ figure he is, but he also sees the humanity of the white and black people who work the farm, and of Mrs. McKinley herself.[27] His vision is a source of hope that grace can break in even in a place where such inhumanity has occurred.

O'Connor's stories remind theologians that the first moral question is one of vision or faith. Though it is no doubt easier to assume one's audience shares one's own convictions, it is more honest to acknowledge the struggles many people have just trying to believe. Creating a compelling vision of Christian faith that can transform people and the lives they lead then becomes a crucial part of a moral theologian's work.

Sin and Finitude

O'Connor's understanding of the difficulty of faith for modern persons is accompanied by a pessimism about human nature that can be seen as a diminishment of gains the church has made since Vatican II. In particular, the church's growing optimism about human persons and its move away from a focus on sinfulness that previously dominated Catholic theology would seem to be at odds with O'Connor's emphasis on human finitude. Catholic theology on marriage in particular has benefited from more attention to the spiritual significance of loving relationships.[28] While few would want to return to pre-Vatican II theology, overly idealized ways of talking about families can be almost as harmful as overly dark descriptions, alienating people because of their distance from reality. Yet, traditional discussions of original sin are difficult for contemporary Christians to hear, because they seem at odds with modern ideas about the goodness and perfectibility of human beings.

O'Connor's stories, however, paint portraits of evil in such a way that Christian teaching about the dual nature of human beings marked by grace and sin is made accessible. Of the novelist, she writes, "His concern with poverty is with a poverty fundamental to man. I believe that the basic experience of everyone is the experience of human limitation."[29] Her characters are stark symbols of limitation rather than realistic depictions. Characters that remind readers of their limits were important to O'Connor, for she believed it is because "we are afflicted with the doctrine of the perfectibility of human nature by its own efforts that the vision of the freak in fiction is so disturbing. The freak in modern fiction keeps us from forgetting that we share in his state."[30]

Contemporary theology centering on family can often fall into the language of perfectibility. In John Paul II's discussion of the family as domestic church, for instance, he writes that, "[T]he Christian family has a special vocation to witness to the paschal covenant of Christ by constantly radiating the joy of love and the certainty of the hope for which it must give account."[31] The language of calling, vocation, and mission animates ethical writings about families and seems to ask of them unanimity, certainty, and constancy, which are often in short supply in the real world.

O'Connor's fiction does not deny the high vocation of families, but it recalls another piece of Christian understanding of human beings—their failures in joy, hope, and love, their experience of being insufficient in themselves. In "The Displaced Person," Mrs. McKinley labors under the illusion that everyone is dependent on her and misunderstands herself as financially rather than spiritually poor, failing to recognize her true needs.[32] In contrast, the priest and the DP are both humble and content to do what they can in imperfect situations. Reading O'Connor's stories schools readers in recognizing human limitation.

Often characters in O'Connor's stories who know they need faith are told by others that they do not, further revealing how human beings struggle to accept their finitude. In "The Lame Shall Enter First," Rufus, foster child of Sheppard, "will not accept explanations of his behavior that omit forgiveness or the need for it."[33] Though Sheppard wants to deny or explain away Rufus's bad behavior, Rufus will not be comforted by cheap grace. He, like many of O'Connor's characters who look evil on the surface, is not willing to change, but at least he knows who he is. What is more, he insists on his need for redemption, even in the face of Sheppard's attempts to convince him that Christianity is standing in the way of his growth. In the end of the story, Sheppard's attempts to reach Rufus are all rejected because they deny Rufus's desire to acknowledge his own finitude.[34] Similarly, in "A Good Man Is Hard to Find," The Misfit who murders the grandmother knows that Jesus "thrown everything off balance," even if he is afraid to truly live with the implications of that claim, and the grandmother realizes obliquely by the end that these things are more important than the manners she has been prattling on about.[35] O'Connor corrected those who saw the grandmother as an unre-

pentant witch, noting that those in the South know many old la-
dies like her.[36] Though deeply flawed, in contrast to those around
them, the grandmother and the Misfit both perceive their needi-
ness, and O'Connor held out hope that both would come around.[37]

The recognition of finitude, so evident in O'Connor's fiction,
should affect the way Christian theologians think about families.
O'Connor offers a reminder of how hard it is for human beings to
see their own weakness. If our theology sounds more appropriate
for people whose faith is always secure, whose understanding and
embrace of the cross are beyond reproach, then something is off-
balance. Even talking about the cross is not enough. Ordinary
people need to be able to visualize what the cross might mean in
an ordinary life, and to think about how they fit into theology
from where they are right now.[38] There has to be a way to express
the finitude at the heart of the human condition and in the midst
of everyday life.

Flannery O'Connor used the grotesque to do this. She explained
that she was "not simply showing us what we are, but what we
have been and what we could become."[39] The power of O'Connor's
stories resides in her ability to portray evil that is so extreme and
yet convince readers that they are not so very different from these
characters. The Misfit is not just a crazy murderer but also someone who knows that if Christ died for us "it's nothing for you to
do but throw away everything and follow Him," yet chooses to
keep doing what he likes.[40] It is a rare reader who cannot see herself in this honest, if brutal, man. Similarly, when Hazel Motes
blinds himself trying to live without Christ, the ordinary struggles
of more normal people are illuminated.[41] Better than sweeping attempts to describe general problems, the use of the grotesque helps
readers see what is wrong with their lives and opens them to the
possibility of grace.[42] Seeing these enlarged characters lends ur-
gency to moral deliberation. If these characters need Christ, do
we? If they have said no, what would it mean to say yes?

Solidarity

Flannery O'Connor is commonly viewed by those who understand her theological perspective as a writer concerned with sin
and grace in general, and not with specific moral issues. Much of
her writing centers on highly unusual situations rather than on
ordinary ethical dilemmas. She professed no responsibility for poli-

tics or social issues. Yet, a close reading of her stories reveals that for most of her characters, evil is associated with pride and exclusion, while grace is linked to humility and reaching out beyond one's social class or race. O'Connor gives flesh to the often amorphous moral value of solidarity, embodying a distinctly Christian sensibility about the responsibility to extend compassion beyond the boundaries of family.

Elsewhere I have tried to establish that contemporary scripture studies, liturgical theology, and social teaching all point toward a Christian family ethic that involves dual callings to serve one's own as well as the broader community.[43] In particular, I would argue that there is a mandate in Catholic family theology to embrace those who are poor and defenseless. Yet, in a society in which family-first seems a necessary message to counter dominant trends encouraging focus on career and the self, it is often difficult to take seriously as a moral failing the mistreatment of needy persons in our own midst.

O'Connor offers specific, penetrating illustrations of pride that impedes connection with others, of genuine if partial and flawed attempts to seek connection, and of overwhelming visions of the good that center on inclusive community. Much more effective than general exhortations to solidarity, her stories invite readers to reach beyond themselves and extend their understanding of family.

Many of O'Connor's stories center on a character who is blissfully ignorant of his or her own self/family-centeredness. Mrs. McKinley of "The Displaced Person" speaks frequently and disparagingly of the poor white and black workers on her farm. Though she takes in the "DP," she is unnerved by his work ethic and worries that he will outgrow his position. When distressed by the DP's attempts to bring his cousin over from a Polish work camp by marrying her off to a black man on her farm, Mrs. McKinley declares, "I am not responsible for the world's misery."[44] Refusing to acknowledge her common bond with the people who work her land, she maintains an illusory independence until the end of the story, when all have left her, and she is alone with worsening health and eyesight, with little hope of ever seeing rightly.[45]

Similarly, Ruby Turpin of the story "Revelation," thinks little of the blacks and poor whites she meets in the doctor's office.[46] O'Connor tells us that Mrs. Turpin occupied herself at night ordering people into classes—colored people, white trash, home owners, home and land owners, rich people.[47] She imagines if Jesus had said, "All right, you can be white-trash or a nigger or ugly," and she cannot come up with an answer.[48] In the climactic scene, a college girl in the doctor's waiting room, who has heard enough of Mrs. Turpin's nonsenshe e, throws a book at her and says, "Go back to hell where you came from, you old wart hog." Mrs. Turpin is stunned because she, "a respectable, hard-working, church-going woman . . . had been singled out for the message, though there was trash in the room to whom it might justly have been applied."[49] O'Connor portrays pride without shame as primary sin.

Conversion, on the other hand, is often represented by a more inclusive or expansive attitude to those normally thought of as outside one's family and class. Near the end of "The Displaced Person," Mrs. McKinley does not change her views completely, but when her physical suffering makes it impossible to maintain her belief in her own independence, she does begin to perceive that she is not so unlike the other displaced persons around her.[50] In "A Good Man Is Hard to Find," the grandmother reaches out for The Misfit, calling him her own son, right before he shoots her.[51] Her ability to see connections between people has greatly improved. In "Revelation," Mrs. Turpin comes slowly to see herself more clearly as the wart hog she clearly is and this opens her to receiving a revelation of the last judgment, in which the last (blacks and poor whites) became the first, and the first (those "accountable as they had always been for good order and common sense and respectable behavior") became the last.[52] The beginning of her conversion is marked by a vision of humanity at odds with her previous racism and classism. The accusations in stories like "Revelation" beg readers to ask, "How am I an old wart hog and who knows it better than I do?" More forceful than exhortations to solidarity, O'Connor's stories cry out for the reader's critical self-reflection.

However, O'Connor does not always leave readers wallowing in guilt. In her own way, she offers a vision of what could be, and usually it concerns solidarity. Ruby Turpin's revelation of all the "classes" of people walking together to heaven is a dream of unity O'Connor's readers could hardly imagine.[53] Solidarity is a crucial part of the mystery O'Connor's best characters come to see, the central ethical ideal she believes is mocked by the way most people live. It is a great deal more than inclusivity or a vague feeling for others. O'Connor's writing concerns "the isolated individual striving toward or resolutely avoiding, true communion with others."[54]

Her stories provide glimpses of grace to encourage the striving, and grace, in almost every case, involves unity among people for whom it does not come easily.

The journey toward communion is a crucial part to a Christian theology of the family. In *Familiaris Consortio* John Paul II speaks about family as communion and conveys the bodily and spiritual coming together of persons with each other in the presence of God.[55] He writes that "the fostering of authentic and mature communion between persons within the family is the first and irreplaceable school of social life, an example and stimulus for the broader community of relationships marked by respect, justice, dialogue, and love."[56] However, we have to know what lack of communion really looks like to understand why it is such a tragedy and to desire its opposite. In her stories, O'Connor gives us a vision of un-communion within and outside families. Without communion, human beings look ugly. More effectively than most moral theologians, O'Connor holds up a mirror and forces readers to confront their own failings, with the hope that they will be moved to keep striving.

Local Ethics

Flannery O' Connor's stories concern solidarity, but they are not "social issues" stories; the solidarity envisioned is distinctively local. While racism and classism were inevitably crucial components of fiction set in the South of the 1950s and 1960s, the central moral issues of O'Connor's work are far less grandiose: humility and the right treatment of those to whom one is closely connected. Some criticize O'Connor's insistence on being apolitical, but her commitment to writing about life in small communities is quintessentially Catholic. As Andrew Greeley claims, "Catholic social theory . . . has espoused decentralization . . . in focusing on the local community, indeed on the family itself, as the essential nucleus of a healthy society."[57] This local focus can be seen in stories revealing "the communal action of grace" that are so common among Catholic writers.[58]

A local focus in Catholic literature does not imply that global or national issues lack importance. Rather, it is an assertion that local issues are *also* significant, that ethical conflicts experienced in families and small communities are meaningful and deserving of attention as well. In Catholic social ethics, advocating decentralization means favoring local control wherever possible and supporting a rich local culture of associations. In Catholic literature, it means paying attention to everyday life in communities. For those who engage in Catholic theology of marriage, it should mean paying attention to morally significant ordinary happenings in family life.

This is precisely what does not happen enough in most theology on marriage. In traditional theological discussions of the husband and wife who image Christ and the church, there is an affirmation of the spiritual importance of the marriage bond, of fidelity, even of the sacrifice a life of fidelity requires.[59] In the more recent theology of John Paul II, there is more attention to the sacramental quality of the self-giving relationship between husband and wife and some thick description of how this plays out in the sexual realm.[60] Still, the language is very general and somewhat disconnected from ordinary married life. The tendency to focus on the marriage dyad and the sexual relationship in particular is limiting, when marriages are situated in families and communities, and sexual contact represents a small part of the life of a married couple. Alternatively, in Catholic social teaching, much attention is paid to economics, human rights, and war and peace. However, there remains a great need to see grace and sin at work and to engage in moral wrestling in other dimensions of life.

Fittingly, the conversions in O'Connor's stories are located in the local moral realm between political ethics and sexual ethics. Ruby Turpin of "Revelation" learns that she needs to substitute humility for the "spiritual vanity" that keeps her up at night sorting classes.[61] At the end of the story, readers are left with the hope that her grandiose vision of a march to heaven led by the least will lead her not to join in political protest but to stop thinking of the poor whites and blacks around her as lesser beings and start treating them with respect. Sheppard of "The Lame Shall Enter First" seems truly moved by Rufus's rejection of him.[62] Although he will not be able to make up for his neglect of his own son, perhaps he will take the spoken needs of the boys he works with more seriously and be open to the idea that he, too, stands in need of something beyond himself. The grandmother in "A Good Man Is Hard to Find" does not survive her attacker, but if she did, she most likely would not have become an advocate for criminals' rights. She might have tried to pass on to her grandchildren a sense of their connection to all people, rather than encouraging them to set themselves apart by their good manners.[63] The small dilemmas at the core of O'Connor's work are not lacking in significance.

Moreover, although O'Connor is viewed more as an observer of communities than families, in fact most of her stories concern how family members treat one another. Mrs. Turpin of "Revelation" fails to appreciate her daughter; Sheppard ignores his own son's grief over the loss of his mother; and the parents in "A Good Man Is Hard to Find" seem blissfully unconnected to their children (which is why the grandmother is left to instruct them in manners and morals). Often O'Connor's stories give us parents shocked into recognition of their misunderstanding and neglect through the intervention of a stranger. Sometimes, there are heartbreaking moments of self-knowledge that lead to change. Sally Fitzgerald once noted that O'Connor was concerned with original sin, and "[I]f she stuck with family relationships and situations as a ground, it was because she wrote of obscure, 'unimportant' people, and some kind of family community is where most of us live, and where even our cosmic dramas are enacted and our souls won or lost."[64] Families, Fitzgerald suggests, are the loci of most people's significant moral struggles and thus they are a crucial part of the local ethics to which O'Connor directs attention.

O'Connor was convinced that social change begins locally. On the civil rights issue of her time, she insisted that laws forcing integration were unhelpful. She supported civil rights for blacks, but was convinced that real change would come, gradually, from below. "The South has to evolve a way of life in which the two races can live together with mutual forbearance. You don't form a committee to do this or pass a resolution; both races have to work it out the hard way."[65] Her stories, which often involve people trying to work it out—sometimes well and sometimes badly—point those who seek social change back to the local realm of family and community.

O'Connor got much of her philosophy from Jacques Maritain who wrote of the habit of art as a virtue that perfects the subject.[66] Sally Fitzgerald proposed that while O'Connor clearly acquired the habit of art, she also strove for the habit of being, "an excellence not only of action but of interior disposition and activity that increasingly reflected the object, the being, which specified it, and was itself reflected in what she did and said."[67] This habit is clearly reflected in her letters, which reveal her very deliberate way of living. Her stories *also* concern the habit of being or how people go about their everyday lives.

O'Connor paid attention to the everyday because she believed in "the essential mystery of a 'here and now,' no matter how superficially devoid of meaning, in which displaced individuals exercise a profound moral freedom."[68] All of her stories raise the question, "What are you going to do with your freedom?" The situations that bring about change are often extraordinary, but the moral changes are small and local, though no less significant. She explained that her work concerned mystery and manners, "The mystery . . . is the mystery of our position on earth, and the manners are those conventions which, in the hands of the artist, reveal that central mystery."[69] That mystery is right in front of us.

Conclusion

What are moral theologians who write about family to take from O'Connor? One of O'Connor's last and best stories provides a helpful compass. In "Parker's Back" an interracial married couple remain faithful but share little warmth or understanding. Parker is distinguished mainly by the tattoos that cover most of his body, except for his back. His wife is notable for her violently strong faith, which Parker does not share. A near-fatal tractor accident shakes Parker up and sends him back to a tattoo artist to ask for a large portrait of Christ on his back. When he arrives home, he expects his wife to understand the change that has come over him, but she does not recognize the face on his back. " 'Don't you know who it is?' he cries in anguish. 'It ain't anybody I know,' " she says.[70] And failing to recognize the image of Christ in her husband, she beats him, leaving red welts on his back, hardening her heart as he cries. Grace goes unrecognized in her partner; the unity that marriage is supposed to embody is destroyed in their estrangement; violence flows directly out of misperception, revealing distance between husband and wife, black and white, faith and practice.

The fiction of Flannery O'Connor offers much wisdom for a Catholic theology of marriage. By portraying human sinfulness in all its intensity, O'Connor reminds us of the human need for God, the depth of human finitude, the fundamentally important struggle for solidarity, and the moral significance of everyday life in family and community where habits of being are cultivated over time. Moral theologians are used to writing about how things ought to be and to speaking with compassion about exceptions to the rules.

O'Connor pushes us to go further. Her stories draw us to sin and call out, like Parker does, "Look at it! Don't just say that! *Look* at it!" Instead of responding, like Parker's wife, "I done looked," we are invited to spend time with imperfection in human relationships, pondering how seeing grace even here can expand our understanding of marriage and aid our journey toward greater faith, humility, and solidarity.[71]

Notes

[1]See, for example, John Paul II, *Familiaris Consortio* (Washington, DC: United States Catholic Conference, 1981), #86.

[2]See Bernard Häring, *Marriage in the Modern World* (Westminster, MD: Newman Press, 1965), who, while admitting the legitimacy of limiting and spacing births by natural means, holds up the sacrifice of families with more than the standard one to two offspring in a world hostile to children (314-23). He cites the *Code familial de l'Union de Malines* #57, which reads, "Properly understood, the law of community demands of every family community the greatest number of children which—all things considered—the couple can not only fittingly have but educate in a fitting manner," and an address of Pius XII to the larger families of Italy (315, 321). See also Ed Willock, "Postscript on Poverty and Marriage," in *Be Not Solicitous: Sidelights on the Providence of God and the Catholic Family*, ed. Maisie Ward (New York: Sheed & Ward, 1953). Willock linked families in the lay Marycrest community to saints who take vows of poverty, saying, "Most families I know who are trying to practice holy poverty have to a great degree solved the problem of luxuries. They haven't any. This happy state is usually achieved by accepting the beggars that God sends whether by way of the door or by way of the womb" (250).

[3]John Paul II, *Familiaris Consortio*, #17.

[4]Ibid., #17.

[5]Flannery O'Connor, "To Cecil Dawkins," in *The Habit of Being: Letters of Flannery O'Connor*, ed. Sally Fitzgerald (New York: Noonday Press, 1979), 326.

[6]Flannery O'Connor, "A Good Man Is Hard to Find," in Flannery O'Connor, *The Complete Stories* (New York: Noonday Press, 1971), 119.

[7]Ibid., 132.

[8]Joseph Fuchs describes the fundamental choice this way, "Grace, therefore, calls, and is accepted or refused in the center of the person . . . grace makes its way from the centre of a man and his basic freedom into all areas of life, in to the many acts of free choice and beyond those into the formation of the world" (see Fuchs, "Basic Freedom and Morality," in *Introduction to Christian Ethics: A Reader*, ed. Ronald P. Hamel and Kenneth R. Himes [New York: Paulist Press, 1989], 197). Richard A. McCormick, drawing on the major moral theologians of his day, agreed that faith transforms the person

at the level of worldview, motivation, and style of life (see McCormick, "Does Faith Add to Ethical Perception?" in *Readings in Moral Theology No. 2: The Distinctiveness of Christian Ethics*, ed. Charles E. Curran and Richard A. McCormick [New York: Paulist Press, 1980], 170). In noting the agreement of most Christian ethicists with the claim that faith is the fundamental moral issue for the person, I am not ignoring the reality of differing views as to how much faith influences ethics, but rather emphasizing the relatively uncontroversial nature of the claim to faith's fundamental status, a reality that is starkly portrayed in O'Connor's stories, if not in most contemporary moral theology.

⁹Flannery O'Connor, "The Fiction Writer and His Country," in *Mystery and Manners: Occasional Prose*, ed. Sally and Robert Fitzgerald (New York: Noonday Press, 1969), 34.

¹⁰Ibid.

¹¹Flannery O'Connor, "The Grotesque in Southern Fiction," in *Mystery and Manners: Occasional Prose*, ed. Sally and Robert Fitzgerald (New York: Noonday Press, 1969), 48.

¹²Paul Elie, *The Life You Save May Be Your Own: An American Pilgrimage* (New York: Farrar, Straus and Giroux, 2003), 153.

¹³Ibid. Not all people feel adrift without faith. O'Connor spoke and speaks primarily to those who already share or come to share her faith and her sense of its significance.

¹⁴Recall John Paul II's plea, "Family, become what you are" (*FC* #17), and his discussion of the situation of the world today, which includes much more darkness than light (*FC* #6). Even the most recent theology on the family rarely addresses unbelief. See Julie Hanlon Rubio, *A Christian Theology of the Family* (Mahwah, NJ: Paulist Press, 2003), as well as Florence Caffrey Bourg, *Where Two or Three Are Gathered: Christian Families as Domestic Churches* (Notre Dame: University of Notre Dame Press, 2004), and David Matzko McCarthy, *Sex and Love in the Home* (London: SCM Press, 2004).

¹⁵Lee M. Williams and Michael G. Lawler, "Religious Heterogamy and Religiosity: A Comparison of Interchurch and Same-Church Individuals," *Journal for the Scientific Study of Religion* 40 (2001): 465-78.

¹⁶Flannery O'Connor, "To John Hawkes," in *The Habit of Being: Letters of Flannery O'Connor*, ed. Sally Fitzgerald (New York: Noonday Press, 1979), 349-50.

¹⁷Flannery O'Connor, *Wise Blood* in *3 by Flannery O'Connor* (New York: Signet, 1983).

¹⁸Ross Labrie, *The Catholic Imagination in American Literature* (Columbia: University of Missouri Press, 1997), describes O'Connor's conception of free will and how it applies to Hazel, who struggles to reconcile divine will with his own will and the wills of others (220-21).

¹⁹O'Connor, *Wise Blood*, 2.

²⁰Flannery O'Connor, "The Displaced Person," in Flannery O'Connor, *The Complete Stories* (New York: Noonday Press, 1971), 194-235.

[21]Ibid., 234.

[22]Labrie, *The Catholic Imagination in American Literature*, 16.

[23]Ibid., 231.

[24]O'Connor, "The Displaced Person," 198, 200. O'Connor, famous for her collection of peacocks and other exotic birds, often uses birds as Christ symbols.

[25]Ibid., 203.

[26]Ibid., 224, 225.

[27]Ibid., 235.

[28]Michael Lawler describes the changes in *Marriage and Sacrament: A Theology of Christian Marriage* (Collegeville, MN: Liturgical Press, 1993), 65-71.

[29]O'Connor, "The Teaching of Literature," in Flannery O'Connor, *Mystery & Manners: Occasional Prose*, ed. Sally and Robert Fitzgerald (New York: Noonday Press, 1969), 131.

[30]Ibid., 133.

[31]John Paul II, *Familiaris Consortio*, #52.

[32]O'Connor, "The Displaced Person," 217, 221.

[33]Labrie, *The Catholic Imagination in American Literature*, 219. See O'Connor, "The Lame Shall Enter First," in Flannery O'Connor, *The Complete Stories* (New York: Noonday Press, 1971), 445-82.

[34]Even more tragically, Sheppard's neglect of his own son leads his son to suicide and Sheppard to despair (481-82).

[35]O'Connor, "A Good Man Is Hard to Find," 132.

[36]O'Connor, "On Her Own Work," in *Mystery and Manners: Occasional Prose*, ed. Sally and Robert Fitzgerald (New York: Noonday Press, 1969), 110.

[37]Ibid., 112-13.

[38]Florence Bourg does an excellent job of talking about the need for attention to moral growth toward moral perfection in her *Where Two or Three Are Gathered*, 66-68.

[39]O'Connor, "On Her Own Work," 118.

[40]O'Connor, "A Good Man Is Hard to Find," 132.

[41]O'Connor, *Wise Blood*, 108.

[42]Granville Hicks wrote that O'Connor used extreme characters to portray reality: "[I]n these times the most reliable path to reality, to the kind of reality that seems to her important, is by way of the grotesque" (quoted in Rosemary M. Magee, *Conversations with Flannery O'Connor* [Jackson: University Press of Mississippi, 1987], 84).

[43]See my *A Christian Theology of Marriage and Family* (Mahwah, NJ: Paulist Press, 2003).

[44]O'Connor, "The Displaced Person," 223.

[45]Ibid., 235.

[46]O'Connor, "Revelation," in Flannery O'Connor, *The Complete Stories* (New York: Noonday Press, 1971), 490.

[47]Ibid., 491.

[48]Ibid., 492.

[49]Ibid., 502.

[50]O'Connor, "The Displaced Person," 235.

[51]O'Connor, "A Good Man Is Hard to Find," 132.

[52]O'Connor, "Revelation," 508.

[53]Ibid., 508-9.

[54]Farrell O'Gorman, *Peculiar Crossroads: Flannery O'Connor, Walker Percy, and Catholic Vision in Postwar Southern Fiction* (Baton Rouge: Louisiana State University Press, 2004), 12.

[55]John Paul II, *Familiaris Consortio*, #43.

[56]Ibid.

[57]Andrew Greeley, *The Catholic Myth: The Behavior and Beliefs of American Catholics* (New York: Scribner, 1990), 258-59.

[58]Labrie, *The Catholic Imagination in American Literature*, 10.

[59]Thomas Aquinas, *Summa Theologiae* III Supp. Q. 42.

[60]John Paul II, *Familiaris Consortio*, #13, 32.

[61]O'Connor, "Revelation," 219.

[62]O'Connor, "The Lame Shall Enter First," 481-82.

[63]O'Connor, in "A Good Man," depicts the grandmother reaching out to The Misfit in recognition of their shared humanity (132).

[64]Sally Fitzgerald, "Introduction," *3 by Flannery O'Connor*, xxiii.

[65]C. Ross Mullins, Jr., "Flannery O'Connor: An Interview," in Magee, *Conversations with Flannery O'Connor*, 104. O'Connor may be justly criticized for not seeing the importance of civil rights laws and even for not appreciating the evil of race relations in the South (Elie, *The Life You Save May Be Your Own*, 327-28). Still, the focus on change from below portrayed in her stories is not thereby discredited. Change must proceed from both ends if it is to be lasting.

[66]Sally Fitzgerald, "Introduction," *Habits of Being*, xvii.

[67]Ibid.

[68]O'Gorman, *Peculiar Crossroads*, 12.

[69]O'Connor, "The Teaching of Literature," 124.

[70]O'Connor, "Parker's Back," in O'Connor, *The Complete Stories* (New York: Noonday Press, 1971), 529.

[71]Ibid., 529.

Hans Urs von Balthasar's Use
of the Dramatic Time of Theater

Responding to a Political-Theological Concern

Randall S. Rosenberg

The Swiss thinker Hans Urs von Balthasar is not regularly invoked for a contribution to liberation or political theology. Thomas G. Dalzell has argued that, while neither the temporal nor the historical is ignored in Balthasar's writings, he does tend to focus on the dramatic relationship between the individual and God, and hence his theology is more interpersonal than it is social.[1] The result is a theology that lacks social drama. Steffen Lösel has labeled Balthasar's theology unapocalyptic. According to Lösel, Balthasar minimizes the impact of God's ongoing engagement in history and God's final advent at the end of the world, because his theology of history portrays the theo-drama as an event between heaven and earth and the cross.[2]

It is my hunch that while there is some validity to these critiques and that they do, indeed, deserve to be answered, Balthasar's theology holds yet untapped resources for those who have political-theological concerns, especially those articulated by Johann Metz.[3] There is no use in arguing that Balthasar is a political theologian in the stripe of Metz, but it is worth noting that they share similar concerns.[4] The concern that I wish to highlight here is the attempt to conceive the human historical drama in terms offered by modernity, namely as evolutionary progress. As the Darwinian evolutionist Michael Ruse suggests, for nearly two centuries, "evolution functioned as an ideology, as a secular religion, that of Progress." At the popular level, Ruse argues, *progress* continues to be the hallmark of most people's encounter with evolution.[5] Ruse writes, "I have yet to find a museum or display or a chart or a book which is not overtly progressionist."[6] It must be said from the beginning that while Metz and Balthasar are helpful in pointing out the dangers of the *ideology* of evolutionary progress, this in no way lessens the importance of more constructive approaches currently being explored in the science-religion dialogue by thinkers such as John Haught, John Polkinghorne, Ian Barbour, and Arthur Peacocke, to name a few.[7] Nor do Metz's and Balthasar's theological critiques offer us a system of explanatory terms and relations, as for instance Bernard Lonergan's does in his analysis of human history as a dialectic of progress, decline, and redemption in the context of a world process marked by emergent probability.[8]

With these limitations in mind, I shall inquire, in light of Johann Baptist Metz's critique of modernity's understanding of time as it relates to the history of suffering, to what degree can Hans Urs von Balthasar's employment of the dramatic time of theater contribute to a political-theological concern for grounding a bounded and apocalyptic understanding of time? In order to answer this question, our investigation will, first, highlight key components of Metz's critique of understanding time in evolutionary terms. Second, it will show how Balthasar's critique of Teilhard de Chardin and embrace of Vladimir Soloviev place him on common ground with Metz. Finally, it will argue that Balthasar's use of the dramatic time of theatrical drama can contribute to the political-theological concern for grounding a notion of bounded and apocalyptic time through its ability to highlight the finite time-span within which human persons are called to struggle for the good, under judgment and in the face of death. This dramatic presentation of time has an ability to draw in the audience and reveal the risk and gravity of human historical life. As Frederick Bauerschmidt notes, "one finds little discussion in Balthasar of such topics as human rights, economics, the environment or other (to our way of thinking) 'political' questions." But this does not necessarily imply "that Balthasar has nothing to offer on this count." The central contribution that Balthasar has to make "lies not on the level of addressing certain issues that we would normally describe as 'political' or 'social,' but on the level of theo-drama as a way of understanding the world."[9]

Metz on Time and the History of Suffering

J. Matthew Ashley has shown that Metz's development of a political theology[10] was in part due to his encounter with post-Enlightenment German philosophers Ernst Bloch, Max Horkheimer, Theodor Adorno, Herbert Marcuse, and Walter Benjamin, to name a few. These thinkers constituted strands of a larger post-Hegelian critique of Idealism. Metz also was coming to grips with the atrocity of the Holocaust.[11] He questioned whether a theology rooted in philosophical idealism was able to address the concrete history of suffering, a paradigmatic example of which is Auschwitz. He writes:

> Because of the way Auschwitz showed up—or did not show up—in theology, it became (slowly) clear to me how high the apathy content in theological idealism is, how incapable it is of taking on historical experiences—despite, or even because of all its talk about history and historicity. It is clear that there is no meaning to history that one can save with one's back turned to Auschwitz, and no God of history whom one can worship with one's back turned to Auschwitz.[12]

In addition to Auschwitz, Metz relays another "dangerous memory," an event that occurred in 1945 while serving in the military. His company commander had sent him to the battalion headquarters to deliver a message. He returned to find all his comrades dead. Metz recounts: "I saw only the lifeless faces of my comrades, those same comrades with whom I had but days before shared my childhood fears and youthful laughter. I remember nothing but a soundless cry. I strayed for hours alone in the forest. Over and over again, just this silent cry! And up until today I see myself so. Behind this memory my childhood dreams have vanished."[13]

Such encounters dramatically call into question an Enlightenment-based hegemonic view of history as a progressive continuum. A history with so much suffering can no longer be understood as innocent or even neutral. An important source for Metz, in his attempt to overcome an understanding of history as progressive emancipation, was Walter Benjamin. Benjamin was able to bring together the "remembrance of the catastrophic past" with "an apocalyptic, messianic hope in the future." Benjamin isolated for

Metz a critique of a "quasi-mythical representation of time which has come to dominate modernity: empty time, time as a homogeneous continuum of moments which have no goal, and finally no subject."[14] In short, evolutionary time. While Metz has no objection to scientific theories of evolution, he rejects their ideological use, namely "the universalization of the model of evolution to encompass our experience of time and history in general."[15]

What are the implications of the dominance of evolutionary time? A presupposition of this view of time is the casting of the human person in Promethean-Faustian terms. Here "the person of the future is depicted without the dark background of mourning and suffering, of guilt and death."[16] Suffering and death are regarded merely as an inevitable part of the world process. For Metz, this inevitability points to the fear not only that everything will catastrophically come to an end, but that there is no end at all, "that everything is sucked into the swell of a faceless evolution that finally rolls over everything from behind, like the sea rolls over grains of sand, and like death, makes everything equi-valent."[17] A consequence of this understanding of time is its potential to create a "cult of apathy." For Metz, an apathetic posture toward the world constitutes a "withdrawal from the danger zones of historical and political responsibility, the clever and adaptational skill of making oneself inconspicuous, of compartmentalized thinking, living life in discrete little pieces: a mentality, finally, that can turn us into voyeurs of our own dissolution."[18]

In response to modernity's evolutionary time, Metz suggests a bounded and apocalyptic understanding of time. From a Judeo-Christian understanding, the world is perceived against a horizon of bounded time. Whether in Job's cry of complaint "How long?" or Jesus's cry of abandonment on the cross, one finds in Judeo-Christianity a kind of faithful questioning from the midst of suffering of a God who is time's end and who comes toward it and bounds it.[19] Bounded time recovers a sense of dignity for the very subjects who have been lost in this faceless evolution; it calls into question the vanishing of persons and their historical world.

Second, this bounded time is apocalyptic time, as it brings God's interruption into proximity. Metz explains:

> In the Apocalyptic's subversive vision, time itself is full of danger. Time is not that evolutionary stretched-out, empty and surprise-free endlessness that offers no resistance to our

projections of our future. Time belongs not to Prometheus or
to Faust, but to God. For the Apocalyptic, God is the one who
has not yet fully appeared, the still outstanding mystery of
time . . . its saving interruption.[20]

Within this vision of the apocalyptic, the continuity of time is
measured by "the trail of suffering." "And respect for the dignity
of the suffering that has accumulated through time," writes Metz,
"impels the apocalyptic to understand nature's time from the perspective of the time of the suffering and, thus, evolution from the
perspective of history."[21] Metz does not ignore the billions of years
of nature's time, but considers it a sort of timeless time. What
modernity has given us is *Zeitlosigkeit*, which can be translated as
an "absence of time." As one commentator on Metz explains,
Zeitlosigkeit is "a loss of time as real presence. Time is devalued
into mechanical process, a continuum inexorably moving from past
to future. All of human history with the many histories of suffering are stuck on this endless evolutionary continuum like so many
dead butterflies on an endless black board."[22]

Now that we have briefly established Metz's critique of mythi-
cal evolutionary time, we shall turn to Balthasar, and explore what
his theology has to offer to our attempt to imagine a bounded and
apocalyptic understanding of time.

Balthasar on Evolution as a Theological Category

As we have seen, Metz criticizes the use of evolution as the
measure of our temporal and historical life. I shall now situate
Balthasar on common ground with Metz by outlining briefly
Balthasar's critique of evolution as a theological category—a critique that is found in his critical remarks on Teilhard de Chardin.[23]

According to Balthasar, Teilhard has "one single conceptual
category for all reality: evolution, which he understands as development upward—progress." For this French Jesuit, "belief in the
Christian God and belief in evolution form an indivisible credo.
Cosmogenesis equals anthropogenesis: the human person can only
be understood as the flowering of the totality of the life in the
cosmos."[24] Balthasar's article is skillfully written and nuanced and
clearly shows a critical appreciation for Teilhard. But for the sake
of the argument, we turn to his strongest claim: "Let us say it
outright: evolution is *the* most inappropriate and unhelpful cat-

egory for explaining *anything* Christian."[25] Leo O'Donovan comments on Balthasar's reading of Teilhard's progressivism that "there seems to be no possible room for a true cross."[26] Balthasar writes that even if "the movement of the *world* can be characterized as a ceaseless ascent, *God's* movement in Christ is absolutely to be characterized as a ceaseless *descent* into what is always below. His is a downward movement of love, an act of humility and self-annihilation *(exinanitio)*, a movement of obedient freedom, even to death on the cross, in shame and godforsakenness."[27]

As with Metz, Balthasar's critique of Teilhard does not necessarily imply that he is hostile to the idea of evolution. In fact, he was favorable to the nineteenth-century Russian thinker Vladimir Soloviev.[28] With Soloviev, Balthasar has found someone who embraced an evolutionary view of the cosmos without eliminating the cross, someone who gave due attention to the fallen, dark side of humanity. Balthasar recognizes that Soloviev accepts the process of the hominization of nature as established fact, the progress of cultural and religious history toward Christ, and consequently the collective evolution of humanity and the cosmos toward "the complete coming into being of God in the world, in the Mystical Body of Christ"—all ideas that Teilhard would embrace.[29] Balthasar writes:

> If Christians eighty years ago had taken Soloviev's world picture seriously, there would be no cause today for all the efforts to refute Teilhard. But, quite apart from Soloviev's incomparably greater speculative power, his picture has this in its favour: at the end of his career, Soloviev was confronted by the apocalypse, by Antichrist; and this serves as a salutary counterpoise to his evolutionism, a counterpoise lacking in Teilhard right up to the end.[30]

Soloviev's theology of the Antichrist was incarnated in the genre of the apocalyptic novel, much akin, as Aidan Nichols notes, to Michael O'Brien's 1996 novel *Father Elijah: An Apocalypse*.[31] Toward the end of his life, Soloviev especially displayed a heightened awareness of what he calls the Kingdom of Death—the evils and injustices that ravage human communities. Soloviev therefore surrenders great parts of his philosophy of cosmic process into the hands of the Antichrist—not the facts of the process itself, but the hegemonic view of progress that has been linked to an evolutionary framework. Balthasar comments: "As regards the *facts* of the process, [Soloviev] has not abandoned a single detail; the one thing he has given up is the idea that the process comes to perfection within history. The harvest of man has been brought home, but not by man; it is brought home by Christ, who alone lays the whole Kingdom at his Father's feet. . . . In this respect, Soloviev humbled himself before the all-conquering Cross."[32] In fact, in his Antichrist novel, "it is only with the slaughter of the last Christians that the Christ appears in apparel to bring the harvest of creation home."[33]

What Balthasar's analysis of Teilhard and Soloviev reveals is his discomfort with importing the category of evolution into theological discourse without simultaneously acknowledging the apocalyptic. The danger of this category, as his discussion of Teilhard shows, is its lack of attention to the cross, and its embrace of continual progress. An over-accentuated emphasis on continual ascent and development hints at an attitude that created the conditions for the emergence of the "political Fausts" of our century. In another place, Balthasar explicitly mentions Stalin and Hitler.[34]

Thus far I have offered Metz's critique of evolutionary time and his corrective in bounded and apocalyptic time. Next, I presented Balthasar's critique of evolutionary thinking and his conviction that it also fails to do justice to the dark side of humanity, to the apocalyptic sense of the Son's descent into the fallen human situation and his forsakenness on the cross. In the final area of investigation, I shall explore Balthasar's use of dramatic categories and suggest that they are helpful in contributing to the grounding of a bounded and apocalyptic sense of time.

Balthasar and the Dramatic Time of Theater

The theme of the apocalyptic holds an important place in Balthasar's thought. His early three-volume work, *Apocalypse of the German Soul*, exhaustively examines in an interdisciplinary manner—poetry, philosophy, and theology—the unveiling of the concrete person's upward movement toward ultimate meaning, from Lessing to Heidegger.[35] Ultimately, the myths of German intellectual history, for Balthasar, find their meaning in the cross of Christ.[36] Our concluding inquiry will draw primarily from what Balthasar started in the *Apocalypse of the German Soul* and treated more thoroughly in *Theo-Drama* 1—namely his exploration of the theater as a theological resource.[37]

Volume one of Balthasar's five-volume *Theo-Drama* serves as a prolegomenon to his theological dramatic theory. Here, the Swiss theologian develops the dramatic resources that will ground his account of the drama of human existence in light of the divine drama. It is breathtaking in its scope. Baltasar offers a history of the church's relationship to the theatre; he explores the idea of the world stage from Ancient Greece, through Christianity, into modernity, referring to figures as diverse as Marcus Aurelius, Plotinus, Augustine, Henrik Ibsen, George Bernard Shaw, and Nietzsche; he discerns key elements of drama—the relationship between author, director, and actor, the drama of human finitude, and the struggle for the good in a tragic-comic context; finally, he analyzes the philosophy and psychology of "role" and "mission" with reference to Freud, Jung, Adler, Fichte, Schelling, and Hegel, among others.

Commenting on Balthasar's work, Donald MacKinnon suggests, "There is a great division between contemporary writers on the kinds of issues that here occupy Balthasar's mind, and that is their awareness or their disregard of the fact that in the terrible twelve years, 1933-1945, six million Jews were deliberately murdered." Similar to Metz's claim that we can no longer do theology with our backs turned to Auschwitz, he comments, "The refusal to reckon with this appalling fact gives to any treatment of fundamental theological issues a sort of shallowness that no modernist expertise can conceal." MacKinnon adds that in Balthasar's work, "there is comparatively little that treats directly of these horrors; but the nervous tension of the whole argument witnesses to the author's passionate concern to present the engagement of God with his world in a way that refuses to turn aside from the overwhelming, pervasive reality of evil."[38] Although MacKinnon is referring primarily to Balthasar's volumes on christology and soteriology, I suggest that this "same nervous tension" and "passionate concern" to acknowledge the "overwhelming, pervasive reality of evil" are also evident in the illumination of the drama of human existence found in *Theo-Drama* 1, especially in its presentation of dramatic time, marked as it is by a struggle for the good—a struggle that is given a certain gravity by the inevitability of death and the reality of judgment.

Why theatrical drama? According to Balthasar, as human beings, we are acquainted with drama "from the complications, tensions, catastrophes and reconciliations which characterize" our lives as individuals in community. The task of the stage is "to make the drama of existence explicit so that we may view it."[39] In the theater the human person attempts "a kind of transcendence, endeavoring both to observe and to judge his own truth, in virtue of a transformation—through the dialectic of the concealing-revealing mask—by which he tries to gain clarity about himself. Man himself beckons, invites the approach of a revelation about himself. Thus, parabolically, a door can open to the truth of the real revelation."[40] Furthermore, theatrical drama often contains an explicitly political dimension. As Balthasar writes in a section entitled "Political Theology," "Ancient drama was essentially concerned with the *polis*, particularly in relationship to the religious dimensions; it is no different in most of the plays of *Shakespeare* and *Schiller*. The great characters are not simply individuals, they carry the burden of the common good; kings, heroes, generals, statesmen, rebels either represent a supra-personal order or else they question it."[41]

Balthasar did not believe non-Christian or even anti-Christian theater was without value. Rather, in this post-Christian era, these plays have the potential to illuminate fragments of Christian meaning. In fact, in a pluralistic context, the theater has a kind of "ecumenical" import and forms a kind of "communion." It is worth quoting Balthasar at length:

> What is it (for surely it cannot simply be amusement) that unites these people who come with active expectation and a readiness to "enter into" the action? Under what denominator does it bring them through the performance? It is a very long time since the theatre had a homogeneous audience, such as the baroque theatre had and on which it could exercise a deliberately didactic influence. . . . Yet it still has the power to place man in acute, inescapable situations that strip him naked and confront him with the unavoidable question: Who is he, this being who exists in terrible finitude? His situation in the world is a dramatic one; even if he were to try to conceal it from himself, the stage would confront him with it. That is no small thing. It is not a cultic event, for the question "What is man?" does not oblige the spectator to give a definite

answer. But it is a public act in which, through the participation of the audience, something like a "communion" is brought about. One could think of the theatre as a kind of ecumenical institution: it does not get too close to any denominational form, nor yet does it aim at a watered down common version; it points the different beliefs forward and up, toward a unity that is at present unattainable . . . a place where every proposal for a solution has to reexamine itself in the face of the publicly posed question.[42]

In order to illustrate Balthasar's discovery of fragments of dramatic meaning in post-Christian theater and in our attempt to ground a bounded and apocalyptic understanding of time, we shall briefly turn to Balthasar's excursus on the twentieth-century German poet and playwright, Bertolt Brecht, and the twentieth-century Romanian-born French dramatist, Eugene Ionesco.[43]

According to Balthasar, the Marxist Bertolt Brecht believed that the theater was not for amusing the middle class or for satisfying their need for empathy. His style was socio-didactic. The dramatic arts, for Brecht, must "leave the stadium where they helped man to interpret the world and enter the stadium where they can help to change it."[44] Brecht's purpose is "not to make the audience into a collective enjoying itself, but to bring the individual spectators to personal decisions." It attempts to polarize the audience and create conflicts in the auditorium.[45] As a Marxist, however, Brecht remains confined to a horizontal horizon and portrays a "humanity obedient to the Marxist program and technically equipped to transform the world."[46] The purpose of the theater is to help the audience experience alienation.

Balthasar juxtaposes Brecht with his critic, Eugene Ionesco. Ionesco rejected communism and every other ideology. Instead of focusing on the fleeting social dimension of existence, Ionesco stresses what (he suggests) is more profoundly common to all—the nonsocial dimension.[47] Ionesco highlights the "I's" upward transcendence, its thirst for absolutes in the face of an inevitable death—a situation that reveals life's "pure contradictoriness." The pure verticality of existence is shown in Ionesco's *Exit the King*, which makes "the sole subject of the play the slow, inevitable death of the king, who, in his regal assumption that he can move things, and in identifying himself with the universe, stands for all ego-consciousness."[48] He knows he will die, but does not want to die; it seems unnatural. Let us allow Balthasar to tell the rest of the story.

> He must be helped to set himself loose, but he keeps on loving himself . . . and stammering "*Moi. Moi. Moi.*" He is told to make himself light; invisible cords holding him to the world are cut, and sacks weighing a ton are lifted from his shoulders. "The dreamer is withdrawing from his dream." He is told to go beyond sound, beyond color; he is to go past the burning, circling wheel (Buddhist image); he is not to be drawn into compassion for the beggar who seizes his hand; he is not to bend, to climb, to look into the imageless mirror or surrender his limbs one by one: "Look, now you'll see: you don't need words any more. Your heart doesn't need to beat. There's no point in breathing any more. All the hurrying was a waste of time wasn't it? Now you can take your place."[49]

What is highlighted here is the ego's confrontation with the absolute, which for Ionesco is death. The answer here to the contradictoriness of existence is a kind of "mysticism of unbecoming."[50] Ionesco's life, in fact, was marked by an obsession with death. As Balthasar points out, Ionesco explicitly envisioned the following taking place in one of his plays: "the announcer begins to address the audience, cries out and is overwhelmed by death; the curtain opens behind him to reveal a table bearing a coffin, in which he is carried away." Balthasar adds: "The menace of death has finally triumphed over the action; now existence can only appear as something that has been terminated."[51]

For Balthasar, the pure horizontality of Brecht and the pure verticality of Ionesco both fail to do justice to genuine persons, in genuine finite time. In anticipation of Balthasar's explicitly theological grounding of time, it is important to note that the terms "vertical" and "horizontal" are key themes in Balthasar's eschatology. They are emphasized, for example, in his analysis of Johannine eschatology: "For John, the Christ-event, which is always seen in its totality, is the vertical irruption of the fulfillment into horizontal time; such irruption does not leave this time—with its present, past, and future—unchanged, but draws it into itself and thereby gives it a new character."[52] Authentic drama reveals characters as limited, mortal beings "locked into a finite time-span within which a meaningful dialogue-action must take place horizontally."[53] But this also occurs within a constant *vertical* presence, which renders the timebound play properly human. Balthasar writes, "Drama, with its horizontal-temporal restriction that calls for the action to be meaningfully brought to a conclusion within it, provides a metaphor of the dimension of meaning in all human finitude, and hence it allows us to discern a (vertical) aspect of infinity."[54] For Balthasar, all genuine drama is a kind of "man-trap" where the actor is put into a "straight jacket" and under the limitations of space and time "is 'caught' in the situation" and "pronounced responsible in it."[55] Furthermore, while all narrative art has the potential to illuminate the finite time-span within which human action must take place, theatrical drama includes the active role of the audience. The audience does not watch the performance from "an uninvolved vantage point" but "must make the effort of entering into the action." The performance presupposes that "we are unreservedly ready to be carried wherever it takes us, even 'where you do not wish to go', into areas that are painful, disturbing and possibly unbearable."[56]

Balthasar argues that theater offers fragments of dramatic meaning for holding together the horizontal and vertical dimensions.[57] This glue, as it were, is the tripartite structure of finitude: death, the struggle for the good, and judgment.[58] For Balthasar, death is the "cardinal point" around which the theater hinges. The "mysterious paradox" of death—that, even though unwanted or resisted, it must be simultaneously affirmed as our destiny—either "imparts ultimate meaning to the play of life, or denies it any meaning."[59] Graham Greene, in *The Living Room*, for instance, accentuates *death as destiny* and portrays the senseless attempt to escape death: "after all the rooms of the house in which a person has died have been locked, those who are trying to avoid death are finally struck by a ray of grace: they will be allowed to die there once the rooms have been unlocked again."[60] Arthur Miller's *Death of a Salesman* illuminates the idea of *death as atonement*. Balthasar writes that "suicide is the only remaining way in which Willy Loman can redeem the failure of his life and at the same time give his family a new start—with the insurance money from his car 'accident.' "[61]

Balthasar draws on various literary authors in order to develop other dimensions of death, such as death as the interpreter of life, death and love, death on behalf of someone else, and death on the borderline (communication between the living and the dead).[62] In an excursus on "The Drama of Generations," Balthasar recognizes that death is both a "most personal, most solitary act" but by no means a private act.[63] Thornton Wilder's one-act play, *The Long Christmas Dinner*, deals with a time-span of ninety years. Balthasar writes, "On the left side of the stage is the brightly decorated door of birth, and on the right the black door of death. Ninety Christmas dinners are summed up in this one, the generations and their characters change, the children grow up, the old pass away, but it is all the same life, trivial but irreplaceable." Balthasar applauds Wilder because he depicts the stream of life "in such a way that the individualities lose nothing of their sharpness of outline."[64] This dramatic tension between death as a personal act and a public act is only disregarded "where a 'purely horizontal', communistic or evolutionist theory of drama prevails, which would allot small significance to personal death and see mankind only as a historical or biological collective."[65] It is fitting in this context to recall Metz's concern that a framework that does not understand evolution from the perspective of human history treats suffering and death merely as inevitable parts of the world process.

But the drama is not reduced to the horizon of death. Death for Balthasar is inseparable from the *struggle for the good*.[66] The tension of drama lies in the ambivalence of the present situation and the future-shaping nature of our free decisions. "In every case the goal of the decision is the Good."[67] Balthasar suggests, however, that the Good exhibits gradations. First, there is the absolute Good indicating the direction toward which we should strive. And second, there is a concrete stopping point on the way—namely the choice for the best course of action under particular circumstances. Balthasar writes: "Only in the catastrophe of tragedy are these two points brought to coincide; that is, in the martyr play, where the total witness of a life coincides with death, which, for the believer, always leads to direct union with the Divinity. It also occurs, however, in non-Christian plays—as in Camus's *Les Justes*— in which some ideal is taken as absolute and is affirmed and vouched for by prior acceptance of death."[68] This depiction of the realization of the human good as a struggle indicates that human progress is not best understood as continuous growth. Human action is marked by both limitation and self-transcendence, by egotistical bias and selfless offering, by social decline and social progress.[69] These tensions—and the moral achievements and failures that result in concrete circumstances—reveal the dramatic nature of our ability to shape history. Theater, for Balthasar, has the ability to illuminate this dimension of the human drama: "This good is something *done*: it cannot be contemplated in pure 'aesthetics' nor proved and demonstrated in pure 'logic.' It takes place nowhere but on the world stage—which is every living person's present moment—and its destiny is seen in the drama of world history that is continually unfolding."[70]

Drama, enacted in the face of death and in light of the struggle for the human good, is also executed in the face of "an ultimate, supra-individual authority that judges between good and evil and is represented in man by the voice of conscience, even if the subject matter that exhibits this distinction is purely secular, entirely unreligious, and even if the horizon is cloaked in anonymity."[71] This is why drama often leads to some kind of external court process. What is crucial here for Balthasar is not the external clarification of the court scene in itself, but "the fact that each play encourages the spectator to make a decision as to whether, in this particular course of events, the right thing had been done; or whether . . . it has *not* been done."[72] Often it is common for the hero to judge himself, especially in tragedies, where no other way is found to re-establish justice than through one's own death. Self-sentencing occurs in plays such as *Othello* and *Antony and Cleopatra*. "Occasionally," writes Balthasar, "a (Christian) path leads out of this self-sentencing, as in Tolstoy's *The Power of Darkness*, where Nikita, overwhelmed by the weight of his guilt, wants to hang himself, but the drunkard, Dimitritch, shows him that a man need not fear other human beings; he resolves to confess and give himself up."[73]

Balthasar also enriches this theme of judgment by bringing it into contact with its paradoxical partner *mercy* in an excursus on "Shakespeare and Forgiveness." After an analysis of Shakespeare's histories; the more ideal and fantastic plots of *Two Gentlemen of Verona*, *As You Like It*, *Measure for Measure*; the tragedies of the middle period, such as *Romeo and Juliet*, *Hamlet*, *King Lear*, *Julius Caesar*; and the late romances, Balthasar concludes that Shakespeare knows the dimensions of the realm of evil. For he has an infallible grasp of what constitutes right action. It can be "ethical," or can translate the ethical into a sphere where, behind the moral squalor, the good heart shines through. We see this in so many of his harlot, pimp, and trickster characters. The action never lacks orientation. In accordance with the Christian principle of forgiving mercy, the dramatist causes the Good to predominate without feeling it necessary to reduce the totality of world events to some all-embracing formula . . . he takes up a position beyond tragedy and comedy, because the world he portrays is a mixture of both elements, so he also rises above justice and mercy by allowing both of them to persist, partly in each other and partly in opposition to each other. But all the time he is utterly certain that the highest good is to be found in forgiveness.[74]

Theatrical drama illuminates the action and pathos of the world stage. Balthasar's purpose in using theater is to show how dramatic action looks from the perspective of finite, time-bound persons, in their subjection to death, their freedom to commit evil, and their implication in the world's suffering. While theater offers a way of parabolically revealing the risk and gravity of human historical life, the drama of human finitude in time only finds an absolute answer, for Balthasar, in the revelation of Christ. Although the central burden of our investigation is to draw on resources from theatrical drama, we shall mention explicitly theological resources as a way of anticipating Balthasar's fuller contribution to this question and as a way of drawing Metz back into the conversation. In *TD 5*, Balthasar writes that hope must not be envisioned

according to the extensions of anthropological time—for in this case Christian hope would extend toward a worldly *futurum*—but primarily according to divine or, rather, christological "time," in which anthropological time is assumed into the divine form of duration. Of course, "assumed" does not mean "annihilated," as if human time is rendered meaningless; but it does mean that this human time and all that takes place in it, and everything of Christian significance that is yet to take place, becomes dependent on Christ's "time" and its unique mode of duration.[75]

Contrary to attempts to "manufacture a redeemed existence" through utopian visions, Christianity offers a different answer. Balthasar writes:

> In an action that man could never have anticipated, [God] steps to his opponent's side and, from within, helps him reach justice and freedom. Finitude, time and death are not negated: they are given a new value in a way that is beyond our comprehension. Indeed, even what is hostile to God, in all its profound abysses, is not abandoned; God does not turn his back on it: it is taken over and reworked. Who is responsible for this, man or God? These alternatives are superseded once the chief Actor appears on the stage. The question *Cur Deus Homo* will be equally vital, equally relevant, as long as the world lasts.[76]

For Balthasar, the divine dramatic *answer* to the concrete histories of suffering has already taken place in the form of a human dramatic *question*: the question that Christ utters in his forsakenness on the cross.[77] "This cry," according to Balthasar, "is the very antithesis of that kind of religious resignation which surrenders to an undramatic, absolute horizon."[78] This abandonment is "more profound than anything we can imagine" and "underpins everything in the world that can be termed 'tragic.' This mystery eludes all literary categories and relativizes them."[79]

It would be important to explore, in this context, the relationship between Metz's mysticism of suffering unto God, of turning the questioning back on God in the face of the history of suffering, on the one hand, and, on the other, Balthasar's theology of the cross, where the God-man takes on this question from within and gives it eternal significance. I am sympathetic with Jan-Heiner Tück's conclusion in this regard.[80] Tück explores Metz's reservations concerning a trinitarian theology of the cross as an answer to the cries and lamentations of history's victims—what Metz has called the "piety of theology." Is this not too easy an answer? Tück concludes that a theology of the cross "need not lead to a quieting of man's complaint." This does not in itself ignore that "the eschatological *fulfillment* of history still lies ahead." "Now, it is just this temporal tension between the already and the not-yet," argues Tück, "that characterizes the fundamental structure of the complaint, which, nourished by grateful remembrance of God's saving deeds in the past, calls upon him to intervene powerfully to redeem in the face of acute experiences of suffering and injustice."[81]

Conclusion

As suggested toward the end of this essay, in order to fully treat Balthasar's contribution to this question, one would have to turn to his christological grounding of time, found chiefly in the christological, soteriological, and eschatological volumes of the *Theo-Drama – Dramatis Personae: Persons in Christ*,[82] *The Action*,[83] and *The Last Act*,[84] respectively. There, he analyzes the tragedy of human finitude in light of the paschal mystery. The limits of the present investigation, however, suggest a more modest conclusion. With Metz, I highlighted the danger of a modern embrace of the idea of continual progress and the temptation to regard the history of suffering as simply part of the evolutionary process. For Metz, only time that is understood as bounded and apocalyptic can do justice to human dignity and especially to the dangerous memories of the victims of history. What I have also shown is the way in which Balthasar's critique of the evolutionary model of time and his appeal to the dramatic time of theatrical drama offer resources for taking seriously the risk and gravity of human historical life. The theater has a way of illuminating the finite time-span within which human action must take place and challenges the audience to enter into the action. This action takes place within the interrupting horizon of judgment and is given ultimate meaning by the interrupting presence of Christ who takes on the human situation and experiences its pathos from within.[85]

Notes

[1]Thomas G. Dalzell, "Lack of Social Drama in Balthasar's Theological Dramatics," *Theological Studies* 60 (1999): 457-75.

[2]Steffen Lösel, "Unapocalyptic Theology: History and Eschatology in Balthasar's Theo-Drama," *Modern Theology* 17:2 (April 2001): 201-25.

[3]Frederick C. Bauerschmidt, for example, has attempted to sketch a "Theo-Dramatic Politics" rooted in a critical appreciation of Balthasar's *Theo-Drama*. See his article "Theo-Drama and Political Theology," *Communio: International Catholic Review* 25 (Fall 1998): 532-52.

[4]In "Theo-Drama and Political Theology," Bauerschmidt notes in passing that on many points Balthasar's views are "in notable harmony with the German political theologian Johann Baptist Metz . . ." (535).

[5] Michael Ruse, *Monad to Man: The Concept of Progress in Evolutionary Biology* (Cambridge: Harvard University Press, 1996), 526.

[6] Ruse points out, for instance, that the "Tower of Time" at the Smithsonian in Washington, D.C., carefully depicts the evolutionary triumph of a black man, an Asian woman, and an aged white male. See *Monad to Man*, 526-27.

[7] See John Haught, *Science and Religion: From Conflict to Conversation* (Mahwah, NJ: Paulist Press, 1995), *God after Darwin: A Theology of Evolution* (Boulder, CO: Westview, 2000), and *Deeper Than Darwin: The Prospect for Religion in an Age of Evolution* (Boulder, CO: Westview, 2003); John Polkinghorne, *Belief in God in an Age of Science* (New Haven: Yale University Press, 1998); Ian Barbour, *Religion in an Age of Science* (San Francisco: Harper & Row, 1990; and Arthur Peacocke, *Evolution: The Disguised Friend of Faith?* (Philadelphia and London: Templeton Foundation Press, 2004).

[8] See Bernard Lonergan, *Insight: A Study of Human Understanding*, Collected Works of Bernard Lonergan, vol. 3, ed. Frederick E. Crowe and Robert M. Doran (Toronto: University of Toronto Press, 1992). For the relevance of Lonergan's system in our contemporary context, see Patrick H. Byrne, "Evolution, Randomness, and Divine Purpose: A Reply to Cardinal Schonborn," *Theological Studies* 67, no.3 (September 2006): 653-66.

[9] Bauerschmidt, "Theo-Drama and Political Theology," 536.

[10] Matthew Lamb helpfully discerns three marks of Metz's political hermeneutics. First, political theology must be grounded not on concepts and ideas, but on the dynamics of historical and social subjects striving to live out the call for conversion. Second, this method recovers the transcendental thrust by understanding it, not as disclosive of human beings "always already" before God but as imperatives to realize their mission to be Christ-like disciples in their own social and historical circumstances. Finally, political theology recovers the concrete history of suffering. See *Solidarity with Victims: Toward a Theology of Social Transformation* (New York: Crossroad, 1982), 120-21.

[11] J. Matthew Ashley, *Interruptions: Mysticism, Politics, and Theology in the Work of Johann Baptist Metz* (Notre Dame: University of Notre Dame Press, 1998), 97.

[12] Johann Baptist Metz, *A Passion for God: The Mystical-Political Dimension of Christianity*, trans. J. Matthew Ashley (New York: Paulist Press, 1998), 39-40.

[13] Metz, "Communicating a Dangerous Memory," in *Communicating a Dangerous Memory: Soundings in Political Theology*, ed. Fred Lawrence (Atlanta: Scholars Press, 1987), 39f.

[14] Ashley, *Interruptions*, 118.

[15] Ibid., 119.

[16] Metz, *A Passion for God*, 50.

[17] Ibid., 51.

[18] Ibid., 51-52. See also 76.

[19] Ibid., 82.

[20] Ibid., 52.

[21]Ibid.

[22]Matthew L. Lamb, "Apokalyptische Unterbrechung und Politische Theologie," in *Befristete Zeit*, ed. Jürgen Manemann (*Jahrbuch Politische Theologie*, Band 3) (Munster: Lit Verlag, 1999): 232-40.

[23]This article will focus on Balthasar's "Die Spiritualität Teilhards de Chardin," *Wort und Wahrheit* 18, no. 5 (1963): 339-50. I thank Edward T. Oakes, S.J., for his English translation. Balthasar has also critiqued Teilhard de Chardin's eschatology in *Theo-Drama: Theological Dramatic Theory*, vol. 5: *The Final Act*, trans. Graham Harrison (San Francisco: Ignatius Press, 1998), 153-68. Leo O'Donovan has critically analyzed Balthasar's treatment of Teilhard de Chardin in "Evolution under the Sign of the Cross," *Theological Studies* 32 (1971): 602-26.

[24]Balthasar, "Die Spiritualität Teilhards de Chardin," 339.

[25]Ibid., 347.

[26]O'Donovan, "Evolution Under the Sign of the Cross," 603-4.

[27]Balthasar, "Die Spiritualität Teilhards de Chardin," 347.

[28]Balthasar devotes a full monograph to Soloviev in *The Glory of the Lord*, vol. 3, *Studies in Theological Style: Lay Styles*, trans. Andrew Louth, John Saward, Martin Simon, and Rowan Williams (Edinburgh: T&T Clark, and San Francisco: Ignatius Press, 1986), 279-352. This volume will subsequently be referred to as *GL 3*.

[29]Ibid., 290.

[30]Ibid.

[31]Aidan Nichols, *The Word Has Been Abroad: A Guide through Balthasar's Aesthetics* (Washington, DC: The Catholic University of America Press, 1998), 118.

[32]*GL 3*, 352.

[33]Nichols, *The Word Has Been Abroad*, 118.

[34]See *Theo-Drama: Theological Dramatic Theory*, vol. 4, *The Action*, trans. Graham Harrison (San Francisco: Ignatius Press, 1994), 144-45. This text will subsequently be referred to as *TD 4*.

[35]Especially relevant to this discussion is *Apokalypse der deutschen Seele III: Die Vergöttlichung des Todes* (Einsiedeln: Johannes Verlag, 1998). For a summary and analysis of this three-volume work, see Aidan Nichols, *Scattering the Seed: A Guide through Balthasar's Early Writings on Philosophy and the Arts* (New York and London: T&T Clark, 2006).

[36]Alois Haas, "Hans Urs von Balthasar's 'Apocalypse of the German Soul,' " *Hans Urs von Balthasar: His Life and His Work*, ed. David L. Schindler (San Francisco: Ignatius Press, 1991), 52-54.

[37]*Theo-Drama: Theological Dramatic Theory*, vol. 1, *Prolegomena*, trans. Graham Harrison (San Francisco: Ignatius Press, 1988). For helpful studies on this theme, see Christopher Denny, "Literature in the Dramatic Anthropology of Hans Urs von Balthasar" (Ph.D. diss., Catholic University of America, 2004) and "Greek Tragedies: From Myths to Sacraments," *Logos* 9, no. 3 (Summer 2006): 45-71.

[38]Donald MacKinnon, "Some Reflections on Hans Urs von Balthasar's Christology with Special Reference to Theodramatik II/2 and III," in *Analogy of Beauty: The Theology of Hans Urs von Balthasar*, ed. John Riches (Edinburgh: T&T Clark, 1986), 164-74; here at 165.

[39]*TD* 1, 17.

[40]Ibid., 12.

[41]Ibid., 37.

[42]Ibid., 322-23.

[43]See Aidan Nichols, *No Bloodless Myth: A Guide Through Balthasar's Dramatics* (Washington, DC: The Catholic University of America Press, 2000), 35, for a brief discussion of Brecht and Ionesco.

[44]*TD* 1, 325.

[45]Ibid., 328.

[46]Ibid., 331.

[47]Ibid., 333.

[48]Ibid., 341-42.

[49]Ibid., 342.

[50]Ibid.

[51]Ibid., 343.

[52]*Theo-Drama: Theological Dramatic Theory*, vol. 5, *The Final Act*, trans. Graham Harrison (San Francisco: Ignatius Press, 1998), 25. Subsequently this volume will be referred to as *TD* 5. Frederick Bauerschmidt, in "Theo-Drama and Political Theology," critically questions Balthasar's understanding of "horizontal" and "vertical": "The horizontal axis is superseded by the vertical, and the eschaton's vertical interruption of history seems to have little historical effect. One might well ask whether this prioritizing of the vertical over the horizontal does not end up slackening the tensions of historical existence, leading to a Christian practice that is so thoroughly internalized that it can avoid the imperative to manifest crucified love to the world by means of a historically and communally embodied tradition" (549).

[53]*TD* 1, 344.

[54]Ibid., 344-45.

[55]Ibid., 346-47.

[56]Ibid., 309.

[57]Nichols, *No Bloodless Myth*, 34.

[58]See ibid., 34-39.

[59]*TD* 1, 371.

[60]Ibid., 374-75.

[61]Ibid., 385.

[62]For Balthasar's full treatment of "death" as a dramatic resource, see ibid., 369-413. See also Graham Ward, "Kenosis: Death, Discourse and Resurrection," in *Balthasar at the End of Modernity*, ed. Lucy Gardner, David Moss, Ben Quash, and Graham Ward (Edinburgh: T&T Clark, 1999), 15-68.

[63]*TD* 1, 408.

[64]Ibid., 412.

[65]Ibid., 413.

[66]See ibid., 413-51.

[67]Ibid., 414.

[68]Ibid.

[69]See ibid., 415-16.

[70]Ibid., 19.

[71]Ibid., 321.

[72]Ibid., 452.

[73]Ibid., 460.

[74]Ibid., 478.

[75]*TD* 5, 56-57.

[76]*TD* 4, 201.

[77]That Christ experienced darkness on the cross is a contested claim. See Bernard Lonergan's argument against this notion in *De Verbo Incarnato*, 3rd ed. (Rome: Gregorian University Press *ad usum auditorum*, 1964), 391-92. See also Matthew Levering, "Balthasar on Christ's Consciousness on the Cross," *The Thomist* 65 (2001): 567-81, for a critique of Balthasar's position from a Thomist perspective.

[78]*TD* 1, 21.

[79]Ibid., 429.

[80]Jan-Heiner Tück, "The Utmost: On the Possibilities and Limits of a Trinitarian Theology of the Cross," *Communio* 30 (Fall 2003): 430-51.

[81]Ibid., 432.

[82]*Theo-Drama: Theological Dramatic Theory*, vol. 3, *Dramatis Personae: Persons in Christ*, trans. Graham Harrison (San Francisco: Ignatius Press, 1992).

[83]*TD* 4.

[84]In *TD* 5. See also his earlier work *Theologie der Geschichte* (Einsiedeln: Johannes Verlag, 1959); translated into English as *A Theology of History* (San Francisco: Ignatius Press, 1994). See especially the section entitled "Christ's Time and Human Time: Faith," 40-50.

[85]I would like to thank the editors of the annual volume and the reviewers for their helpful criticisms and suggested revisions.

Part IV

AESTHETICS AND EDUCATION

Profound Learning, Theological Aesthetics, and AIDS

Assessing the Effectiveness of Service-Based Pedagogies

Kimberly Vrudny

In her 2003 documentary, *Pandemic: Facing AIDS*, Rory Kennedy profiles the presence of HIV/AIDS in the lives of a formerly drug-addicted couple in Russia, a prostitute in Thailand, a gay man in Brazil, an adulterous husband in India, and two orphaned children in Uganda.[1] The poignancy of the film derives from the manner in which the filmmaker identifies tragedy coming into contact with love and yielding hope in each individual story. Through their advocacy work, Sergei and Lena find redemption; through her family's introspection, Lek finds reconciliation; through his country's social system and family's acceptance, Alex finds hope for a prolonged life; through his repentance, Nagaraj prevents contagion to his offspring; and through her music therapy, Margaret becomes a mother to dozens of children orphaned by the disease. In each instance, a thoughtful response encounters AIDS and yields beauty. Could a class on theological aesthetics, I wondered, accomplish the same? Through partnership with a community organization preparing meals for, and delivering meals to, people living with and affected by HIV/AIDS, could students begin to see beauty in what is not necessarily pretty?

Theologians have received service learning unevenly. On the one hand, service learning seems to have a natural affinity with theology. Since the inception of the academic journal *Teaching Theology and Religion* in 1998, one monograph and three articles have considered the merit of using service-based pedagogies in classrooms of theology or religious studies.[2] All of these have appeared since 2002. On the other hand, there are real tensions between service learning and theology that merit attention. When I speak with colleagues, they express concern about the academic rigor of service-based learning. In a discipline often misunderstood and impugned by the larger academy, some professors of theology tend to resist less established pedagogical techniques, dismissing them as "lightweight," "fluff," or "trendy." Certainly, academics in other disciplines share this concern. In their article in the *Michigan Journal of Community Service Learning,* researchers Abes, Jackson, and Jones found that there were "four factors that most strongly deter faculty from using service-learning."[3] These include uncertainty regarding logistics and techniques in using service learning effectively, as well as concerns regarding relevancy and provision of release time. "Lack of relevance was . . . a strong deterrent for respondents from the arts. . . ."[4] Despite their misgivings, some of these respondents were open to learning how to use service learning effectively. One commented: "Some examples of service-learning technique, applied to [courses in my discipline] would be helpful to me and might provide a stimulus for action on my part."[5]

In order to address the concern about academic rigor, as well as the desire among educators for ideas about how to use service-based pedagogies in discipline-specific courses, I would like to present two experiences of teaching a course in theological aesthetics. The differing results between the two courses, as evidenced in journal entries, final-paper thesis statements, and course and instructor evaluations are so dramatic that they indicate I taught the abstract, theological content more effectively with a service-learning component than without it. My intention in this presentation is twofold. First, I shall provide an example of how a service-based pedagogy was implemented in a course on theological aesthetics. Second, I shall attempt to prove from available evidence that students achieved a higher mastery of abstract theological content in my theological aesthetics course when I taught with a service-based pedagogy than when I taught the same course without such a component.

Most simply stated, theological aesthetics is the study of the theological dimension of beauty. When teaching theological aesthetics as an upper-level undergraduate course at a Catholic university, one central course objective I have is to challenge the idea that "beauty is in the eye of the beholder" by untangling the beautiful from "the pretty," and by considering the possibility that "the beautiful" may have an objective nature that is convertible with "the good" and "the true." That is, by reference to the theological tradition, we explore how these words may point to a single reality—to love, to existence itself, insofar as existence can be known. We also consider the implications this has for a life of faith. Thus, in the course we explore the possible relationships between the aesthetic, the rational, and the ethical. As we work through the primary readings, we begin to see how historical figures like Thomas Aquinas associated Beauty with the second person of the Trinity. Readings from voices of a twentieth-century liberation perspective enable us to focus on Jesus's ministry of compassion, his concern for those the world neglects, and the integrity of his position of non-violence that carried him all the way to the cross. Through these readings, we begin to examine the meaning of "beauty," drawing into question its American Heritage Dictionary definition as "A pleasing quality associated with harmony of form or color, excellence of craftsmanship, truthfulness, originality, or another, often unspecifiable property."[6] Instead, we begin to ask questions about what it means for Jesus to be identified with Beauty, particularly in reference to the crucifixion. Was Beauty forsaken by God in the distortion and disfigurement of the cross, or realized—or still something else? If Beauty was realized through crucifixion, does Christianity glorify suffering? Does such glorification of suffering and violence by necessity perpetuate its existence? Was Beauty realized through crucifixion, or only through resurrection? If realized through resurrection, what implications are there for Beauty in the "already," and the "not yet"?

These are among the questions we explored when I first taught two sections of the course "Art, Beauty, and the Revelation of the Divine" as an adjunct professor, teaching at the undergraduate level in a rural Catholic institution just outside Minneapolis during the spring semester of 2003. One section met on Tuesday nights, the other on Thursday nights, each for three-and-one-half hours. Because the course satisfied a core requirement in the Judeo-Christian heritage as well as an upper-level requirement for theology majors, twenty-one students enrolled in the first section, and seventeen in the second. I used the same syllabus in each course, treating a different philosopher or theologian each week, beginning with Plato's *Symposium*, before entering Christianity with Augustine's *De Musica*.[7] Plato's understanding of beauty was foundational for what we were trying to accomplish in this course, for he outlines how we might understand material things to lead us in stages from forms to actions to the notion of Beauty absolute, which is the same "essence of beauty" Augustine will proclaim to be the trinitarian God. In order to be more certain that students were seeing that, in this class on beauty, we were discussing things quite other than fair sunsets and the latest fashions, I required them to prepare outlines of each primary reading we covered. In addition to Plato and Augustine, our reading list included the writings on images and icons of John of Damascus,[8] Thomas Aquinas's treatment of the divine names with a consideration of Umberto Eco's analysis of Thomas's understanding of beauty,[9] Kant's *Third Critique*,[10] and Jonathan Edwards' interrelation of beauty and virtue,[11] before turning to more recent thinkers such as Barth,[12] Tillich,[13] Weil,[14] Balthasar,[15] and Tracy.[16]

From time to time throughout the semester, in addition to studying these primary readings together in class, we discussed works of art in order to probe more deeply into particular issues we faced in the texts. For example, when we read John of Damascus's *On Divine Images*, which argues that incarnational theology establishes a theological basis for the use of images in prayer, a Benedictine monk and iconographer came to our class to demonstrate the method and theology of creating an icon. When we read Simone Weil on the relationship between beauty and human rights, I showed charcoal drawings by Weil's contemporary, German artist Kathë Kollwitz, who depicted workers protesting unfair labor practices. We discussed how both texts, written and visual, communicated parallel theologies while each provided unique insights.

It was during one such session in "looking at art" that I realized, for the majority of students, definitions of beauty had not shifted much from "what is pretty." Midway through the semester, we considered documentary photographs by Sebastião Salgado of the 1980s famine in Ethiopia and posed the question: "Are these images, in any sense, beautiful?" These were images of emaciated children hanging in baskets at weighing stations, fathers carrying bodies of their limp children to feeding centers, and mothers breastfeeding twin babies from shriveled breasts. Even after we had engaged in a review of the perspectives so far encountered in the course—perspectives that might have enabled us to recognize Beauty in these images—one student said, "You will never get me to say those images are beautiful." I sensed that student spoke for many in the classroom who were not yet willing to engage theological questions probing the possible mystical, sacramental, or iconic presence of Christ in such images and some were unwilling to investigate the formal qualities of the work that make Salgado's photographs visually compelling—a maneuver that would have enabled us to engage critiques of his work by Susan Sontag.[17] These obstacles prevented us, too, from examining possible implications of naming Christ "Beauty," particularly as these implications intersect with human suffering.

Though it appeared that the terms "beautiful" and "pretty" remained synonymous for most of the students at mid-semester, I hoped their final papers would indicate more of a shift. Put succinctly, the assignment for their final papers asked students to "Write an eight- to ten-page paper in which [they] state[d] [their] theological aesthetic"; that is to say, they were to write "about [their] definition of beauty, its relation to God, and its relation to art." They were asked to do this by identifying a work of art they considered beautiful, and to reflect on the piece through an engagement with the thinkers we had read in class. When the results started coming in, I was alarmed. Despite questions supplied on the assignment sheet pointing to a specific investigation of beauty and its (potential) contraries of deception, evil, and deformity, and despite the centrality of these questions in our conversations about the readings, very few of the papers addressed these questions to any significant degree. The students wrote about why the works they chose were pretty.[18]

My overall reaction to the experience was one of dissatisfaction. I knew that I had not met my central course objectives adequately. For the most part, students had not wrestled with the identification of Christ with Beauty in their final papers, and had not recognized the relationship between Beauty and the love of neighbor—particularly of those the world neglects. They did not wrestle with these issues because I did not adequately make the connections between them in the course. If Christ is the personification of Beauty Absolute, in what direction does his life and ministry point his disciples? What does his violent death mean for Beauty? Was Beauty forsaken by God? Or might God as Beauty Absolute abide with humans even in their moments of greatest physical, psychological, and spiritual turmoil? If so, what does Beauty *look* like? These questions, for the most part, went unexplored in the final papers of 2003.

The opportunity to teach the course again came sooner than I had imagined. Even while I was teaching the class as an adjunct, I was offered a tenure-track position in the fall in the Department of Theology at the University of St. Thomas in St. Paul, Minnesota. Among my courses would be "Art, Beauty, and the Theological Imagination," to be offered in the spring semester of 2004. Because I had pinpointed the central course objectives to be consideration of the possible trinitarian nature of existence in the true, good, and beautiful, and exploration of the implications of such an understanding for living a beautiful life attentive to the suffering of those the world neglects, I redesigned the course with such objectives in mind.

Even while I was pondering how to do so, I enrolled in a faculty development workshop about "best practices of service learning." Service learning is a pedagogy that requires students to learn discipline-specific course content in collaboration with a community partner, and is intentional in its emphasis on socio-economic and/or ecological justice. The week-long seminar had as its goal the implementation of a service-learning component in a new or reconfigured course of our own choosing. It occurred to me during the week that a service-learning activity might be precisely the sort of pedagogy I needed in order to help students see that our readings in theological aesthetics, which wanted us to equate Christ with beauty, did not enable us to continue defining beauty as "what is pretty."

As these thoughts solidified in my mind, I was confronting the question—Where would I have my students work, and how precisely would their service work help them to process the content of theological aesthetics? They were not engineers who could design a piece of equipment to perform a particular function, nor were they computer science students who could help immigrant business people design databases for their particular entrepreneurial needs. In order for students to gain a richer perspective into contemporary theologies addressing the person of Christ, and the role of the church or the believer in relation to populations marginalized by ethnicity, class-status, and/or gender, I wanted our community work to be at a place where we could examine systems that perpetuate poverty, as well as a place where students would recognize implications of privilege and its lack. When the facilitator suggested that faculty draw on their own interests and passions when identifying potential partnerships, it was as if all the pieces fell together. I would have students partner with Open Arms of Minnesota, an organization that prepares meals for, and delivers meals to, people living with or affected by HIV/AIDS in the Twin Cities. This was an organization that my son and I had been involved with since he was three. I thought if I could ask my students to deliver meals on an Open Arms route four or five times during the semester and work at the headquarters once or twice, reflecting afterwards on specific journal questions about the presence or absence of God in the experience of suffering, they might begin to make the sort of connections I had struggled to facilitate when I initially offered the course. By the end of the workshop, I had the master plan for "Art, Beauty, and the Theological Imagination." It would be a service-learning course.

I was particularly concerned about focusing on the dimension of *learning* in service learning and was pleased to discover, upon approaching the Open Arms staff about a possible partnership, that they were well-equipped to help manage the logistics of a service-learning arrangement with a class our size. They were in the process of hiring a person (who had previously worked in the service-learning office at another local university) specifically to work with colleges, churches, and other community organizations. Because we wanted to be sure the relationship was authentically reciprocal, we realized during our discussions that research in theological aesthetics was not exactly a necessity for Open Arms! However, they were short on volunteers to deliver meals and to help with office tasks. We determined together that Open Arms could accommodate our students six times each, an acceptable amount to equip them with material for reflection in their journals about the connection of their service to theology and beauty. The students might call themselves volunteers, but I wanted to be confident that when they delivered those meals and worked at office tasks, they were appropriating content from the course. To ensure such learning was happening, two class sessions were designated as service-learning "check-in" days. A staff person from Open Arms attended those sessions to help us navigate questions concerning HIV/AIDS, Christian belief, and beauty. In addition, one session at the beginning of the semester was conducted by Open Arms staff, and was entirely devoted to training the class about HIV/AIDS, the work of Open Arms, and the work the students would undertake there. At that session, Open Arms staff emphasized we would be engaging with a vulnerable population. They asked the students to protect the confidentiality of the clients and to maintain an atmosphere of professionalism by not crossing the threshold into the clients' homes. Clients were not to be interviewed for the purposes of the course.

Because of these important restrictions, students were forced to process course content strictly through observation. A number of questions guided their journal reflections, including questions to help identify their own perspectives as they conducted their research: "How does your experience at Open Arms impact the way you understand the concept of 'beauty' and the 'beauty of the AIDS experience,' as we have been examining these concepts in class?" I also asked them to think about issues of blame and responsibility, and directed them away from simplistic accusations rooted in sexual mores of individual people, asking them, instead, to think about systemic causes that perpetuate the spread of AIDS among the poor. I urged them to focus on the community's collective responsibility for responding to the pandemic locally as well as globally. I also asked them to reflect on appropriate and inappropriate employment of language concerning the virus and people living with HIV/AIDS.

I hoped their service work would contribute deeper insight into the larger research project required of students in their third-level theology courses. Instead of requiring students to write about a work they found beautiful, they were assigned to answer, in eight to ten pages, "What is the beauty of the AIDS experience"? In addition to reflecting on course texts in order to describe their own theology of beauty, they were asked to research an artist whose work has touched the issue of HIV/AIDS in some way. In their papers, they were to discuss the artist's biography, analyze one of the artist's works about AIDS, and tie the work into their own construction of beauty. I required that they meet with me twice before they presented their research.

In terms of designing the course, little else changed. Requirements were redistributed to give service learning its legitimacy in the course.[19] By the time all the dust settled, fourteen students had enrolled. None was a theology major; all were enrolled in the course to satisfy the third-level theology requirement ("Faith and the Catholic Tradition") in the core curriculum. There was nearly equal distribution of Catholic and Protestant students, as well as a number (up to four) of students who categorized themselves as either agnostic or atheist. They were scheduled to meet three times a week for sixty-five minutes rather than one night a week. For the most part, though, I conducted the class as I had previously. I assigned the same readings, with only a couple of slight modifications. In order to accommodate the service-learning component, a few readings were eliminated, and one additional reading was assigned. Students were asked to read *Sing Me to Heaven: The Story of a Marriage*, written by theologian Margaret Kim Peterson about her marriage to a man who was HIV-positive.[20] Several class sessions were devoted to our work with Open Arms, where we reflected together about student experiences, and the relationship of those experiences to theological aesthetics.

Those conversations gave me the first hints that the course objective of examining the relationship between beauty and suffering was being met. A stronger indication came as I read the journal entries upon which the class discussions were based. I collected journals from students on the last day of class, after hearing their formal presentations. I was not prepared for the level of reflection I encountered. Eight prevalent themes emerged: 1) stereotypes were challenged; 2) blame for the virus was assigned or questioned; 3) empathy was aroused; 4) self-reflection was induced; 5) the impact of the Open Arms organization was assessed; 6) theological questions were raised; 7) the presence or absence of God in the experience of suffering was explored; and 8) beauty was defined. The final three are the most relevant here.

Theological questions were raised when students encountered people living with, and dying from, complications associated with HIV/AIDS. Some blamed God directly, wondering to what extent suicide is an issue upon diagnosis. "How could you keep hope, keep faith in a God that would do this to you?" Another wondered where God was, given so much suffering and death. "I just cannot understand. If there was ever a time to wonder where God is, now is it." Another was indignant at God's complicity:

> What is God trying to do with these people? Shouldn't he give some kind of antidote or is he just letting them die because it was their fault decided through free will? To me, God should be a fair God. He must look at the goodness vs. the evil in one's life. He should help give more to one's good and less to the evil. But life does not go that way. People die, suffer, starve, no matter what they do in life. God is too inconsistent. People that are diagnosed with AIDS must ask themselves

why they suffer when millions of others have unprotected sex and do drugs and live normal, happy lives. God's unfairness is one reason I turned my back on him.

Others, though, found positive theological meaning in their experiences. One wrote, "I like to think that, through us and others, humanity is doing the work of Christ." Another wrote of a man who struggled to the door, and of helping him back down the steps to his apartment. "For this man, we were God that day. We were goodness, hope, truth, beauty, and love. . . . I now know there to be beauty in this thing we are doing. I have seen it with my own eyes, known it in my mind, and felt it in my soul." Another wrote, "I was at first skeptical that I could have any experience of the divine and/or beautiful by doing this. After actually doing it, it would seem that this kind of experience is completely inevitable." Later in the same entry, this student wrote,

> There is incredible beauty in this thing we are doing. I do not know if, as of yet, I am able to articulate it effectively but it is there undeniably. I feel it and sense it, spiritually. Can it be a true experience of the divine? It would seem so in some respects. I know that we are doing good, and I know it is appreciated. I also know that it makes life happier and easier for these people in some way. Although this way may be small, in the larger scope of things it lacks nothing in significance.

These theological issues led directly to questions of God's presence or absence in the experience of suffering, with which the students were grappling for the purpose of their final research projects. One simply wrote, "I didn't see anything today that would encourage me to think that God is somehow present." One student struggled with the tendency to glorify suffering. Another decided against God's existence in the face of such profound suffering:

> I just cannot understand. . . . To try and justify the situation with God's greater purpose or some hidden meaning seems incredibly unethical. Why should he suffer if I do not? How can God pick those to experience pain and not provide them with any comfort? These people are living through hell with little regard or recognition. As to God's existence throughout

this tragedy, I cannot explain. If He is somehow involved, I do not think I can fully view Him as omni-benevolent. The sorrows of some are far too great.

Through such sincere questioning, some students arrived at the positions they would present in their final papers. One student argued against the presence of beauty in the experience of suffering. "The lack of beauty that I have experienced in the world has nothing to do with what is pleasing to me and my eyes; I have come to conclude that it is a full and complete absence of goodness, and God." Others disagreed. One discovered beauty to be "true happiness, which is obtained by love," even "love for the victims of AIDS." Another related his thesis to the experience at Open Arms directly. "Open Arms has been an amazing experience. It has exposed me to the beauty that can be experienced when I am fully present, even in the face of suffering."

When I met in my office independently with students about their research, I was finally convinced that I had successfully met my course objectives. These meetings were valuable opportunities for me to hear more about the students' perceptions of beauty, of AIDS, of art, and of the interrelatedness of the three in their minds. What I heard was nothing short of stunning. Students were making the connections I hoped they would make as they wrestled with questions of beauty and suffering.

The thesis statements from their papers alone indicate that the assignment forced them to grapple with this most difficult question of the relationship between beauty and suffering. They ended up articulating four different positions: 1) implicating God in the suffering; 2) finding God's presence with those who suffer; 3) finding God's presence in those who compassionately serve others who suffer; and 4) extricating God from the suffering altogether.

Drawing on the theologies of Augustine and Thomas Aquinas, two students articulated in differing ways the understanding that God sends the disease for a purpose, and is able to draw good from it. One wrote that God works beauty through the illness: "The beauty of the AIDS experience is how God, through the affliction of the disease, provides an opportunity to control its destructive nature by its potential for beauty, which transforms the experience for the afflicted, as well as for those who accompany them." Another wrote that, through suffering, humankind comes to deeper understanding of beauty than is otherwise possible: "The beauty of the AIDS experience is that, through the grace of God, humankind is able to obtain greater understanding of the beauty that exists in oneself, in other humans, and in the surrounding world."

Basing their opinions on the theology of Jonathan Edwards, by distinguishing primary from secondary beauty, six students in the course found beauty in those who, like Christ, served those who suffered, rather than finding beauty in the suffering itself. One argued, "The beauty present in the AIDS experience exists in Christ-like acts of love, kindness, and charity which are able to shine through the rampant terror of the virus, much as redemption emerged from the horrors of the cross." Another wrote, "The beauty of the AIDS experience is the presence of the Trinity standing silent but empowering in our presence, transforming the human heart, and providing the courage to be concerned about the well-being of others." A third argued, "The beauty of the AIDS experience is found in the capacity for humans to be fully present to one another, which makes the Sacred manifest to humankind."

Others found the theologies of such divergent voices as John of Damascus and Paul Tillich compelling. Five students found beauty in the suffering itself, often articulating contingencies upon which such an experience must be based. Referencing Tillich, they understood beauty as, in some way, equivalent to existence, or the ground of being. One student wrote, "When we are able to be fully attentive in the present moment, even in the face of immense suffering, we become more like Christ and experience the true beauty of an ultimate reality." The student here qualifies the statement by asserting that the ability to be a manifestation of beauty and to experience beauty in the midst of AIDS is dependent on one's ability to be attentive.

Only one student argued that beauty was absent from the experience of AIDS. His fellow students recognized during the presentation that he, like they, was articulating grounds for empathy and compassion in the face of AIDS: "Beauty is absent from the AIDS experience, for that which is most beautiful is that which is most fully actualized; God, as a force which opposes suffering and wills benevolence, inspires us to alleviate suffering by restoring hope to the hopeless, accompanying the lonely, restoring beauty to deformity, and loving thy enemy."

The students evaluated both the course and its instructor highly. They gave the course an average rating of 4.64, and the instructor a 4.93 out of 5.0 points, noting the challenging yet life-changing nature of the course. Such sentiments were confirmed one year after the course was offered. Nine of the fourteen students (64 percent) replied when asked to participate in a post-experience survey. Some tied beauty to suffering directly in their recollections of the course: "I learned about the idea of beauty and its role in the arts as expression in the dynamic context surrounding loss, struggle and political action," and "I have used AIDS as an example when I have described to other people about what beauty is." Others reflected more purposefully on the aspect of service learning: "The service learning was directly applicable to the class discussions. In fact, it provided a much more solid context than the texts could provide. To me, the service learning was the heart of the course and the texts were supplemental. I can't even imagine the course without the service learning, it would seem so devoid of content and context." Another remarked, "This kind of experience gives a perspective that one could not possibly obtain in a classroom [alone]."

Perhaps most rewarding are student responses to the question, "Do you sometimes think of beauty, and reflect on it in terms that we discussed in class, even now that you are no longer in the course?" All nine students responded to this question. Three were especially thoughtful in terms of the content of the course. One wrote, hearkening back to Thomas Aquinas, "Yes. . . . If God is ultimate beauty, and God created everything—there is somehow a degree of beauty in everything." Another wrote, "Yes, I do. I look at art, models, events, and experiences and I wonder where grace plays its part, where the revelation of God is." Still another wrote, "Absolutely. The class opened my eyes to the beauty of God's presence in our world, even in horrible situations."

Clearly, service learning was integral to the acquisition of the content of the course in theological aesthetics. I asked a statistician on campus to compare results from 2003 with those from 2004 by reference to three parameters: student overall ratings of the course, student overall ratings of the instructor, and student total scores in coursework.[21] Minitab output shows that, for the course and instructor ratings, the mean score in 2004 was significantly higher than in 2003. This is interpreted as saying that the differences in means were too large to be reasonably ascribed to the luck of getting particular groups of students by randomly drawing from populations of students who would have given the same sets of results. It is standard practice to call the differences significant if the probability of such differences in random drawing is less than 0.05. The two-sample T-test on the course showed a probability of 0.000 that the numbers would increase to the degree they did between 2003 and 2004 unless something about the course changed; the two-sample T-test on the instructor also showed a probability of 0.000 that the numbers would increase to the degree they did between 2003 and 2004, unless something about the course changed.[22] This suggests there was something different about the offering in 2004—a change in the course that contributed to its greater success in terms of student satisfaction and, I believe, student outcomes. Because so little else changed about the course, it is clear from the evidence accumulated here that the service-learning component was vital to its success—not only because students responded favorably, but more importantly because service-learning was central to their acquisition of the abstract theological content of the course, as witnessed in their journals, final papers, and post-experience surveys.

Professors of Christian theology might be apt to think that service-learning is an uneasy fit with courses at the undergraduate level, where we are not training priests or pastors how to be ministers, counselors, or liturgists. Instead, we are typically helping young adults to reconcile faith and reason within a Christian framework. Nevertheless, the lesson I carry away from these two experiences of teaching theological aesthetics is that, when approached creatively and courageously, service learning can be a legitimate, academically rigorous pedagogical strategy for teaching upper-level, even abstract theological content. Concepts in the minds of such thinkers as Plato, Augustine, John of Damascus, Thomas, Edwards, Kant, Barth, Tillich, Weil, and Balthasar came alive for students in my 2004 seminar, leading one to comment, "I hardly ever use the word 'beauty' in my conversations and in writing unless I am trying to convey something extremely powerful. To me it is a word that has very strong connotations and it is something that I can only whisper for I fear it will vanish instantly. Sounds kind of corny, but it is true." By contrasting the two experiences of teaching the course, I hope more professors of theology and religion will consider service-based strategies as academically rigorous and legitimate approaches to pedagogy. Indeed, I cannot imagine teaching theological aesthetics again without incorporating service-learning. The evidence presented here of its greater efficacy over classroom learning alone is strong. The ability of service to reach students and to transform their lives is profound. My students would recognize that, even in the ten seconds it takes me to type this sentence, there has been another infection somewhere in the world. Recognition raises the question: Has there likewise been a response of Beauty?

Notes

[1]Rory Kennedy, producer, *Pandemic: Facing AIDS* (Docurama: 2003).

[2]The monograph is Richard Devine, Joseph Favazza, and F. Michael McLain, eds., *From Cloister to Commons: Concepts and Models for Service-Learning in Religious Studies* (Washington, DC: American Association for Higher Education, 2002). The articles are Fred Glennon, "Experiential Learning and Social Justice Action: An Experiment in the Scholarship of Teaching and Learning," *Teaching Theology and Religion* 7, no. 1 (2004): 30-37; Gerald Oakley West, "Beyond the 'Critical' Curtain: Community-based Service Learning in an African Context," *Teaching Theology and Religion* 7, no. 2 (2004): 71-82; and Alicia Batten, "Studying the Historical Jesus Through Service," *Teaching Theology and Religion* 8, no. 2 (2005): 107-13.

[3]Elisa S. Abes, Golden Jackson, and Susan R. Jones, "Factors That Motivate and Deter Faculty Use of Service-Learning," *Michigan Journal of Community Service Learning* (Fall 2002): 11.

[4]Ibid., 12.

[5]Ibid., 12.

[6]*The American Heritage Dictionary,* Second College Edition (Boston: Houghton Mifflin Company, 1982, 1985).

[7]W. F. Jackson Knight, "Book VI," *St. Augustine's De Musica: A Synopsis* (London: The Orthological Institute), 85-125.

[8]St. John of Damascus, *On the Divine Images: Three Apologies Against Those Who Attack the Divine Images* (Crestwood, NY: St. Vladimir's Seminary Press, 2000), 13-30, 50-67, 71-90.

[9]Thomas, "Whether the perfections of all things are in God?," in *Summa Theologica* I.4.2., and "The names of God," in *Summa Theologica* I.13.1-12; Umberto Eco, *The Aesthetics of Thomas Aquinas*, trans. Hugh Bredin (Cambridge: Harvard University Press, 1988), 49-63, 190-201.

[10]Immanuel Kant, *Critique of Judgment*, trans. J. H. Bernard (New York: Hafner Press, 1951), 37-81. In 2004, I assigned Kant's earlier but more accessible work, *Observations on the Feeling of the Beautiful and Sublime* (Berkeley: University of California Press, 1991, 1960).

[11]Jonathan Edwards, *The Nature of True Virtue* (Ann Arbor: University of Michigan Press, 1960), 1-41.

[12]Karl Barth, *Wolfgang Amadeus Mozart* (Grand Rapids.: Eerdmans, 1986), 25-59.

[13]Paul Tillich, *On Art and Architecture*, ed. John Dillenberger (New York: Crossroad, 1989), 11-41, 139-57.

[14]Simone Weil, "The Needs of the Soul," in *Simone Weil: An Anthology*, ed. Siân Miles (New York: Grove Press, 1986), 85-120.

[15]Hans Urs von Balthasar, *Heart of the World*, trans. Erasmos Leiva (San Francisco: Ignatius Press, 1979), 91-153.

[16]David Tracy, "The Religious Classic and the Classic of Art," in *Art, Creativity, and the Sacred: An Anthology in Religion and Art*, ed. Diane Apostolos-Cappadona (New York: Crossroad, 1992), 236-49.

[17]See Susan Sontag, *Regarding the Pain of Others* (New York: Farrar, Straus and Giroux, 2003).

[18]In order to assess the overall success of the course in meeting the objectives of challenging the idea that beauty is in the eye of the beholder by associating beauty with Christ rather than what is pretty, on the one hand, and the potential presence of beauty in the experience of suffering, on the other, student papers would need to be coded in order to determine statistics regarding how many students addressed these dimensions. Because I did not retain a copy of every paper for my records, I am unable to compile such statistics.

[19]Service learning accounted for 20% of the points available in the course. Text outlines and reflections now accounted for 30% of the course grade. Presentation of a text was 20%, allowing the paper to account for 20% of the final grade, and the final presentation of research counted for the last 10%.

[20]Margaret Kim Peterson, *Sing Me to Heaven: The Story of a Marriage* (Grand Rapids: Brazos Press, 2003).

[21]Admittedly, there were other variables between the courses. In 2003, I was a first-time adjunct instructor living over sixty miles from the institution where we met for a three-plus hour block at night without frequent meetings about research, whereas in 2004 I was in my second year as a full-time tenure-track instructor at a familiar institution where we met for sixty-five minutes three times a week and held frequent meetings about research.

[22]The statistical tests were two sample T-tests, without assuming equal population variances. Graphs of the data did not appear normally distributed, but Minitab recommends the two sample T-tests rather than a nonparametric test, when the shapes of the sample distributions differ from each other, as they did here. Two-sample T-Test and CI: Course 2004, Course 2003. Estimate for difference: 0.945887. 95% lower bound for difference: 0.574214. T-Test of difference = 0 (vs >): T-Value = 4.28; P-Value = 0.000; DF = 42. Two-sample T-Test and CI: Instructor 2004, Instructor 2003. Estimate for difference: 0.891827. 95% lower bound for difference: 0.625680. T-Test of difference = 0 (vs >): T-Value = 5.64; P-Value = 0.000; DF = 42. Two-sample T-Test and CI: Student Scores2004, Student Scores 2003. Estimate for difference: 19.7556. 95% lower bound for difference: -13.6101. T-Test of difference = 0 (vs >): T-Value = 1.01; P-Value = 0.161; DF = 26. I am grateful to Drs. Robert Raymond and Mari Heltne of our Quantitative Methods and Computer Science Department for their help with the statistical analysis provided here.

Beauty in a Rahnerian Key?

Some Reflections on the Perception of the Beautiful in Transcendental Experience

Ki Joo Choi

As any one familiar with Rahnerian scholarship is well aware, little attention has been devoted to the topic of aesthetics in Rahner's thought.[1] Even less attention has been given to the more specific topic of beauty. This is not entirely surprising since Rahner, unlike his contemporary Hans Urs von Balthasar, seldom refers to beauty in his vast theological corpus. Yet it would be too hasty to conclude that Rahner does not, at the very least, provide the groundwork for a theologically substantive account of beauty.

I want to propose the following interrelated claims. Some of the more prominent and intriguing references to beauty appear in Rahner's short reflections on poetry. They are few in number and may appear relatively trivial, but they nevertheless alert us to the prospect that beauty is linked to a hierarchical ordering of mediating objects. In other words, these references suggest that for Rahner certain worldly objects, realities, or locations constitute privileged mediators of self-transcendence in knowledge and freedom, and it is in these privileged mediating objects—such as poetry—that one perceives beauty. The second claim builds on the first. Simply put, linking beauty to poetry as a privileged mediator of self-transcendence offers a framework within which to suggest that beauty can also be perceived in the encounter with the neighbor. While there are no obvious or explicit connections between beauty, poetry, and love of neighbor in Rahner's writings, we can propose one, given that Rahner's later essays on the love commands intimate that self-transcendence is *necessarily* mediated through the personal other;

the neighbor is not merely *a* "worldly object" that mediates our
self-transcendence, but more properly *the* privileged mediator of
our self-transcendence among worldly objects. Such a claim, I propose, pushes us to consider the possibility that beauty can also be
encountered, and perhaps most fully, in and through interpersonal
relationship. As such, it may very well be the case that from a
Rahnerian perspective the beautiful is tied fundamentally to the
ethical.

It bears emphasizing from the outset that the advancement of
these two claims will be developmental and perhaps provisional at
best. Again, we need to keep in mind that Rahner does not offer
an account of beauty himself, at least not in any direct manner.
But there are a number of textual sites that suggest a theological
perspective from which a more explicit and systematic, Rahnerian
account of beauty can be developed. While such an exploration is
far from a comprehensive account of Rahner's understanding of
beauty, my hope is that it will show why the theme of beauty in
Rahner deserves greater attention. It not only offers a more focused understanding of various aspects of Rahner's theology, but
also encourages a renewed look at his ethics.

To advance the claim that beauty is linked to a hierarchical
ordering of worldly objects requires that we first take specific note
of the contextual nature of Rahner's transcendental anthropology.
We can then consider the question of whether Rahner suggests, or,
at the very least, assumes the notion that some worldly objects
mediate our self-transcendence more powerfully than others. Toward this consideration, Rahner's less known articles on the theological significance of both verbal and nonverbal art constitute a
promising point of departure. They also provide the context that
motivates a consideration of the relationship between beauty and
neighbor love.

Rahner's Contextual Transcendental Anthropology

Central to exploring the theme of beauty in Rahner is recognizing the particular significance he gives to certain worldly objects
with respect to the mediation of our self-transcendence in knowledge and freedom. This claim necessarily presupposes that Rahner's
transcendental anthropology is, to begin with, contextual. Such a
premise, however, is not necessarily an obvious one. We need, therefore, to begin our inquiry by making a few observations about the

contextual nature of Rahner's transcendental anthropology.

First, a basic and familiar feature of Rahner's thought is the claim that a pre-thematic awareness of God is intrinsic to human beings, intrinsic, however, in the sense that it is graced, implanted by God in the depths of the human spirit so that we have a real potency for receiving supernatural grace or God's self-gift.[2] Second, just as a pre-thematic awareness of God is intrinsic to human beings, so is human freedom. Freedom belongs to our potency for receiving God's self-gift. As such, human freedom is properly the graced capacity to respond to the spiritual dynamism of the human person, her transcendental openness to God. To the extent that we are free, Rahner maintains that "there can be no possibility of a 'neutral' knowledge of God."[3] In our knowledge or awareness of our own transcendence toward the absolute value, our transcendence confronts us with the responsibility of either disposing ourselves to God or saying no to God's self-communication. This leads us to a third observation. While freedom presupposes awareness of our transcendence, this awareness is founded on the fact that we recognize ourselves not simply as the products or compilation of finite causes, effects, or objects but as grounded in the fullness of being itself and as the gift of that fullness. In other words, it is in experiencing oneself as *subject* that one is able to experience oneself as an addressee of God and thus experience freedom, that is, assume responsibility for the sort of person one will become, either for God or not.[4]

In light of these observations, we can now add a fourth: to experience oneself as subject, that is, as more than the product of finite objects and thus as transcendent spirit, *requires finite objects*. While this claim sounds paradoxical, it reflects the extent to which for Rahner our self-transcendence in knowledge and freedom is thoroughly contextual. In other words, it underscores the sort of seriousness Rahner ascribes to the peculiarities of *human* perception.[5] While the human person is open to the infinite God in her transcendence, "[t]here is for human beings no purely transcendental experience."[6] This by no means implies that the human person can grasp God conceptually, that is, as anything other than the holy mystery. But it does mean that God is known to human persons in a unique *mode*.[7] That is to say, our awareness of transcendence toward the infinite appears as a horizon, even though we are spirit in transcendence. This is so because we can never completely distance ourselves from the finite, worldly factors of our existence; we are not absolute spirit.[8] Since we cannot step outside the finite world in which we exist in some absolute sense, we can never grasp the totality of the ground of our transcendental-ity, "which is pure being, God."[9] Therefore, the awareness of God that constitutes our openness to absolute being and thus the capacity to receive God's self-communication is not a purely internal or wholly mystical reality of human existence. Rather, this awareness is realized through what Rahner refers to as the objects of human history. Historicity is a central dimension of human beings as spirit. As Rahner states, "The place of our transcendence is always also a historical place."[10] "We must understand historicity as belonging to our basic nature."[11]

If Rahner insists on the mediating nature of history with respect to the experience of God, it is to a large extent a reflection of his methodological commitment to starting with the peculiarities of human existence as such, that is, to examining the structure of human subjective activity.[12] But his emphasis on the mediating nature of history is also a reflection of his scholastic foundations, more precisely, his commitment to providing a more modern reading of Thomas's epistemology. The complexity of Rahner's appropriation of Thomas's approach to human knowing, especially as found in his dense and highly technical text *Spirit in the World*,[13] prohibits any thorough discussion of it here. However, we can, for our purposes, note a few general claims. Following Thomas's answer to question 84, article 7, of the prima pars of the *Summa Theologiae*, Rahner maintains that "[e]very act of knowledge involves an act of the senses."[14] Stephen Fields notes that the importance Rahner places on the sense powers or *phantasmata* for human knowing is tied to Thomas's claim to an intrinsic unity between the body and the soul.[15] In accordance with this unity, Rahner sees the senses as underscoring the importance of worldly experience with respect to the spiritual nature of human existence. How is this so?

We can begin by noting Rahner's statement that "man is essentially ambivalent. He is always exiled in the world and is always already beyond it."[16] What this means more precisely is that the awareness of ourselves as spirit involves engagement *with* the world. The human person is not, as Thomas Sheehan explains, "a self-contained monadic subject, entirely present to himself over against the world."[17] Rather, as human persons, we are self-present or self-luminous, in Rahner's technical vocabulary of metaphysics, when we grasp another object different from ourselves, when "we step outside ourselves toward another reality distinct from us."[18] Only then do we know or possess any knowledge, both mundane and supernatural, about ourselves and God, when we turn toward another finite reality.

For Rahner, knowing as a dynamic process involving engagement with the world is exactly what is entailed in human sense experience. At the level of daily experience, the senses in their simplest definition refer to bio-chemical mechanisms and activity. At a deeper level, the function of the five senses underscores a more "complex reality."[19] Sensibility entails activity, not passivity: acts of inquiry, judgment, synthesis, and conceptualization. Such activity entails detecting, encountering, or reaching out toward objects that are seemingly distinct or apart from us. Common experience reveals as much. For example, hearing is hardly self-referential, but always presumes relationality. That is, we hear *something*; our hearing is an act of awareness evoked by some object distinct from ourselves. These objects constitute the world in which we exist. And to the extent that we know by grasping these objects, that is, through the phantasm or sense experience, we can say that these worldly objects mediate us to ourselves.

A Hierarchy of Worldly Mediums?
The Case of the Visual Arts and Poetry

There is certainly much more that can be said about Rahner's transcendental anthropology. But it should be clearer by now that a contextual dimension is far from lacking in Rahner's thought. The human person, as revealed in the experience of subjectivity, is "spirit in a peculiar way."[20] The human person is spirit in the world, and for Rahner this means that human transcendence "is necessarily reached by an intuition that depends on sensory, and therefore also historical experience."[21] The emphasis on sensory and historical experience serves to underscore the reality of our experience of God as mediated through those objects or realities that constitute our worldly, temporal existence. It is not as if the human subject exists "outside history, society, and the world."[22] Thus in "*every* experience of an object" the experience of God in our transcendental openness is possible.[23] Otherwise, it would mean that divine grace is strictly an inner moment of the human person. But then that would suggest a God who desires to be in relationship with us in a way that is indifferent to our humanity in its peculiarities.[24]

Be that as it may, not all worldly objects or realities are of equal mediatory weight. This is at least one inference from Rahner's belief that the experience of God will be informed by one's particular circumstances. More is at stake than apologetics in this position. Certainly, as Fergus Kerr rightly remarks, one task Rahner sets out to accomplish is to emphasize that Christian faith, or the experience of God more generally, is "at least plausible, or at any rate less bizarre and esoteric, to people brought up in post-Enlightenment culture."[25] Thus the experience of God is not merely something intelligible but also intimately meaningful. This is what is assumed when referring to God as a personal God; we "allow God" to be present to us "in a way in which he in fact wants to encounter us and has encountered us in our individual histories. . . ."[26] The objects of our horizon that mediate its ground to us are ones that are significant to us, to our personal concrete life. Subjectively speaking, then, some objects will mediate human transcendence and its ground more than others.

Yet in some of his lesser known writings on the arts, Rahner suggests that we can also make more normative or formal determinations about the mediatory function of worldly objects. Rahner's short article, "Art Against the Horizon of Theology and Piety," is particularly insightful. Here, he sets out to consider the theological status of art forms, particularly, as he states, "architecture, sculpture, painting, music."[27] These nonverbal (or nonliterary) art forms are expressive of the transcendental realities of the human person as spirit. While he never explicitly claims that such a characterization of nonverbal art forms is a strict or proper definition of the arts or art in general, Rahner, in making the characterization, proposes that there is a link between the arts and transcendence beyond a mere affinity. This is clear given his claim that the arts and theology "are mutually related." Just as Rahner does not affirm merely an affinity between theology and the experience of God's self-communication, there exists something more than an affinity between the arts and transcendence. Theology, according to Rahner, "is the conscious self-expression of persons about themselves from the point of view of divine revelation." And if the arts are an expression of the human person as spirit, then the arts must be considered an "integral part" of theology, if there is to be "the most perfect kind of theology."[28] The arts can

and must be a critical source of theology because both are conscious expressions of the experience of "the human being as a creature of transcendence always directed to the experience of the
mystery and transformed by grace."[29] "[I]t is only because we are
transcendental beings that art *and* theology can exist," says
Rahner.[30]

There is little doubt that Rahner's approach to art hinges profoundly on his transcendental anthropology.[31] He states rather
unequivocally that "[w]hatever is expressed in art is a product of
that human transcendentality by which, as spiritual and free beings, we strive for the totality of all reality."[32] Rahner further remarks, "*[g]enuine* art is the result of a well determined historical
event of human transcendentality [of the individual artist]";[33] it is
an expression of her "own religious experience."[34] "Of their very
nature artists are discoverers of a concrete situation in which persons concretely realize their transcendental being in a new way,
one that differs from former ways. This does not entail an opposition between historicity and transcendence, but rather their necessary mutual relationship. *Real* artists undoubtedly announce what
is eternal in truth, love, and eternal yearning."[35] Such self-expression, Rahner tells us, is accomplished through the use of images
and metaphors, among other things.[36]

What is particularly interesting to note in the foregoing citations is Rahner's reference to "*genuine* art" or the artwork of "*real*
artists" and not merely to art or art in general. The distinction
suggests that while art in general is a profound expression of the
transcendentality of human persons, particularly that of the artist,
it may be more accurate to say (though Rahner does not say this
explicitly) that art in general is *potentially* expressive, in the sense
that some works of art will more fully express or embody the
transcendentality of the artist than other art objects. This appears
to be the inference in Rahner's reference to genuine art. While art
in general *can* be self-expressive of the artist and therefore the
existential reality of human transcendentality, it is only genuine
art that *is* authentically self-expressive.

That there is a significant distinction to be drawn between art
in general and genuine art is reinforced by Rahner's suggestion
that some works of art are more mediatory than others. In "Art
against the Horizon of Theology and Piety," Rahner claims that
an artwork is not merely a self-expression of the artist's religious
experience but also that which can mediate a religious experience

for those who are its audience, such as the one who gazes at the artist's drawing or listens to the composer's score. However, Rahner suggests that not all artworks succeed in mediating such an experience, acknowledging that there is such a thing as "religious *Kitsch*." Such art objects may explicitly entertain religious themes, but may not necessarily mediate transcendental experience. In some cases, a work of art that is not explicitly religious may in fact "do" what religious artwork is intended to do, "to evoke in those who see it a genuine and deep religious reaction." So, Rahner surmises, "it is quite possible that a Rembrandt painting, which is not intended as religious, moves people so deeply, bringing up the question of life's ultimate meaning, that it is, strictly speaking, a religious painting."[37]

For Rahner, it must be the case that some art objects are able to mediate religious experience more powerfully than others, and it is not a matter of whether a work of art's original intent is religious or non-religious. Instead, that some works of art are more mediatory than others further underscores Rahner's belief in the mutual relationship between theology and art. "[T]heology," Rahner claims, "must somehow be 'mystogogical,' that is, it should not merely speak about objects in abstract concepts, but it must encourage people really to experience that which is expressed in such concepts."[38] And theology must do so because concepts and words can only be understood if they engage the full range of the human senses: "[m]etaphysical knowledge depends on sense experience. . . . [I]n the final analysis, even in the religious domain, concepts and words can only be understood if and insofar as they contain a sensory moment."[39] This is no less the case for art. It is striking that Rahner proposes that so-called religious paintings are only religious kitsch—"not truly religious paintings"—so long as they are unable to elicit a profound sensory experience; "they do not *affect* us deeply enough to elicit religious feeling," says Rahner.[40] When a work of art, religious or non-religious in theme, brings about a sensory experience of transcendence, it may then be properly described as religious artwork.

"Art," Rahner acknowledges, "offers the possibility of transcendence," as Gesa Elsbeth Thiessen rightly remarks.[41] *Genuine* works of art, however, do not only offer the possibility of transcendence, they also actualize or mediate authentically and more powerfully our self-transcendence in knowledge and freedom.

Rahner's references to genuine art are not arbitrary and haphazard, but accentuate a real difference between the mediatory capacity and status of different artworks. His reference to genuine art, then, is a revealing instance of the contrasting mediating function of worldly objects. This contrast underscores his claim that "[t]he statement 'God is everywhere with his grace' does not mean that every reality has the same relation to me or to God."[42] For all art objects—and all worldly experiences for that matter—to be deemed equally mediatory of transcendental experience would assume a too indiscriminate understanding of divine grace in the world.

The thesis that certain art objects more than others evoke or mediate a greater, more profound awareness of one's original transcendental experience continues in his reflections on the verbal arts, and poetry in particular. His most sustained discussion of poetry appears in "Priest and Poet," originally published as a foreword to a collection of poems on the priesthood by Jorge Blajot, S.J. "To the poet is entrusted the word," declares Rahner.[43] Then, following a comment about the substantial unity of spirit and matter, he proposes, sounding like a poet himself, that the words of the poet "are like sea-shells, in which can be heard the sound of the ocean of infinity, no matter how small they are in themselves."[44] These words, he declares, are "gifts of God" and thus "bring light to us."[45] They are "primordial words."[46] And like the nonverbal arts of architecture, painting, sculpture, and music, they are mediatory; they too make known to us the infinite God in our transcendentality.

The mediatory nature of primordial words is underscored in Rahner's reference to the primordial word as symbol. The reference allows us to think of the experience of God as the experience of grace made symbol in that primordial word. A symbol is that which makes present the reality it signifies.[47] Thus, the primordial word as symbol does not only point to or signal the reality it signifies: "It is not merely the sign of something whose relationship to the hearer is no way altered by it. . . . [I]t brings the reality it signifies to us, makes it 'present,' realizes it and places it before us."[48] In signifying the reality of the mystery of being, the primordial word "transfers" this reality "into man's sphere of existence,"[49] rendering the presence of God to the human creature in the awareness of her transcendence as spirit.

It is important to note that Rahner does not claim the primordial word is *a* symbol or *any* symbol. In "Behold This Heart!," a shorter version of "Priest and Poet" that considers the implication of the primordial word for a theology of the devotion to the Sacred Heart, Rahner claims emphatically that any word that counts as a primordial word—"heart" for instance—is "not an arbitrary symbol, not a conventional sign, but a genuine, original symbol, a primordial symbol."[50] A common inference of the word primordial is unique or original, and it is one that gains momentum in the contrast Rahner makes between the primordial word and what he refers to as mere words. It is "more than a mere word," Rahner says of the primordial word.[51] As such, the primordial word "intimately and truly" grasps reality as such.[52] This is not the case with mere words, insofar as they grasp reality as such only to a certain extent. More specifically, Rahner observes: "They [primordial words] are *deeper* and *truer* than the worn-down verbal coins of daily intellectual intercourse, which one often likes to call 'clear ideas' because habit dispenses one from thinking anything at all in their use."[53] The comparatives "deeper and truer" indicate that mere words may evoke an awareness of one's transcendence as spirit and thus mediate an experience of God, but not to the degree that primordial words can and do. As Rahner states, "the redeeming mission of the word is true in some way of every word. But it is *especially* true of the primordial words," which particularly, or *more* powerfully and fully, mediate our transcendence as spirit; they render the presence of God in the experience of our transcendence as spirit in a manner that mere words cannot.[54]

Rahner thus places special significance on the mediating function of the primordial word in referring to it as the primordial symbol. Curiously, however, he does not make use of the terms primordial symbol when talking about the primordial word in "Priest and Poet," nor in "Poetry and the Christian."[55] (The scant references to the language of symbol in his other essays on the arts are curious; in fact, one would be hard pressed to find any sustained discussion of symbol in any of these texts.) But as the foregoing presentation indicates, insofar as the primordial word is mediatory of the experience of God in ways beyond the mere word, it is appropriately a genuine or real symbol. Why then is the reference to primordial symbol absent in two of his most sustained discussions on the meaning and significance of the primordial word?

Rahner's persistent reference to primordial word rather than primordial symbol in both "Priest and Poet" and "Poetry and the Christian" suggests that his primary concern is focusing attention on the primordial word as specifically the symbolic words of the poet. As he tells us, "wherever a primordial word is really pronounced, wherever a thing appears in word in its positive freshness there a poet is at work."[56] Poetry is not a mere application of linguistic forms and techniques, a compilation of only rhymes and verse, for example. Poets who write in this way are poets in the common sense of the word but really "no poets at all" in Rahner's mind, just "rhymers and versifiers."[57] Techniques and forms are employed by "true poets" in such a way that reality as such is communicated to human persons.[58] We might consider a common theological statement juxtaposed to a more artistic, poetic rendering of it. "When I say for instance, 'We must love God,' " according to Rahner, "I have said something very profound in a simple statement, but in the shallow dullness of life I have not really brought it home. However, when I read a lyrical poem in the style of John of the Cross or a novel by Julian Green, . . . my own religious experience may be evoked. . . ."[59]

"[G]reat poetry only exists where man radically faces what he is," asserts Rahner. The words of a true poet, therefore, confront and challenge us, taking "us beyond the two-legged creature which pre-occupies us only too often and too long in our everyday life. . . ."[60] As such, "great poetry" or "real poetry" entails risk.[61] The person encountered by great poetry "may be entangled in guilt, perversity, hatred of self and diabolical pride, he may see himself as a sinner and identify himself with his sin." In all this, however, in confronting and struggling with what he is, "[t]he more deeply great poetry leads man into the abysses which are the foundation of his being." Therefore, "he is more exposed to the happy danger of meeting God, than the narrow-minded Philistine who always skirts cautiously the chasms of existence, to stay on the superficial level where one is never faced with doubts—nor with God."[62]

These moving, stirring reflections on the power and significance of poetry verge on the poetic themselves. The poetic word, unlike the mere "abstract concept" or "sentimental torrent of words,"[63] possesses a particular, if not unique, capacity to evoke our sensibility and reach the human heart, thereby mediating a profound awareness of our transcendental openness to the divine mystery. It is in this sense that the mediatory function and status of great poetry complements what we earlier said about the mediatory function of genuine art (the nonverbal arts), but there are substantial differences to be drawn between poetry (great poetry) and genuine, nonverbal art.

Rahner suggests that poetry's capacity to mediate the awareness of the absolute God is authoritative in a way that genuine art is not. For the most part, Rahner refers to the primordial word in terms of great poetry and not genuine art. In fact, in "Priest and Poet," Rahner makes explicit that it is the word and not the image or song that is the primordial word: "But among all the modes of expressing himself that man uses in all the arts, the word alone possesses something which is not shared by any other creation of man: it lives in transcendence. . . . The word alone is the gesture which transcends everything that can be represented and imagined, to refer us to infinity."[64] Moreover, the elevation of poetry over other works of art is heightened in its capacity to transform and release these other works of art into mediators of the infinite. As Rahner remarks, "It alone [poetry] can redeem that which constitutes the ultimate imprisonment of all realities which are not expressed in word: the dumbness of their reference to God."[65]

But why is poetry ascribed such a special or privileged status? Why is poetry the primordial word and, correlatively, the primordial symbol, or the *highest* worldly reality or representation that renders God present to us in our transcendence?[66] The answer is fundamentally theological. The poetic word, says Rahner in "Poetry and the Christian," is particularly mediatory insofar as it is through the Logos, or "the Word become flesh," that God the Father makes himself known to the human creature:

And therefore and since then and in this Word made flesh the word of man has become full of grace and truth. It is not just a sort of silently signaling finger, pointing away from what it delimits and illuminates into the infinite distance, where the incomprehensible itself, as grace and mercy, has entered the human word. In the region encompassed by the human word, infinity has built itself a tent, infinity itself is there in the finite. The word names and truly contains what it apparently only hints at by a silent signal, it brings on what it proclaims, it is the word which really only attains the full realization of its being in the sacramental word, where it really becomes what God's grace made it as he *uttered* his eternal Word itself in the flesh of the Lord.[67]

It is interesting that Rahner refers to God as one who has "uttered" his Word. The reference recalls his several comments about God's self-revelation and speech in "Priest and Poet." God's self-revelation to humanity is something that is *spoken* to us in creation;[68] God reveals himself by speaking to us in word, through the spoken word. Christianity is, after all, "the religion of the word proclaimed," according to Rahner.[69] In this way, the notion that God reveals himself in the Logos or the Word become flesh includes the reality that God reveals himself to us by uttering or speaking words of himself in the world. It is by virtue of God speaking words of himself in the world that the human word of poetry is made efficacious; poetry "produces an effect. . . . [I]t is not merely discourse *about* something that would remain equally real and effective if it were not talked about."[70] When the poetic word is spoken, God is made present in the world, for it is the continuation of God's utterance of himself in the world: "For the presence-to-us of the reality of the divine self-revelation as expressed in this word always remains dependent upon this word being spoken and repeated. If it cannot be spoken by Christ himself until the end of time, then it must be carried on by others."[71] Because God's self-revelation to us is itself proclaimed *in* the world, God's self-revelation is embodied proclamation, an embodied event.[72] Such a declaratory event (noting the connotation of speech and the use of words in declaration or proclamation) takes place wherever the poetic word is really pronounced.

So important, then, are the words of poetry that the mediation of our transcendentality in knowledge and freedom would be made difficult without it. As Rahner states, "the poetic word and the poetic ear are so much part of man that if this essential power were really lost to the heart, man could no longer hear the word of God in the word of man."[73] Therefore, "[w]e Christians must love and fight for the poetic word, because we must defend what is human, since God himself has assumed it into his eternal reality,"[74] that is, through the Logos. Poetry is an indispensable, necessary worldly medium through which God makes Godself known to the human creature, and this indispensability belongs singularly to poetry. Any mention of the primordial word as including genuine, nonverbal art is conspicuously absent in both "Priest and Poet" and "Poetry and the Christian."

Encountering "Real Beauty" in Poetry and in the Personal Other?

While Rahner does not speak directly to a hierarchy of worldly objects in the mediation of our self-transcendence in knowledge and freedom, it is noteworthy that he makes distinctions between those worldly objects that authentically mediate the experience of God and those that do not. As discussed previously, the mediatory function of genuine art, whether in the form of architecture, painting, sculpture, or music (the nonverbal arts), is to be distinguished from art in general. Additionally, it appears that for Rahner the mediatory function of genuine, nonverbal art can be distinguished from the primordial word or the verbal art of poetry. A unique status is ascribed to poetry: it is primordial, or the highest worldly reality that mediates the experience of the holy mystery in our transcendental openness. It is in this context that we encounter Rahner's use of the word beauty.

In "Priest and Poet," Rahner refers to beauty in only a few passing instances.[75] The more intriguing references appear in the concluding paragraph of the first section. He states that if poets "speak primordial words in powerful concentration," these words then "are beautiful."[76] The primordial words of genuine poetry are not merely beautiful, however. Poetry is indeed something beautiful, but Rahner does not suggest that poetry *is* beauty. More precisely, he claims that "real beauty *is* the pure appearance of reality as brought about principally in the word."[77] When the poetic word is pronounced and thus heard, real beauty is present, encountered, or experienced. Real beauty as the pure appearance of reality *is* the revelation of God himself, which Rahner further describes as the appearance of "the radiant, intimate clarity of the absolute fullness of God."[78] That said, it is striking that, at the conclusion of "Priest and Poet," he states that what is proclaimed in poetry is "radiant beauty." Poetry, as the primordial word, mediates our self-transcendence in knowledge and freedom, but this means more specifically that it mediates an experience of the radiance of God as mystery, "the luminous darkness of [the] Father."[79] This experience is an experience of real beauty.

We must not forget, however, that Rahner claims the experience of God's radiance as the experience of real beauty is "brought about principally in the word."[80] More specifically, it is mediated *principally* in *poetry*. Again, we see that Rahner draws contrasts between the mediatory function of various worldly objects or realities. While he claims that he does not wish to trivialize the power of music with respect to the experience of God as the holy mystery, he advises that "theologians might give thought to the fact that God revealed himself in word and not in purely tonal music."[81] While "the other arts" can mediate the experience of God in his radiance, poetry surpasses other art forms in such mediation, so that this radiance is real beauty or appears to us as beautiful, particularly in and through poetry.

Does this mean that real beauty is only perceivable in and through the poetic? This is hardly a simple question to attend to, given Rahner's few explicit statements on beauty. But we may be able to see how he implies or assumes an answer to the question if we first take note of what he says about the relationship between artistic talent and holiness in "Art Against the Horizon of Theology and Piety." While he maintains that art which deeply affects us is mediatory of religious experience, Rahner wonders whether this means that those who are holy—"genuine saints, who love God and their neighbor in a radically unselfish way"—are necessarily artistic. That is, are artists and/or those who love art *necessarily* saints? Rahner resists definitive conclusions on the matter. He does say that, empirically or observationally speaking, it appears the answer is negative. As he remarks, "there are those who have developed an extraordinary artistic sensibility without being saints." He further observes that there are also saints who "nevertheless, have hardly developed any artistic capacities, who in matters of art are real lowbrows, capable of rudimentary reactions."[82] The potential force of these observations is that although art is mediatory of transcendental experience, this does not mean that the encounter with God in our transcendence is necessarily dependent on being deeply affected by art. Or, on the other hand, this does not mean that in appreciating or being profoundly affected by art one *will* encounter God or that it will *necessarily* lead one to be a saint.

If holiness is not necessarily dependent on artistic capacities or sensitivities, then we may infer that the mediation of the experience of God in our transcendence is not necessarily dependent on seeing an image. Nor may the mediation of the experience of God in his radiant beauty be necessarily dependent on hearing the poetic word. Rahner appears to suggest as much in "Poetry and the Christian." He asserts that one "must be schooled" in the poetic word or "practice listening" to the poetic word; we are not readily receptive to hearing the poetic word in all its mystery.[83] But if this capacity and readiness require training, Rahner asks whether "a man [can] be fundamentally unreceptive to this word and still be a Christian?"[84] One can read a sense of hesitation in his answer to the question, but ultimately it is a yes.[85] He finally concedes that "poetry is *one way* of training oneself to hear the word of life," although he thinks that once a person learns to notice, hear, and appreciate the poetic word, he is more capable of being, or more likely to be, affected by its evocation and presentation of the eternal mystery: "he begins to be a man who can no longer be totally unreceptive to every poetic word."[86]

It appears that our experience of the holy mystery is not necessarily dependent on the mediating function of the poetic word. More specifically, it seems that the radiant beauty of God as mystery does not have to appear to us in the poetic word. Certainly, Rahner maintains that if we are trained well enough to be open to the evocative power of the poetic word, then the poetic word indeed becomes a presupposition to our hearing the divine word, to encountering the radiant beauty of the holy mystery in our transcendence. However, such an encounter is not necessarily dependent on whether one in fact perceives the poetic word. Only artists or the aficionado would then be counted as Christian. We then face the possibility that the radiant beauty of God as mystery can be experienced or can appear in and through something other than the poetic word.

The possibility gains momentum or, at the very least, greater plausibility when we bear in mind that the appearance of real beauty is linked to poetry's *privileged* status as mediator of the divine mystery. Poetry, we recall, is the *primordial* word and thus not just any symbol. It is in this primordial word or symbol that true beauty appears to us. Yet poetry for Rahner is not the only privileged mediator. In fact, he claims unequivocally that the experience of God is definitive of the encounter with the personal other. If this is so, then it may indeed be appropriate to suggest that the experience of God in his radiant beauty is also possible in our relationships with the neighbor.

To be more specific, we may consider a few passages from Rahner's "Experience of Self and Experience of God." Here he reiterates a familiar feature of his transcendental subjectivity: when the human person experiences herself as subject, she sees herself as transcendence or as "contain[ing] an absolute orientation towards the infinite," even though she is and remains a finite creature.[87] Such an experience of self is an experience of God, for it entails acknowledging that the infinite is in fact the "enabling condition" of the experience of self as open to the infinite.[88] Accordingly, Rahner thinks that the experience of self and God is best described in terms of unity; in experiencing oneself as spirit, one is *also* experiencing God as the ground of all being. Yet he also claims that one comes to experience the reality of one's transcendentality insofar as one comes to experience a worldly entity. What this means is that the experience of self and experience of God in unity is, according to Rahner, "conceivable in connection with an individual piece of material 'subject-matter.' "[89] But Rahner continues, "the experience of self in the concrete has, in relation to its 'pieces of subject-matter,' a structure in which *not every item has an equal value.*"[90]

This last statement—that "not every item has an equal value"—appears to confirm our earlier reflections on the mediatory significance of poetry. Certain worldly objects or realities mediate the experience of God in our transcendentality *more* than others. Poetry is not of "equal value" with some other finite objects in this respect, for it is "where the silent mystery makes itself *unmistakably* heard as the foundation of existence."[91] However, Rahner pushes us to qualify such a claim about poetry in an important way.

To be sure, he makes no reference to poetry or its privileged mediatory status in "Experience of Self and Experience of God." Yet given the prominence he attributes to the mediatory reality of interpersonal relationship, it would be too hasty to conclude that poetry is the only privileged mediator of the radiant beauty of the holy mystery. Appealing to the reality of daily, human experience, Rahner thinks that the experience of self as spirit and thus of God is more connected with the human other, perhaps in a non-negotiable way. The human other or "[o]ne's fellow man is not any 'piece of subject-matter,' one of many in which the experience of self can be achieved," Rahner tells us.[92] Instead, "the experience of life is an experience of one's fellow men, one in which material

objects are encountered as elements connected with and surrounding concrete persons and not otherwise."[93]

The last statement is a difficult one. For Rahner, the experience
of God in our transcendentality is constitutive of interpersonal
mediation. But does this mean that one cannot through "material
objects" (worldly realities other than interpersonal relationships)
achieve the experience of self as spirit and thus the experience of
God? A plain reading of the foregoing citation does not necessarily negate the mediatory potential of material objects or realities
other than interpersonal relationships. But if material objects can
mediate the experience of God in our transcendentality, they can
do so only in relation to "other persons in dialogue, in trustful and
loving encounter." This must be the case so long as Rahner insists
on the primacy of interpersonal relationship with respect to transcendental experience: "The only way in which man achieves self-
realization is through encounters with his fellow man, . . . who is
not a thing or a matter, but a man. . . . Man experiences himself by
experiencing the other *person* and not the other *thing*."[94] It is primarily in relationship with the neighbor that one experiences self
as spirit, which for Rahner is the experience of God. This is why
he can claim that love of neighbor is love of God.[95]

The link between love of neighbor and love of God is given more
systematic expression in "The 'Commandment' of Love in Relation
to Other Commandments" and "Reflections on the Unity of the
Love of Neighbour and the Love of God."[96] In these two substantial
reflections on love, Rahner claims, without qualification, that the
encounter with the neighbor or personal human other is the finite
arena within which our original transcendental experience takes
place. He thus dispels any possibility that interpersonal relationship
has only incidental significance with respect to the experience of
God in our transcendentality; the encounter with neighbor is no
occasional "place" of such experience. This must be the case, because the human person possesses an "essential *a priori* openness to
the other human being" and not to *any* worldly entity or reality.
Such openness "[belongs to the] most basic constitution of man and
is an essential inner moment of his (knowing and willing)
transcendentality."[97] As such, one's encounter with the human other
is "the *necessary mediation* of the knowing subject to itself."[98]

Because to be human is by definition to exist in an environment
of persons (we are social creatures after all), it is our sociality that
mediates us and who we will become in the face of the holy mys-

tery. This is not to say that our *cultural* environment does not also contribute to the mediation of our return to self and thus experience of God as mystery. In "Poetry and the Christian," Rahner claims that by virtue of God's grace operative in the world, "human culture . . . wherever it still exists, revives, proves itself true and displays itself *radiantly*. . . ."[99] Accordingly, poetry, as an essential dimension of human culture, possesses a particular power to refer us to the radiance of the infinite mystery, so much so that this radiance appears to us as beautiful. Yet, if we are to take Rahner seriously when he claims that the mediation of our self-transcendence and thus of God is possible only in relationship with the human other, then we also need to take seriously the prospect that the radiant beauty of the holy mystery is not only perceivable in poetry but also in the encounter with the human other. And perhaps more radically, we need to consider the possibility that *unless* we discover the neighbor and really allow the neighbor to encounter us, we cannot know and encounter God in his radiant beauty.

The last consideration challenges us to re-imagine poetry's relationship to our perception of radiant beauty in the world. To be more specific, we need first to recall and bear in mind a statement cited earlier. "[M]aterial objects," says Rahner, "are encountered as elements connected with and surrounding concrete persons *and not otherwise*."[100] We should also note the additional, complementary statement that the human person, "could not achieve a self-withdrawal from a world consisting *exclusively* in material objects any more than he could from his own body. . . . He who fails to discover his neighbour has not truly achieved realization of himself. . . ."[101] Though Rahner makes no reference to poetry in commenting on "material objects," I do not see why it cannot be counted as a material object in this context, insofar as poetry belongs to the materiality of human culture. And if it is indeed the case, as the foregoing citations strongly suggest, that encountering material objects *alone* cannot mediate the experience of self as spirit and thus the experience of God, then it may indeed be the case that material objects, including poetry, can mediate successfully only in the discovery of the neighbor. What I am proposing, more specifically, is that loving the neighbor is perhaps requisite to perceiving the word of God—the radiant beauty of God—in the human word of poetry. We cannot *learn* to be receptive to, and ultimately to love the poetic word, unless we can and indeed love the neighbor in the first place.

Conclusion

The human person is a being whose transcendental nature or openness to absolute being is made possible by virtue of God's infinite love and freedom. But because this human person, though spirit, is and remains a finite creature, her experience of God in her transcendentality is an event that is mediated in and through the world. God approaches us in the thick of our ordinary, mundane life. But an important elaboration of this claim must be made if we are to gain an understanding of beauty in Rahner's thought.

This elaboration begins with the acknowledgment that while the movement of our dynamic spiritual nature, and thus our experience of God, takes place within the world, all worldly objects do not have equal status and significance when it comes to the mediation of our encounter. Rather, there are particular objects of this world that take on unique mediatory significance. It is in these objects that the radiant beauty of God as holy mystery appears to us. Genuine poetry is such an object, but the neighbor must be included as well, for we cannot overlook the extent to which Rahner maintains and elevates the vital importance of interpersonal relationships with respect to our self-transcendence in knowledge and freedom. Such an emphasis on interpersonal relationships raises the question of whether Rahner assumes a kind of ordering with respect to the mediation of the experience of God in the world.[102] It is in loving the human other that we encounter the silent mystery "which is behind expressible reality in its deepest depths."[103] Moreover, it is in such encounter that the efficaciousness of the poetic word can be felt in its fullness. Encountering and loving the neighbor is the condition for our openness to poetry as those human words in which the word of God, that is, the radiant beauty of the holy mystery appears, and is perceived. Accordingly, the poetic word, as that which makes visible radiant beauty, deepens, concentrates, and fully realizes the fundamental, original experience of the ineffable mystery that is "present from the outset in everyday life," in our daily encounter with the human other.[104]

Notes

[1]See Gesa Elsbeth Thiessen, "Karl Rahner: Toward a Theological Aesthetic," in *The Cambridge Companion to Karl Rahner*, ed. Declan Marmion

and Mary E. Hines (Cambridge, UK: Cambridge University Press, 2005), 225.

[2]See Jean Porter, "Salvific Love and Charity: A Comparison of the Thought of Karl Rahner and Thomas Aquinas," in *The Love Commandments: Essays in Christian Ethics and Moral Philosophy*, ed. Edmund N. Santurri and William Werpehowski (Washington, DC: Georgetown University Press, 1992), 242.

[3]Brian Linnane, S.J., "Dying with Christ: Rahner's Ethics of Discipleship," *The Journal of Religion* 81, no. 2 (April 2001): 208. See also Karl Rahner, *Hearer of the Word*, trans. Joseph Donceel (New York: Continuum, 1994), 86.

[4]Karl Rahner, *Foundations of Christian Faith: An Introduction to the Idea of Christianity*, trans. William Dych (New York: Crossroad, 1978), 37.

[5]Rahner, *Hearer of the Word*, 94.

[6]Richard Viladesau, *Theological Aesthetics: God in Imagination, Beauty, and Art* (New York: Oxford University Press, 1999), 93.

[7]Ibid., 92.

[8]See Karl Rahner, "The Concept of Mystery," *Theological Investigations* IV (Baltimore: Helicon Press, 1966), 50-52.

[9]Rahner, *Hearer of the Word*, 84.

[10]Ibid., 94.

[11]Ibid., 95.

[12]See Roger Haight, S.J., *The Experience and Language of Grace* (New York: Paulist Press, 1979), 120.

[13]Karl Rahner, *Spirit in the World*, trans. William Dych (New York: Continuum, 1994).

[14]See Miguel H. Díaz, *On Being Human: U.S. Hispanic and Rahnerian Perspectives* (Maryknoll, NY: Orbis Books, 2001), 87.

[15]See Stephen Fields, "Balthasar and Rahner on the Spiritual Senses," *Theological Studies* 57, no. 2 (June 1996): 4.

[16]Rahner, *Spirit in the World*, 406.

[17]Thomas Sheehan, *Karl Rahner: The Philosophical Foundations* (Athens: Ohio University Press, 1987), 8.

[18]Rahner, *Hearer of the Word*, 97.

[19]Karl Rahner, "The Theology of the Religious Meaning of Images," *Theological Investigations* 23 (New York: Crossroad, 1992), 152.

[20]Ibid., 106.

[21]Ibid., 150.

[22]Rahner, *Foundations of the Christian Faith*, 38.

[23]Rahner, "The Theology of the Religious Meaning of Images," 159, emphasis added.

[24]See Karl Rahner, "The Word and the Eucharist," *Theological Investigations* 4 (Baltimore: Helicon Press, 1966), 259.

[25]Fergus Kerr, *Immortal Longings: Versions of Transcending Humanity* (Notre Dame: University of Notre Dame Press, 1997), 179.

[26]Rahner, *Foundations of Christian Faith*, 74.

[27]Karl Rahner, "Art Against the Horizon of Theology and Piety," *Theological Investigations* 13 (New York: Crossroad, 1983), 162.

[28]Ibid., 163.

[29]Thiessen, "Karl Rahner," 226.

[30]Rahner, "Art Against the Horizon of Theology and Piety," 165, emphasis added.

[31]Thiessen, "Karl Rahner," 226.

[32]Rahner, "Art Against the Horizon of Theology and Piety," 165.

[33]Ibid., 166, emphasis added.

[34]Ibid., 164.

[35]Ibid., 166, emphasis added.

[36]Ibid., 164.

[37]Ibid., 167.

[38]Ibid., 164.

[39]Rahner, "The Theology of the Religious Meaning of Images," 150.

[40]Rahner, "Art Against the Horizon of Theology and Piety," 167, emphasis added.

[41]Thiessen, "Karl Rahner," 229.

[42]Rahner, "Art Against the Horizon of Theology and Piety," 167.

[43]Karl Rahner, "Priest and Poet," *Theological Investigations* 3 (Baltimore: Helicon Press, 1967), 294.

[44]Ibid., 295-96.

[45]Ibid., 296.

[46]Ibid.

[47]See Karl Rahner, "Theology of the Symbol," *Theological Investigations* 4. Rahner claims that symbol refers to one reality representing another or rendering another present. While the reality that represents (the symbol) and the reality rendered by the representation (the signified) are not identical, they are necessarily related (225).

[48]Rahner, "Priest and Poet," 299.

[49]Ibid.

[50]Karl Rahner, " 'Behold This Heart!': Preliminaries to a Theology of Devotion to the Sacred Heart," *Theological Investigations* 3 (Baltimore: Helicon Press, 1967), 327.

[51]Rahner, "Priest and Poet," 298.

[52]Ibid.

[53]Ibid., emphasis added.

[54]Ibid., 301, emphasis added.

[55]Karl Rahner, "Poetry and the Christian," *Theological Investigations* 4.

[56]Rahner, "Priest and Poet," 301.

[57]Ibid.

[58]Ibid.

[59]Rahner, "Art Against the Horizon of Theology and Piety," 164.

[60]Rahner, "Poetry and the Christian," 365.

[61]Ibid., 365 and 366, respectively.

⁶²Ibid., 365.

⁶³Rahner, "Priest and Poet," 309 and 301, respectively.

⁶⁴Ibid., 302.

⁶⁵Ibid. It is important to note that while Rahner ascribes such an elevated status to poetry, he does not think that *only* poetry can mediate the transcendence of the spirit in knowledge and freedom. This is so given his insistence that all the human sense powers are important to such mediation. As he states in "The Theology of the Religious Meaning of Images," "if religious images may exist, it must be possible for them to have such a mediating function with regard to the absolute God. Such a function should not belong exclusively to the word. This assumption is implicitly present in our basic thesis, which holds that all peak experiences of *every* sense domain, and not only those of the sense of hearing, may be the basis and element of a religious act . . . every act of the sense powers as such implies some experience of transcendence" (158). However, Rahner insists, for reasons we shall discuss in more detail below, that the mediating function of the word does have normative priority over the image, for "[w]e must grant," he says, "that such a function is more immediately and easily understandable in the case of words than in that of images. . ." (158).

⁶⁶See Rahner, "The Theology of the Symbol." Here, Rahner refers to the "most primordial manner in which one reality can represent another" to really be present as "the highest" (225).

⁶⁷Rahner, "Poetry and the Christian," 361-62, emphasis added.

⁶⁸Rahner, "Priest and Poet," 303. The reference to the word spoken is made several times here.

⁶⁹Rahner, "Poetry and the Christian," 357.

⁷⁰Rahner, "Priest and Poet," 305.

⁷¹Ibid., 304.

⁷²Ibid.

⁷³Rahner, "Poetry and the Christian," 363.

⁷⁴Ibid., 364.

⁷⁵In fact, among his several articles on both verbal and nonverbal art forms, the word beauty appears only in his "Priest and Poet."

⁷⁶Rahner, "Priest and Poet," 301.

⁷⁷Ibid., emphasis added.

⁷⁸Ibid., 302.

⁷⁹Ibid., 297.

⁸⁰Ibid., 301.

⁸¹Ibid., 302.

⁸²Rahner, "Art Against the Horizon of Theology and Piety," 168.

⁸³Rahner, "Poetry and the Christian," 362.

⁸⁴Ibid., 363.

⁸⁵As he finally states, without ambiguity, "One can of course be a good fellow and a good Christian in the common-place sense of the term and still be a miserable poet" (ibid., 365).

[86]Ibid., 364.

[87]Karl Rahner, "Experience of Self and Experience of God," *Theological Investigations* 13 (New York: Seabury, 1975), 125.

[88]Ibid.

[89]Ibid., 27.

[90]Ibid., 127, emphasis added.

[91]Rahner, "Poetry and the Christian," 360, emphasis added.

[92]Rahner, "Experience of Self and Experience of God," 127.

[93]Ibid.

[94]Ibid.

[95]Ibid., 128.

[96]Karl Rahner, "Reflections on the Unity of the Love of Neighbour and the Love of God," *Theological Investigations* VI (London: Darton, Longman, Todd Ltd., 1974); Karl Rahner, "The 'Commandment' of Love in Relation to the Other Commandments," *Theological Investigations* V (London: Darton, Longman, Todd LTD, 1966). See also Karl Rahner, *The Love of Jesus and the Love of Neighbor*, Robert Barr, trans. (New York: Crossroad Publishing Company, 1983).

[97]Rahner, "Reflections on the Unity of the Love of Neighbour and the Love of God," p. 241.

[98]Ibid., p. 240, emphasis added.

[99]Rahner, "Poetry and the Christian," 358, emphasis added.

[100]Rahner, "Experience of Self and Experience of God," 127, emphasis added.

[101]Ibid., 127-28, emphasis added.

[102]To that extent, Rahner may indeed imply a kind of ordering that is not unlike (but certainly not identical to) von Balthasar. See Christopher Steck, S.J., *The Ethical Thought of Hans Urs von Balthasar* (New York: Crossroad, 2001), 136.

[103]Rahner, "Poetry and the Christian," 363.

[104]Rahner, "Experience of Self and Experience of God," 124.

Fictitious Worlds and Real Unrealities

The Aesthetic Imagination in Søren Kierkegaard and Herbert Marcuse

Jennifer Elisa Veninga

"But the world of a work of art is 'unreal' in the ordinary sense of this word: it is a fictitious reality. But it is 'unreal' not because it is less, but because it is more as well as qualitatively 'other' than the established reality. As fictitious world, as illusion, it contains more truth than does everyday reality . . . only in the 'illusory world' do things appear as what they are and what they can be."—Herbert Marcuse[*]

"When the imagination is allowed to rule in this way it prostrates and anesthetizes the soul, robs it of all moral tension, and makes life a dream."—Søren Kierkegaard[**]

From their disparate positions, Marcuse and Kierkegaard reflect the perennial debate about the very nature of the imagination. The early Greek suspicion of the imagination (the Greek *phantasia*, associated with the unreliability of the senses) exemplified in Plato's banishment of the artists from the Republic and his distrust of imitation and illusion is still alive and well for many today. Particularly for those who interpret imagination as a syn-

---

[*]*The Aesthetic Dimension: Toward a Critique of Marxist Aesthetics*, trans. Herbert Marcuse and Erica Sherover (Boston: Beacon Press, 1978), 54.

[**]*The Concept of Irony*, trans. Lee Capel (New York: Harper and Row, 1965), 308.

onym for fantasy, that which "makes life a dream," this human capacity can signal a dangerous divorce from reason. At the same time, reverence for the imagination has been central for so many artists, who view the imagination as *the* faculty or capacity that allows for meaningful creative existence. The history of religious and theological discourse undoubtedly reflects this tension regarding the imagination as well. In both the Jewish and Christian traditions, for example, the use of images has been regarded with ambivalence—viewed as either the divine connection between God and humans, or the ultimate source of idolatry.[1] Finally, the imagination has been a central issue in modern Western philosophy since Kant's *Critique of the Power of Judgment* reserved a crucial position for the imagination in the concepts of taste, the beautiful, and the sublime.[2] A positive interpretation of imagination can certainly be traced up through the Idealists and Romantics who saw the capacity as fundamental; such thought is exemplified by writers such as Percy Bysshe Shelley, who called the imagination "the great instrument of the moral good."[3]

One of the central issues underlying the historical ambivalence toward the imagination is the relation of imaginative production to "reality." While the imagination plays a crucial role in aesthetics, it is frequently regarded as the faculty that removes the human being from the conditions of reality and thus has little to do with ethics, praxis, or "real-life" decisions. There are those, however, who argue that imagination does have an intrinsic relationship to reality, and therefore provides possibilities of social and ethical transformation. In this essay, I shall explore the disputed relationship between the aesthetic imagination and reality, and shall examine the role of the aesthetic imagination in an unlikely pair of bedfellows—Danish philosopher Søren Kierkegaard (1813-1855) and Marxist philosopher Herbert Marcuse (1898-1979).

Despite their disparate positions, Kierkegaard and Marcuse both give significant attention to the realm of the aesthetic. While they interpret the meaning of the aesthetic in dissimilar ways, both agree that the imagination is its central capacity, and that the aesthetic imagination does, in fact, produce illusion and fictitious realities. The implications of this fictitious reality, however, vary between the two philosophers. For Marcuse, the illusion produced by the imagination has the potential to critique and transform reality. For Kierkegaard (or his pseudonymous counterparts), on the other hand, the imaginary reality of the aesthetic frequently seems to draw the individual away from actuality. This presentation will explore these ostensibly competing interpretations of the aesthetic imagination, giving particular attention to the ability of art to represent reality, the role of communication in the aesthetic, and the implications for the role of the individual in light of aesthetic imagination. Despite their contrary interpretations, the aesthetic theories of Kierkegaard and Marcuse can be held to share a striking number of commonalities. I turn first to Søren Kierkegaard, who provides a complex (and often misunderstood) interpretation of the human imagination.

Anesthetizing the Soul:
Kierkegaard's Criticism of the Imagination

In his posthumously published work, *The Point of View*, Kierkegaard summarizes the central aim of all his writings—to manifest the illusion of what he calls "Christendom" and illuminate what it means to become an authentic Christian in his age.[4] For him, the official church in Denmark, the exemplar of "Christendom," had become a bastion of bourgeois ideology that had turned Christianity into empty, easy, and irrelevant rituals. Throughout his works, Kierkegaard seeks to recover individual subjects in relation to God—subjects he believed had been abstracted into a mass of uncommitted so-called Christians. This kind of abstraction was for him characteristic of the sickness of the "present age."

For Kierkegaard, this sickness manifested itself in what he calls "leveling," a symptom caused by the press and the church in which the individual is subsumed into the whole of society. The dialectic of the present age finds fulfillment in this leveling, he explains, "as the negative unity of the negative reciprocity of all individuals."[5] Furthermore, the present age has abolished what he calls the "principle of contradiction."

Rather than critiquing the established reality, individuals had simply settled into the illusion that their church and society were nearly perfect entities. Without the principle of contradiction, Kierkegaard saw little hope for Christians to challenge this bourgeois mentality of leveling. In order for individuals to have any promise of change, they must present an ideal that also contains contradiction: "The ideal will include the qualitatively opposite possibility."[6]

It is from the standpoint of Kierkegaard's critique of his "present age" that one can interpret his theory of the three spheres of life—the aesthetic, the ethical, and the religious, and more specifically, his thoughts on the imagination.[7] Most critics believe that Kierkegaard disparages this human capacity, interpreting it as the source of empty fictitious reality. There is certainly ample evidence for this position, one instance of which is found in Kierkegaard's comment that the imagination, when left on its own, simply makes life a dream devoid of ethical and moral tension. Nor does he appear to give credence to the *aesthetic*, the sphere he predominantly associates with the imagination.[8]

Indeed, for Kierkegaard, one of the worst fates a person could suffer would be to "get stuck" in an aesthetic existence that involves no ethical or religious commitment. The first volume of Kierkegaard's *Either/Or* makes this point exceedingly clear. Written pseudonymously, the book is presented as a fragmented collection of reflections by a young "aesthete," an artist and seducer of women, who constantly lets himself be taken into a flight of the imagination. The many stories and vignettes reveal what the author believes to be the immediate, accidental, and fantastic world of music, drama, romantic love, and poetry—all of which characterize the aesthetic realm for Kierkegaard. Without grounding in ethics and religion, such activities perpetuate a life of indecision and unfulfilled possibility. One immersed in this kind of existence becomes divorced from actuality, ensuring an escape from the reality of pain and the suffering of life. "The image of perfection that the imagination depicts always looks so easy, so persuasive," Kierkegaard writes.[9] In truth, he maintains, becoming a Christian is the task of a lifetime and involves ongoing personal struggle.

Furthermore, the aesthete's unrelenting pursuit of the ideal obscures the infinite qualitative difference between humans and God. Through acts of imaginative creation, the artist attempts to represent the unrepresentable divine. For Kierkegaard, however, one of the crucial marks of being an authentic Christian is to become *unrecognizable*, following the example of Christ as a lowly servant whose Godhood for him was virtually inconspicuous. Following this example, the Christian message itself can only be communicated *indirectly*. Thus, when an artist believes that he or she has directly represented the Absolute, the creation is essentially a material idol.

> Could I be motivated to lift my chisel in order to represent Christ in color or to carve his figure? That I cannot do . . . I do not comprehend this calmness of the artist in this kind of work, this artistic indifference that is indeed like a callousness toward the religious impression of the religious. . . . The point of view of the religious is completely dislocated; the beholder looked at the picture in the role of an art expert: whether it is a success, whether it is a masterpiece . . . the artist has somehow turned into money and admiration.[10]

Within the larger framework of Kierkegaard's theology, then, the imagination appears to be only a tool of bourgeois Christian ideology that desensitizes the human subject to suffering and paralyzes decision-making. Given these accusations that the imagination is entirely divorced from reality, it seems that the human capacity to imagine has little or no constructive value for Kierkegaard. In typically Kierkegaardian paradoxical fashion, however, this criticism is only half of the story.

"The Capacity for All Capacities":
Kierkegaard's Positive Assessment of the Imagination

Thus far we have only explored Søren Kierkegaard's distaste for the realm of the aesthetic. In turning to Kierkegaard's actual *definition* of the imagination, however, we can begin to see the positive role that it plays within his theology. In *The Sickness unto Death,* he makes the illuminating distinction between the fantastic and the imagination.[11]

> The fantastic, of course, is most closely related to the imagination (*Phantasie*), but the imagination in turn is related to feeling, knowing, and willing. As a rule, imagination is the medium for the process of infinitizing; it is not a capacity, as are the others . . . it is the capacity *instar omnium* (for all capacities). When all is said and done, whatever of feeling, knowing, and willing a person has depends upon what

imagination he has, upon how that person reflects himself—
that is, upon imagination.[12]

Rather than leading one away from actuality—as in the case of
the young aesthete in *Either/Or*—here the imagination, as the "capacity for all capacities," is the very power that grounds feeling,
knowing, and willing. Thus, Kierkegaard writes, the imagination
is "a power that is the first condition for what becomes of a person."[13]

That the imagination is the capacity *instar omnium* and the
very foundation for selfhood suggests, I believe, the need for a
more nuanced interpretation of the relationship between the aesthetic, ethical, and religious spheres in his thought. While it is clear
in Kierkegaard's corpus that the religious life is qualitatively different from the purely aesthetic, it is not so evident that the leap
into the religious involves an absolute negation of the aesthetic
sphere. Rather, both the aesthetic and the ethical are brought into
the religious experience and remain necessary for a truly integrated
existence. "If you cannot manage to see the esthetic, the ethical,
and the religious as the three great allies," writes the ethical pseud-
onym Judge William, "if you do not know how to preserve the
unity of the different manifestations everything gains in these different spheres, then life is without meaning."[14]

Thus the aesthetic does not have to be abandoned—it is rather
"dethroned" or transfigured. Consequently, to imagine, to feel, or
to experience sensuous or aesthetic pleasure, one does not have to
leave behind aspirations of an ethically or religiously decisive life.
What Kierkegaard does insist upon is that those aesthetic experiences not be absolutized, lest they become idolatrous themselves.
John W. De Gruchy, in *Christianity, Art, and Transformation*, notes
that rather than leaving the aesthetic behind, for Kierkegaard,
"What is rejected is a particular understanding of the aesthetic,
not the aesthetic as such. The aesthetic, is, rather, continually rein-
terpreted within the sphere of the ethical and religious."[15] Such a
distinction reflects a broader theme for Kierkegaard, that the task
of existing is "to practice absolute relation to the absolute τέλος
in such a way that the individual strives to reach this maximum: to
relate himself simultaneously to his absolute τέλος and to the
relative—not by mediating them but by relating himself absolutely
to his absolute τέλος and relatively to the relative."[16]

Kierkegaard's contemporaries, however, had in his opinion failed to find a balance of the three spheres. Rather than recognizing that becoming a Christian takes a lifetime, they believed that they were already genuine Christians and needed to do little more, for example, than bury their beloved in a Christian cemetery or baptize their children, without ever giving Christ a second thought. The diagnosis that Kierkegaard gives for the bourgeoisie is that they lack possibility: they are "bereft" of imagination. "In order for a person to become aware of his self and of god," he writes, "imagination must raise him higher than the miasma of probability, it must tear him out of this and teach him to hope and to fear."[17]

Despite Kierkegaard's ambivalence toward the imagination, his critique suggests that imaginative capacity is somehow *essential* to a fully realized religious and Christian existence. Therefore, the imagination is also an agent or catalyst for change, the initial force behind his famous "leap" into the religious life. Perhaps if the imagination can teach the bourgeoisie to "hope and fear," it may teach a *universally* valuable lesson about how to live deeply and meaningfully. This message shares more than a few similarities with that of Marxist philosopher Herbert Marcuse.

Herbert Marcuse: Imagination as Real Unreality

Like Søren Kierkegaard, Herbert Marcuse was a complex figure who held multiple and diverse roles throughout his career. Born in Germany and an immigrant to the United States, Marcuse was one of the first-generation critical theorists of the Institute for Social Research in Frankfurt.[18] A philosopher, Marxist cultural theorist, and political activist, he applied psychoanalytic theory to his critique of advanced technological society, exemplified in his 1955 work, *Eros and Civilization*. Later Marcuse would explore the role of the aesthetic in what he called the current "one-dimensional society."[19]

Thus, like Kierkegaard, he was a critic of his own "present age." In the reality of one-dimensional, advanced industrial society, he maintained, there is a proliferation of false needs created through excessive capitalist impulses in which "people recognize themselves in their commodities" and "social control is achieved by new needs."[20] Marcuse believed that the individual had become identified with her class or with society as a whole, a process that devalued subjectivity. Just as the individual had become unrecognizable amidst the masses, virtually all opposition to hegemonic power was canceled out. Advanced industrial society "silences and reconciles opposition"[21] as "all established reality militates against the logic of contradictions."[22]

For Marcuse, however, there is hope for liberation from this one-dimensional universe. As evidenced in his later works, Marcuse believed that the role of the *aesthetic* dimension was crucial in a utopian vision that could provide an alternative to the oppressive order of society. He proposes a socialist utopia marked by a "new sensibility," which would challenge injustice and suffering, and increase the standard of living for all people. What he calls an "aesthetic ethos" is central to the new sensibility. "The term 'aesthetic,' in its dual connotation of 'pertaining to the senses' and 'pertaining to art,' " Marcuse writes in *An Essay on Liberation*, "may serve to designate the quality of the productive-creative process in an environment of freedom. Technique, assuming the features of art, would translate subjective sensibility into objective form, into reality."[23] His emphasis on the importance of sensory experience reflects his critique of advanced technological society in its uncontrolled commitment to rationality and technology at the cost of subjective emotion, inwardness, and imagination.

In his final work, *The Aesthetic Dimension*, Marcuse challenges orthodox Marxist aesthetics by arguing that the transformative potential of art lies in "art itself," in its very form. For him, art both *protests* and *transcends* given social relations, subverting the dominant consciousness.[24] He believes that Marxist aesthetics has committed the same mistake of advanced industrial society—it devalues the subject. Subjectivity has been "dissolved into class consciousness," thereby eliminating a potentially subversive resource for revolution.[25] The inwardness of subjectivity is indeed a kind of escape, but it is an escape that frees the liberative potential of the human being's passion, imagination, and conscience.

These subjective potentialities find their home in the aesthetic dimension and in the promise of art. "Art transcends its social determination and emancipates itself from the given universe of discourse and behavior while preserving its overwhelming presence. Thereby art creates the realm in which subversion of experience proper to art becomes possible: the world formed by art is recognized as a reality which is suppressed and distorted in the given reality." [26] These subjective potentialities find their home in the aesthetic dimension and in the promise of art. Art subversively indicts the established reality, but does not allow for mere escapism. At the heart of the revolutionary potential of art, of course, lies *the imagination*.

During times of great historical revolution, Marcuse asserts, the imagination found freedom to create "a new social morality," but over time, it was "sacrificed to the requirements of effective reason" in the advanced industrial society. [27] When the imagination is given its full rights, he argues, reconciliation can occur between the individual and the whole, desire and realization, and happiness and reason. [28] The imagination retains its revolutionary potential despite the destruction of this original unity; it remembers the liberation that failed and the promise of a different and better reality. Marcuse argues that the critical function of phantasy is "its refusal to forget what *can be*." [29] Only in the imagination—as a refusal of reality—he tells us, can the rebellion and its uncompromised goals be remembered. [30]

In recalling the possibility of an alternative to the established reality, the imagination helps to *shape* this new order of things. "The imagination, unifying sensibility and reason, becomes 'productive' as it becomes practical: a guiding force in the reconstruction of reality." [31] Like Kierkegaard, Marcuse admits that in the reconstruction of this new world, the imagination does in fact create an illusion—a fictive reality. Yet he is also careful to insist as well that this fiction is perhaps more real than actuality:

> Art opens the established reality to another dimension. To be sure, this is illusion, *Schein*, but an illusion in which another reality shows forth. And it does so only if art wills itself as illusion: as an unreal world other than the established one. And precisely in this transformation, art preserves and transcends its class character. And transcends it, not toward a realm of mere fiction and fantasy, but toward a universe of concrete possibilities. [32]

For Marcuse, the aesthetic imagination provides the possibility of a *qualitatively different* social order. In language remarkably congruent with Kierkegaard's, he makes clear that an authentic socialist revolution would have to involve a "rupture with this universe, the *qualitative leap.*"[33] Through the imagination, art represents the suffering and injustice of the world, but it also transcends the "inhumane reality of want and need" by contradicting it.[34] The world of art, Marcuse asserts, contains nothing that does not already exist in the given reality: "the actions, thoughts, feelings and dreams of men and women, their potentialities and those of nature." Yet, the aesthetic realm of art is " 'unreal' in the ordinary sense of this word: it is a fictitious reality. But it is 'unreal' not because it is less, but because it is more as well as qualitatively 'other' than the established reality."[35] The power of the imagination lies in its dialectical nature—by imagining the qualitative difference, the tension between the "is" and the "ought" is revealed, which allows for the possibility of this kind of qualitative leap.

Like Kierkegaard, Marcuse believes that the established reality cannot be challenged directly. In terms of the aesthetic, this means that subversive art cannot take the form of an explicitly political novel, painting, or poem. The radical nature of art can be communicated only through the pure *form* of art itself, not by political content. "In order to come into their own [forms of art] would have to abandon the direct appeal, the raw immediacy of their presentation."[36] Direct representation and efforts to communicate the possibility of qualitative change through content and not form repress the imagination and stunt the potential for authentic revolution. Marcuse critic Stephen Eric Bronner summarizes: "In the same way that advanced industrial society subverts the cathartic experience, it attempts to absorb the negative, critical potential of traditional forms. Art will therefore necessarily be forced to transvalue and alienate itself from alienated society. . . . Only through its estrangement from the given order will art remain able to preserve itself as the negation of that order."[37]

The indirect communication of artistic truth—that which presents alternatives to the established society of commodity—is necessary during a time when the public media have been reduced to one dimension. In the realm of public discourse, Marcuse says, "speech moves in synonyms and tautologies; actually, it never moves toward the qualitative difference."[38] For Marcuse, it is specifically in the imaginative art form as such that the qualitative difference can be successfully communicated in a world where opposition and contradiction have been flattened out. Put simply, art "communicates truths not communicable in any other language: it contradicts."[39]

Kierkegaard and Marcuse:
An Imaginative and Unlikely Congruence

The preceding discussion has suggested means by which Søren Kierkegaard and Herbert Marcuse arrive at their respective positions on the imagination from their extremely dissimilar perspectives. Kierkegaard's entire corpus was directed toward discerning the nature of the Christian life, a journey that was as much about his own personal faith as it was about the church in general. He gave little thought to politics or economics, asserting that the central concern of existence was the individual's relationship with God. Marcuse, on the other hand, generally regarded religion with suspicion, viewing it as one aspect of a destructive bourgeois mentality.

In regard to the aesthetic imagination, initially it appears as though Kierkegaard and Marcuse exemplify the opposing positions in the debate about the imagination and its relationship to reality. Kierkegaard's biting comment that the imagination anesthetizes the soul certainly reflects his ambivalence about, and concern with, the elevation of the imagination. Much of his work, after all, details the existential choices that must be involved in leaping out of the aesthetic, into the ethical, and finally into the religious. *Either/Or* embodies these contrasts, as Kierkegaard demonstrates the destructive potential of an aesthetic life without ethical commitment or religious conviction. Similarly, *Fear and Trembling* posits the concept of the "knight of faith," exemplified by Abraham, who refuses to remain in either the aesthetic or the ethical realm, but rather makes the leap into the religious.[40] These and other examples seem to demonstrate that the aesthetic imagination, without grounding in reality, is to be surpassed if not conquered altogether.

Yet, as mentioned earlier, the aesthetic imagination retains an important function for Kierkegaard, not entirely unlike its role in Marcuse. As the "capacity for all capacities," the imagination is the faculty that brings together thought, will, and emotion. It is the faculty of possibility, without which an individual has little hope of transcending a meaningless existence apart from God. Furthermore, while Kierkegaard does separate the aesthetic from the ethical and religious, he suggests that the aesthetic is certainly not to be eliminated. Rather, it takes on a new and constructive function for the individual who seeks to come into right relation with God.

Drawing from Kierkegaard's positive interpretation of the aesthetic imagination, it becomes clear that he shares some striking similarities with the Marxist Marcuse. The genesis of both philosophers' projects is a critique of their respective "present ages." The object of Kierkegaard's scrutiny is the nineteenth-century Danish Lutheran Church, while Marcuse directs his critique to twentieth-century advanced industrial society as well as Marxist orthodoxy. Both believe that reason has assumed a hegemonic role over the individual conscience, whether it is in the form of reflective philosophy for Kierkegaard, or technology for Marcuse.

At the center of their critiques is the belief that the individual subject has been subsumed into "the masses," leading to a devaluation of subjective inwardness, passion, emotion, and decision-making. Kierkegaard and Marcuse use almost identical language to describe the obliteration of distinctive individuality; the present age is one of leveling, or flattening. The loss of the possibility of a "qualitative other" or "qualitative difference" is frequently decried in the work of both philosophers. Both stress the need for contradiction in the quest for authentic subjectivity and social transformation, and both suggest the same problem with the present age—a lack of the dialectical presence that holds the tension between the already and not-yet, as well as the promise of change. Furthermore, Kierkegaard and Marcuse insist that the language of this kind of dialectic cannot be expressed *directly*. For Kierkegaard, the need for indirect communication follows from Jesus himself, who communicated truth indirectly in his life as a lowly servant. Marcuse, on the other hand, argues that explicit political content simply does not have the same impact as artistic imaginative form. This leads him to suggest, for example, that "there may be more subversive potential in the poetry of Baudelaire and Rimbaud than in the didactic plays of Brecht."[41]

Although they relate the imagination to reality in different ways, Kierkegaard and Marcuse find its liberating potential in its ability to re-present the actuality of existence and, at the same time, to transcend that reality and provide the possibility of a qualitatively different universe. The imagination provides an abstraction from the given social, political, or religious order, which allows for possible change. At the same time, they recognize that perhaps precisely *because* of its power to depict and form reality, the imagination is easily manipulated. Marcuse demonstrates the way in which the imagination has been thwarted and twisted in one-dimensional society—"Imagination has not remained immune to the process of reification. We are possessed by our images, [we] suffer our own images." He further notes, "To liberate the imagination so that it can be given all its means of expression presupposes the repression of much that is now free and that perpetuates a repressive society."[42]

In the end, Kierkegaard and Marcuse do not deny the tension between the imagination and reality, between art and revolution. Qualitative change must ultimately involve the decision and the struggle of individuals, whether they are working for political change or committing themselves to an absolute relation with the absolute God. However, for both, the aesthetic imagination, with its power to critique the given reality, to transcend it, and to provide the possibility of a new and liberating universe, is an essential aspect of hope itself. Such hope, I believe, is not only *applicable* to what Kierkegaard would call our own "present age," but is also *necessary* for both individual and social change.

While being wary of imposing my own twenty-first-century lens upon either Kierkegaard or Marcuse, I do submit that the historical situations of each, which called for transformative aesthetic imagination, have similarities to our own. The one-dimensional industrial society that became the object of Marcuse's critique has "advanced" into our new millennium of multinational capitalism and ubiquitous globalization. If Marcuse were writing today, perhaps his argument would necessitate a more nuanced interpretation of the economic and political order, particularly regarding the role of Marxist aesthetics in a world where Marxism is no longer the viable political force it was during his lifetime. A twenty-first-century Kierkegaard would certainly find a different set of challenges for the individual in a Denmark where the "established order" of the state church simply does not elicit the participation it once did.

Yet the fundamental questions asked by both philosophers are still relevant for assessing and improving life in the Western world. Where, for example, does individual subjective agency reside in a commodity-driven, multinational, corporate society? Given that the imagination itself is so easily colonized by the images and rhetoric of materialism, where can one find resources that liberate and nourish the imagination in responsible and life-giving ways? The

Kierkegaardian perspective, too, compels us to reevaluate our own relationships to the communities of which we are a part. Whether we are speaking of a religious community, a political party, or even a nation, Kierkegaard pushes us to consider the relationship between our individual identity and the identity of the groups to which we belong. How does one register responsible criticism of one's nation and its practices, and at the same time, call oneself patriotic? Or in terms of membership in a religious community, how can we balance our doubts and dissent with the desire to find theological commonality? The answers to these kinds of questions involve moves of aesthetic imagination for conceiving human identity and our relationship to others.

There is, of course, the undeniable historical ambivalence toward the imagination made clear in the discourse of Marcuse and Kierkegaard. Marcuse's warning that imagination can become reified, and Kierkegaard's critique of its ability to take us away from the real, are not to be dismissed. Despite the imagination's extraordinary life-giving power, one can easily cite instances of its capacity to incite oppressive philosophy and practice. Theologian William T. Cavanaugh has sought to "expose some of the false theological imaginings of modern politics" in his fight against torture. Likewise, political scientist Benedict Anderson has classified violent nationalism as "the shrunken imaginings of recent history"; and Eva T. H. Brann argues that the dystopia of political totalitarianism "puts the imagination in the service of dread." [43]

Nonetheless, I maintain that this ambivalence does not suggest that we utilize human imagination less, but rather that we use it more responsibly and in the service of constructive individual and social transformation. Marcuse and Kierkegaard remind us that it is human imagination that allows us to hold in tension both the already and the not-yet; it is this same capacity that allows us to see both the reality of suffering and an alternative to that suffering. Perhaps in the end, the imagination *does* produce only fictitious worlds, but as our philosophers suggest in their different ways, these worlds may be the most "real" of all unrealities. And there is, finally, exceptional power and promise in these unreal worlds. "To be sure, the aesthetic transformation is *imaginary*," Marcuse writes. "It must be imaginary, for what faculty other than the imagination could invoke the sensuous presence of that which is not (yet)?"[44] And, without eschewing any of his characteristic existential commitment to the here and now, I have my suspicions that Kierkegaard might well have asked the very same rhetorical question.

Notes

¹See, for example, Genesis 1:27: "So God created humankind in his image, in the image of God he created them" and Deuteronomy 27:15: "Cursed be anyone who makes an idol or casts an image, anything abhorrent to the Lord, the work of an artisan, and sets it up in secret."

²For Kant, the imagination is the "faculty of *a priori* intuitions" that cooperates with understanding in the process of judgment and has the capacity for representation and productive creativity. See Immanuel Kant, *Critique of the Power of Judgment,* ed. Paul Guyer, trans. Eric Matthews (New York: Cambridge University Press, 2000).

³Percy Bysshe Shelley, *The Selected Poetry and Prose of Percy Bysshe Shelley,* ed. Carlos Baker (New York: Random House, 1951), 502.

⁴Søren Kierkegaard, *The Point of View,* trans. and ed. Howard V. Hong and Edna H. Hong (Princeton: Princeton University Press, 1998).

⁵Søren Kierkegaard, *The Present Age,* trans. Alexander Dru (New York: Harper and Row, 1962), 52.

⁶Ibid., 70.

⁷The three spheres or "stages," as Kierkegaard calls them early in his work, are detailed in Kierkegaard's *Stages on Life's Way: Studies by Various Persons,* trans. and ed. Howard V. Hong and Edna H. Hong (Princeton: Princeton University Press, 1988).

⁸Cultural critic Terry Eagleton writes of Kierkegaard: "Of the major philosophers from Kant to Habermas, he is one of the few who refuse to assign [the aesthetic] any predominant value or privileged status. He thus stands stubbornly askew to the aestheticizing currents of the modern European mind, which is not to say that the aesthetic is not from first to last one of his central preoccupations" (Terry Eagleton, *The Ideology of the Aesthetic* [Malden, MA: Blackwell Publishing, 1990], 173.)

⁹Søren Kierkegaard, *Practice in Christianity,* trans. and ed. Howard V. Hong and Edna H. Hong (Princeton: Princeton University Press, 1991), 187.

¹⁰Ibid., 255-56.

¹¹Kierkegaard's distinction between the imagination and the fantastic is similar to Samuel Taylor Coleridge's distinction between the imagination and fancy, which he defines as "no other than a mode of Memory emancipated from the order of time and space; while it is blended with, and modified by that empirical phenomenon of the will. . . . Fancy must receive all its materials ready made from the law of association" (Samuel Taylor Coleridge, *Biographia Literaria* in *Selected Poetry and Prose of Coleridge,* ed. Donald A. Stauffer [New York: Random House, 1951], 263).

[12]Søren Kierkegaard, *The Sickness unto Death: A Christian Psychological Exposition for Upbuilding and Awakening,* trans. and ed. Howard V. Hong and Edna H. Hong (Princeton: Princeton University Press, 1980), 30-31.

[13]Kierkegaard, *Practice in Christianity,* 186.

[14]Kierkegaard, *Either/Or,* Part 2, trans. and ed. Howard V. Hong and Edna H. Hong (Princeton: Princeton University Press, 1987), 147.

[15]John W. De Gruchy, *Christianity, Art and Transformation: Theological Aesthetics in the Struggle for Justice* (New York: Cambridge University Press, 2001), 81.

[16]Søren Kierkegaard, *Concluding Unscientific Postscript to Philosophical Fragments,* vol. 1, trans. and ed. Howard V. Hong and Edna H. Hong (Princeton: Princeton University Press, 1992), 407. This criticism of mediation echoes Kierkegaard's anti-Hegelian rhetoric that appears throughout his authorship.

[17]Kierkegaard, *The Sickness unto Death,* 41.

[18]Robert Feenberg, Robert Pippin, and Charles P. Webel, eds., *Marcuse: Critical Theory and the Promise of Utopia* (London: Macmillan, 1988), ix-xiv.

[19]Noted in Marcuse's works, *One-Dimensional Man* (1964), *An Essay on Liberation* (1969), *Counterrevolution and Revolt* (1972), and his final work, *The Aesthetic Dimension* (1978).

[20]Herbert Marcuse, *One-Dimensional Man: Studies in the Ideology of Advanced Industrial Society* (Boston: Beacon Press, 1991), 9.

[21]Ibid., 11.

[22]Ibid., 142.

[23]Herbert Marcuse, *An Essay on Liberation* (Boston: Beacon Press, 1969), 24.

[24]Marcuse, *The Aesthetic Dimension: Toward a Critique of Marxist Aesthetics* (Boston: Beacon Press, 1978), ix. Marcuse also challenges six theses of Marxist aesthetics, including the idea that the only authentic art is produced by the ascending class, or the proletariat; that the writer or artist has the obligation to express the needs of the proletariat; and that the declining class, or bourgeoisie, is only capable of producing decadent art (1-2).

[25]Ibid., 3.

[26]Ibid., 6.

[27]Marcuse, *An Essay on Liberation,* 29.

[28]Herbert Marcuse, *Eros and Civilization: An Inquiry into Freud* (New York: Vintage Books, 1955), 130.

[29]Ibid., 135.

[30]Marcuse, *An Essay on Liberation,* 44.

[31]Ibid., 31.

[32]Herbert Marcuse, *Counterrevolution and Revolt* (Boston: Beacon Press, 1972), 87.

[33]Ibid., 16. Italics mine.

[34]Marcuse, *Eros and Civilization,* 171.

[35] Marcuse, *The Aesthetic Dimension*, 54.

[36] Marcuse, *An Essay on Liberation*, 47. By "form," Marcuse refers to the total qualities (harmony, rhythm, contrast, etc.) that make the artwork a self-contained and structured whole with its own style.

[37] Stephen Eric Bronner, "Between Art and Utopia: Reconsidering the Aesthetic Theory of Herbert Marcuse," in *Marcuse: Critical Theory and the Promise of Utopia*, ed. Robert Feenberg, Robert Pippin, and Charles P. Webel (London: Macmillan, 1988), 117.

[38] Marcuse, *One-Dimensional Man*, 88.

[39] Marcuse, *The Aesthetic Dimension*, 10.

[40] Søren Kierkegaard, *Fear and Trembling*, trans. and ed. Howard V. Hong and Edna H. Hong (Princeton: Princeton University Press, 1983).

[41] Marcuse, *The Aesthetic Dimension*, xiii.

[42] Marcuse, *One-Dimensional Man*, 250.

[43] See William T. Cavanaugh, *Theopolitical Imagination* (New York: T&T Clark, 2002), 7; Benedict Anderson, *Imagined Communities: Reflections on the Origin and Spread of Nationalism* (New York: Verso, 1983, 1991), 7; and Eva T. H. Brann, *The World of Imagination: Sum and Substance* (Savage, MD: Rowman and Littlefield Publishers, 1991), 723.

[44] Marcuse, *Counterrevolution and Revolt*, 96.

Part V

CONTEMPORARY FORMS

Wind, Water, Fire, and *Chocolat*

Playing with Film Images for Feminist Pneumatology

Frances M. Leap

Over the last decade there has developed a growing interest in studying religious imagery in popular cinema. Films about the life of Jesus, especially, have inspired new texts and in some cases even vigorous public discussion.[1] But beyond such clearly religious subject matter, there is also a recognition that in our culture cinema provides a primary forum in which discussions of value and meaning can occur, more effectively perhaps than in our houses of worship.[2] John Paul II identified the world of communications as the "first Areopagus of the modern age," recognizing that for many it provides a "chief means of information and education, of guidance and inspiration."[3] Films offer some of our culture's most significant opportunities for reflection on the "ancient and perennial question of human life: How should we live?"[4] In this sense a film might be rightly understood as religious on levels other than its immediate subject matter.[5] I shall explore here a few thoughts on film images of what could be called sacred taste, Divine sweetness, and the theology of life in the Spirit.

My text is the 2000 film by Lasse Hallstrom, *Chocolat*, based on the 1999 novel of the same title by JoAnne Harris.[6] When *Chocolat* hit the theaters, whether critics gave it thumbs up or down, they all seemed to miss or misread its religious themes.[7] I suggest that we can find in *Chocolat* images of a pneumatology that are illustrative of feminist insights regarding the activity of Spirit in the world and the *metanoia* toward which Spirit beckons.[8]

We can't really blame the secular press for missing the images—

it is rarely attuned to theological themes at all and even less to pneumatology (a term unrecognized even by spell check). The religious reviewers can hardly be held accountable either, for, as Elizabeth Johnson has observed, classical theology itself had all but forgotten Spirit, substituting instead the role of Mary or the church.[9] Johnson suggests that it may be the affinity of Spirit's activities to those traditionally associated with women's work that kept pneumatology and its theological reflection marginalized in patriarchal experience.[10] Perhaps the same dynamic was at work here, making it easy to miss the presence of Spirit in a "chick flick," as many of my students have titled the genre to which they consign this film.

Reviewers generally characterized *Chocolat* as a "war between the forces of paganism and Christianity"[11]; a "condescending, self-congratulatory attack on provincial sanctimony . . . against the twin evils of organized religion and institutional patriarchy";[12] "pitting the forces of liberation against the forces of repression."[13] "The Catholic church looms as a major joy killer, against . . . a kind of liberation chocology."[14] Even those who were not offended by the film still bought into the dualism of opposition: "Can the liberating virtues of pleasure . . . triumph over well-meaning but closed-minded small-town zealots?"[15]

What the reviewers failed to recognize, and so mislabeled as conflict, is what might be identified as the energizing dialectic between institution and charism, the single activity of the same Spirit in creative tension between the ecclesia, the official assembly, and *koinonia*, a community of loving fellowship.[16] Far from being a war between opposing sides, it is rather the single work of Spirit in mutual influence and transformation that we see in *Chocolat*, for both ecclesia and *koinonia* are changed by the film's end. The insight of Yves Congar in regard to the dialectic of institution and charism is embodied through the main characters of the film. "Some things are codified, some are experienced."[17] The Comte de Raynaud vigorously defends the institution of Spirit's codified presence while Vianne Rocher offers the experienced charism of Spirit's activity. But unlike the more readily identifiable image of Jesus, the action of Spirit in church, in world, and in film manifests itself in ways more subtle and diverse and so requires of us some consideration.

Throughout the film, we find the use of images that scripture associates most strongly with Spirit: the blowing wind, flowing water, and fire. Each in its turn brings the grace of challenge and change to the characters, but it is Hallstrom's use of the wind, especially in the opening scene, that indicates this not a struggle of opposition but the dialectic of transformation. He provides images for what Elizabeth Johnson has termed a "feminist envisioning of reality in patterns of wholeness that undercut dualism" and "serve an integrative rather than divisive function."[18]

As the film opens, the people of Lansquenet enter their village church, greeted at the door by their mayor, the Comte de Raynaud; the narrator explains that this is a town of villagers who have "held fast to their traditions." The camera moves through the church and we hear the congregation singing: "Come, Holy Ghost, Creator come/From Thy bright heavenly throne/Come take possession of our souls/And make them all Thine own."

The people of Lansquenet are in some way like the apostles in the upper room after Jesus' ascension—a people possessed of a transforming message, but lacking the experiential ability to proclaim its truth. Lansquenet knows the good news but has forgotten how to live it. This ecclesia, like the stone building in which it gathers, has ossified its charism, losing the vitality of the tradition to which it holds. Yet the very request made in their hymn will soon be met with an unexpected Pentecost.

"A sly wind . . . from the north" drives two figures, caped in bright Pentecost red, uphill to the village, and we hear the voice-over of Père Henri in his sermon for this first Sunday of Lent. As he asks, "Where will we find truth?" the same gusting wind circles the church in a camera pan and, as if in answer, the Spirit of truth blows the church doors open wide. It is the Comte de Raynaud who rises to close and bar them against further encounter as the scene cuts to the arrival of those Pentecost figures, Vianne and her daughter Anouk, at the house of Armande. Thus does Hallstrom suggest that the blowing Spirit that brings Vianne to Lansquenet is the same Holy Ghost of the hymn, who seeks entry to the lives and the ecclesial institution of the townspeople; in this encounter all sides will find transformation.

Reviewers who see organized religion as the "bad guy" seem to react to the plot of the novel and have missed the fundamental changes made by scriptwriter Robert Nelson Jacobs. While the antagonist of the novel is the single dark character of the village priest, for the film the work of this character is divided and thereby redeemed. The aggressive negativity of the priest is now thoroughly disarmed in sweet-faced Père Henri, the new curé of the parish. The tension is instead transferred to the Comte de Reynaud, a new character created for the film. He becomes the rigid moral crusader controlling the young priest and seeking the ouster from the town of Vianne and her chocolate temptations. The banishing of evil, which occurs in the novel when the priest leaves the village disgraced, is displaced onto the eviction of Serge, the abusing husband. Thus, rather than organized religion waging its battle against "liberating pleasure," we see the official assembly drained of inspiration by a rigid domination. Ultimately, Hallstrom seems to suggest, it is not the institution itself, but its empty interpretation and sclerotized codification that are the problem. The doors of the ecclesia have been closed to Spirit by the Comte and by Père Henri's predecessor who, it is revealed, had served the parish for five decades. But Spirit is breathing in new life. The window of *aggiornamento* has been opened with the arrival of Père Henri, and now the sly north wind, Spirit's creative presence, will blow in the charism of living community. It is significant that the characters drawn to the *chocolaterie* are the same characters attending mass each Sunday and expressing their hearts in the confessional. This is not a case of either/or but a process of transformation. Hallstrom illustrates Congar's insight that "The Church is not just an establishment where past forms are preserved. It is Tradition, and true Tradition is criticism and creativity as well as the handing-down and preservation of identical realities."[19]

   Elizabeth Johnson has identified three key insights for feminist pneumatology: the transcendent God's immanence, divine passion for liberation, and the constitutive nature of relation.[20] We see these themes developed in the film through the work of Vianne as she opens her *chocolaterie* in town. Vianne becomes an envoy of Spirit to Lansquenet, bringing close the presence of the Divine in vivifying, renewing, empowering,[21] especially the marginal and vulnerable of the town. Her generous, accepting presence gathers a small community of quirky townspeople to the *chocolaterie*. Spirit's presence in grace may be seen in Vianne's ministry of offering to others their "favorite" chocolate. Every soul, known by name and called to life, encounters the grace necessary in particularity to invite healing. Chocolate becomes both a symbolic and an efficacious presence of grace as the *chocolaterie* becomes a *koinonia*, growing in the shadow of the stone ecclesia, the transcendent God immanent in Spirit's loving fellowship. Through this *koinonia* the villagers will "encounter the mysteries of personhood, grace, sexuality, suffering, love, forgiveness, and communion," which are, as Catherine LaCugna reminds us, the mystery of divine life "active in history and human personality."[22]

Many of Vianne's customers are the marginal of the town and the words of Luke 4:18 echo in her work; she brings good news to the poor, release to captives, recovery of sight to the blind, freedom to the oppressed. Her landlady, Armande, is a bitter old woman of the village. Her home is the edge of the town wall; she does not attend the church; she is rejected by her daughter and forbidden to see her grandson. Within the *koinonia* of the *chocolaterie*, though, Armande regains her laughter, sees her grandson, and reaches out to Josephine, the battered wife of Serge.

In Josephine's story we see vividly the divine passion for liberation and the constitutive nature of relationship through which liberation is achieved. Josephine's liberation might be characterized as a *metanoia*. Rosemary Ruether has identified sin as both "the capacity to set up prideful antagonistic relations to others . . . and in the passivity of men and women who acquiesce" to them.[23] In this understanding, Josephine is a woman in sin, a woman who has acquiesced to the brutal control of her husband and the alienation of the town. Her liberation is as much deliverance from her own sin as it is from her abusive situation. *Metanoia* for women, Ruether tells us, "involves a turning around in which they literally discover themselves as persons, as centers of being upon which they can stand and build their own identity." This *metanoia* becomes possible, she explains, by a conversion to community, "an alternative upon which we base ourselves."[24] The constitutive nature of relationship becomes the grounding of liberation. The transformation of Josephine illustrates this understanding of *metanoia*. From the gift of self, grounded in the emerging community of the *chocolaterie*, Josephine draws courage to leave the abusive marriage. Her growth is made visual by the shades of red Hallstrom chooses for her clothing, vividly identifying her with the life of Spirit.

In superb contrast, Hallstrom compares the life-giving conversion of Josephine with the emptiness of the conversion the Comte imposes upon Serge. Having witnessed in her bruises the abuse Josephine has suffered, the Comte responds that, "your husband will be made to repent for this." He literally drags Serge through institutional forms of repentance in the ecclesia. But Hallstrom's

inter-cutting of scenes indicates that the problem is not the institutional form, but rather its lack of vitality. Père Henri protests that
confession must be made "in a spirit of sincere repentance," but
the Comte shoves Serge into the confessional, assuring the little
priest that he is ready. This contrasts to Josephine quietly confid-
ing her cowardice to Vianne. Serge is shown in a children's cat-
echism class replying with faulty answers to Père Henri's inquiries
and the scene cuts to Josephine correctly responding to Vianne's
queries on the proper way to prepare chocolate. We see Serge receiving the eucharistic host from Père Henri and the scene cuts to
Anouk feeding Josephine a chocolate wafer—taste and see how
sweet is the Lord. With this scene chocolate itself moves to identification with the eucharistic presence.

Hallstrom communicates that the ecclesia has form and message, but in the *koinonia* Spirit brings it to embodiment. In imposing the disciplines of repentance, the Comte succeeds in changing
the outward form of Serge but neglects his true *metanoia*, ironi-
cally remaking Serge in his own image, like the statue of the Comte's
ancestor that stands in the square before the church, a frozen and
rigid form, forgetful of the human flesh it seeks to evoke. Out-
wardly Serge is cleaned up, but inwardly, like the Comte, he is full
of anger at his rejection and wild to control his wife again. In an
inebriated rage, Serge forces his way into the *chocolaterie* to re-
claim Josephine and attacks Vianne for sheltering his wife. He is
knocked out cold by a skillet-wielding Josephine and deposited by
the women at the base of the statue in front of the ecclesia—a
judgment on its rigid and empty failure. In the *koinonia*, however,
Spirit fills the life of the chocolate shop and draws its people to
live more fully at the table of gracious love. The eucharistic presence is shared in chocolate, its grace vivifying, renewing, and empowering the community. Josephine continues to grow in the grace
of Spirit in the *koinonia,* and Vianne announces her plans for a
chocolate festival to be held on Easter Sunday.

The activity of Spirit intensifies as Lent deepens. Scripture's
image of flowing water carries a fresh invitation from Spirit as the
river Tannes brings gypsies traveling by boat—a new challenge to
the townspeople, to the Comte, and also to Vianne herself in unexpected ways. There is a gentle humor to the film as Spirit leads
the Comte and Vianne more deeply toward their own *metanoia*.

The villagers join the Comte in the boycott he organizes to deny
services to the river gypsies and drive them out of town, while

Vianne befriends them and their leader, Roux. As the Comte's efforts seem to succeed and Vianne's business declines, Armande insists that Vianne serve for her a seventieth birthday party. It is on Wednesday of Holy Week that gypsies and friends of the *chocolaterie* are invited to Armande's home for a magnificent meal and repair afterward for dessert on Roux's boat. The dinner and its preparation are an agape celebration; like the wedding feast of Jesus' parables, Spirit gathers the marginal for rejoicing. LaCugna's description of the *koinonia* Spirit gathers is vividly portrayed: "a place in which everyone is accepted . . . irrespective of how the dignity of a person might otherwise be determined."[25] The joy of God's reign overflows in food, music, and dancing. Images of grace and Spirit abound: in the chocolate flowing in rich abundance through the meal, in the water that brought the gypsy boats, in the fire lighting the evening activities, and in joyful dancing, a *perichoresis* of the human community mirroring the divine dance in which it partners.[26]

It is on the water that Roux takes up the work of Spirit and invites the process of *metanoia* for Vianne. After the meal, agape continues as Roux draws Vianne away from Martha ministry (clean-up) into dance, and later in gentle conversation challenges her wandering life and its effect on Anouk. As Vianne begins to face her own vulnerability this night, they are suddenly threatened by a frightening fire on the river boats, secretly started by Serge. Though ultimately no one is hurt, Vianne, her weakness exposed, draws back from Roux. When Armande is found dead of diabetic shock, Vianne feels isolated and responsible. Immediately following the Saturday funeral, she suddenly packs and again prepares to move, abandoning her chocolate festival. Vianne herself falls back into a dualism—while she is excellent in offering the grace of Spirit, the challenge and support of mutual relation, she recoils from receiving it herself. She remains in bondage to the wandering of her own gypsy mother, symbolized by the urn of ashes she has carried with her; and, like her mother, she flees her own fears, refusing her own needs and the need of Anouk for the grace of a home and a stable community of relation.

Hallstrom returns here to the imagery of a powerful wind storm, and Spirit blows in Easter transformations. As a great wind rattles the house, we see a protesting and resentful Anouk struggling with Vianne down narrow stairs, when suddenly, from their luggage, the urn of ashes falls and its contents are poured out. With frightened apologies Anouk seeks to gather them again. But it is precisely in the emptying of her mother's urn that Vianne begins to empty of her fear, to lift her mask as giver, and receive herself the gift she has previously offered. The sound of voices leads Vianne into her own kitchen, where Josephine has gathered the friends of the *chocolaterie* to work and provide the festival. "The *koinonia* of the Spirit leads to *diakonia* on the part of all, not just some, members of the community constituted by the Spirit."[27] Message and ministry do not depend on the minister. The question with which Josephine greets Vianne is virtually the same question that Vianne had addressed to her in first offering the grace of mutual relationship. Now Vianne herself is graced with *metanoia*, turning to receive back again the care and community that she has offered. The eschatological longing expressed in Anouk's apology that, "The next time will be better, won't it, Mama?" is unexpectedly and graciously fulfilled in community present. The Easter vigil of the *koinonia* kitchen incarnates the grace of eucharistic presence. Hallstrom confirms this by cutting the scene to Père Henri saying, "Christ is risen," as he practices the Easter sermon the Comte is writing for him.

Meanwhile, the Comte's journey to *metanoia* becomes the culmination of Spirit's work in Lansquenet as charism is returned to ecclesia. Throughout the film Hallstrom visually links the suffering of the Comte de Reynaud over his wife's abandonment of their marriage with the suffering of Jesus. Several times the elements of a scene include the Comte, a crucifix, a picture of, or question about, the missing wife, even a reference to truth. The Comte lives a long Lenten agony in the garden as he avoids truth, refusing to accept the cup of suffering and admit his wife will not return. He evades the *kenosis* of his cross by substituting instead the empty belly of a strict Lenten fast.

On this same Holy Saturday evening, Serge visits the Comte to confess it was he who set the boat fire a few days earlier. Though Serge expects the Comte's approval for this work, the Comte instead is horrified and banishes him from the town.[28] This unforeseen consequence of his efforts at moral reform shakes the Comte and is compounded later that evening when he sees his lovely secretary, who had supported him faithfully in his moral crusade, enter the *chocolaterie*. She has experienced her own *metanoia* in events surrounding the agape dinner and has been recruited by Josephine to prepare for the festival. This friendless moment of

Judas betrayal for the Comte begins his journey toward *metanoia*.

Hallstrom shows us the Comte, deep in the night, before the large crucifix of the church as he prays in despair: "All my efforts have been for nothing. . . . I feel so lost. I don't know what to do. Tell me what to do." Significantly, the very crucifix before which the Comte prays is clothed in a red loincloth, suggesting the promise of Pentecost fire. As an idea enters his mind, the Comte leaves the church with a dagger-like letter opener in hand. Unlike Serge, it is not people he aims to hurt, but the temptation he seeks to destroy. The chocolate is his target, but grace itself will offer his salvation.

The Comte breaks into the *chocolaterie* and enters the display window where he encounters a large chocolate figure of a woman. Unlike the statue of his ancestor in the square, this likeness is both form and substance. If we can take our cue, as Johnson does,[29] from images of Native American experiences of God, she is Chocolate Woman, God embodied in life-giving, sweet confection. The Comte stabs violently at the chocolate, slashing the figure and bringing ruin. But in this last desperate act of control the hungry soul of the Comte is touched by the taste of grace as a fragment of chocolate falls on his lips. The death of Chocolate Woman brings redemption. Like Eucharist broken, she is more than symbol, she is efficacious Presence. As the fasting Comte loses control and fills himself with pieces of chocolate in the window, he is overcome with tears. He literally falls, not into sin as he had feared, but into the sweet presence of God herself surrounding him in wildly generous abundance. Cradled in chocolate, eating and weeping his vulnerability, his tears become the orgasm of his grief, the emptying of his hopes, the cross of his *kenosis*. Though he came to the *chocolaterie* bringing death, he is drawn instead into his own death. The display window becomes the tomb of his control, and the kiss of grace brings him weeping to empty sleep.

That Père Henri, with the dawn of Easter morning, is the first to see the Comte at the windowed tomb is significant. Like Mary Magdalene, he brings the news to Vianne, who rouses the dazed and contrite Comte to the grace of mutuality, promising that she "will never tell a soul." But charism is risen, and with Père Henri it enters the ecclesia once more. At mass, a humbled Comte sits at the back, listening to the little priest speak a sermon in his own words, as the narrator tells us that "the parishioners felt a new sensation that day—a lightening of the spirit, a freedom from the

old *tranquillité*. Even the Comte de Reynaud felt strangely released." The doors of the church are thrown open to a carnival of
Easter and Pentecost presence as the square is filled with images of
Spirit: enormous white wings of a costumed dancer, fire breathing,
chocolate in abundance, a red balloon attached to the statue, which
seems now to smile.

In a final and noteworthy scene the wind speaks to Vianne "of
towns yet to be visited, friends in need, yet to be discovered." But
Vianne sustains her conversion to community and remains in
Lansquenet, offering her mother's ashes instead to the wind, knowing that the wide work of Spirit does not depend solely on her
ministry. Thus does stability ground charism, and the constancy
of ecclesial institution embrace *koinonia*. Inclusiveness, community, and freedom: for a moment the work of Spirit is in harmony
at Lansquenet, and all sides have found Spirit's transformation.[30]

It is a fable after all. That we have laughed and come to a happy
ending with the moral of the story neatly summarized by Père Henri
should be no surprise. Even a writer of the gospels felt the need to
add verses 9 through 20 to the original ending of Mark 16. In this
sense, *Chocolat* can be termed a religious film as well: it brings us
to the joy of Easter laughter—*risus paschalis*—the unexpected and
surprising reversal, the great joke that God has played on death.[31]
The foundation of Christian existence is the joy made possible in
Easter, a "liberated and redeemed joy which breaks down barriers
and brings integration . . . especially in the interests of those who
are marginalized and excluded."[32] Like the parables of Jesus,
Chocolat does the work of Spirit, telling a simple story to change
our perception. It uses holy humor to reveal to us a wholly embodied God who will, Père Henri tells us, "measure goodness by
what we embrace, by what we create and who we include." Perhaps as a reflection on the "ancient and perennial question" this is
an answer well-offered to our culture today.

Notes

[1]The *Journal of Religion and Film* was founded in 1997; several new texts
dealing with Jesus in film have appeared: Lloyd Baugh, *Imaging the Divine:
Jesus and Christ-figures in Film* (Kansas City: Sheed & Ward, 1997); W.
Barnes Tatum, *Jesus at the Movies: A Guide to the First Hundred Years* (Santa
Rosa, CA: Polebridge Press, 1997); Richard C. Stern, Clayton N. Jefford, and
Guerric Debona, *Savior on the Silver Screen* (Mahwah, NJ: Paulist Press,

1999); Richard Walsh, *Reading the Gospels in the Dark: Portrayals of Jesus in Film* (Harrisburg, PA: Trinity Press International, 2003). The impassioned public debate surrounding Mel Gibson's film *The Passion of the Christ* and some years earlier Martin Scorsese's *The Last Temptation of Christ* are examples.

[2]Margaret R. Miles, *Seeing and Believing: Religion and Values in the Movies* (Boston: Beacon Press, 1996); Clive Marsh and Gaye Ortiz, eds., *Explorations in Theology and Film* (Malden, MA: Blackwell, 1997); John May, ed., *New Images in Religious Film* (Kansas City: Sheed & Ward, 1997).

[3]John Paul II, *Redemptoris Missio* (1990) [cited 4 November 2006]. Available from http://www.vatican.va/holy_father/john_paul_ii/encyclicals/documents/hf_jp-ii_enc_07121990_redemptoris-missio_en.html.

[4]Miles, *Seeing and Believing,* 25.

[5]Wendy M. Wright, "Babette's Feast: A Religious Film," *Journal of Religion and Film* 1, no. 2 (October 1997) [cited 6 March 2006]. Available from http://www.unomaha.edu/jrf/BabetteWW.htm.

[6]JoAnne Harris, *Chocolat: A Novel* (New York: Penguin Books, 1999). Special thanks to Christine Blaney for introducing me to the film and to Daniel Frescura and Rosa Snyder-Boyd for sharing generously of their insights.

[7]This includes the review on the website of the USCCB, which describes the film as an "unpalatable fable . . . in which a single mother arrives . . . to open an enticing chocolate shop during Lent, causing bitterness and opposition from the townsfolk tempted by her rich confections during a season of penance. . . . (The) film insults with its disingenuous rallying cry for tolerance while it mocks faith traditions, religious tenets and Catholic sacraments" (United States Conference of Catholic Bishops, Office for Film and Broadcasting [cited 22 May 2006]). Available from http://www.usccb.org/movies/c/chocolat2000.shtml. In striking and exceptional contrast is the assessment of the Religious Communicators Council, which presented a Wilbur Award to *Chocolat* in 2001. Wilbur Awards "recognize excellence in the communication of religious issues, values and themes in the secular media." A specific review of the film did not accompany the award (Religious Communicators Council, Wilbur Awards [cited 6 March 2006]). Available from http://www.religioncommunicators.org/wilbur.html.

[8]Spirit is used without a definite article throughout to convey more clearly this person of the Trinity rather than a title.

[9]Elizabeth A. Johnson, *She Who Is: The Mystery of God in Feminist Theological Discourse* (New York: Crossroad, 1994), 128.

[10]Ibid., 130.

[11]Roger Ebert, "*Chocolat,*" *Sun Times,* 22 December 2000 [cited 6 March 2006]. Available from http://rogerebert.suntimes.com/apps/pbcs.dll/article?AID=/20001222/REVIEWS/12220303/1023.

[12]Dennis Lim, "That Slack Magic," *Village Voice,* December 13-19, 2000 [cited 6 March, 2006]. Available from http://www.villagevoice.com/film/0050,lim,20595,20.html.

[13]David Ansen, "Twice as Sweet as Sugar," *Newsweek*, 18 December 2001, p. 19 [cited 7 April 2006]. Available from http://atgbcentral.com/choconewsweek.html.

[14]Rand Richard Cooper, "Hallucinogens for All," *Commonweal* 128, no. 3 (2001): 19.

[15]Elvis Mitchell, "*Chocolat*: Candy Power Comes to Town," *New York Times*, 15 December 2000 [cited 6 March 2006]. Available from http://query.nytimes.com/gst/fullpage.html?res=9F02E2DD1F3FF936A25751C1A 9669C8B63.

[16]I am using these terms suggestively, drawing on discussions from *The New Dictionary of Theology*, ed. Joseph Komonchak, Mary Collins, and Demont Lane (Collegeville, MN: Liturgical Press, 1987), 186, 557. The Greek and Hebrew roots of ecclesia as "a convoked assembly" imply the official institution. The Greek *koinonia* refers both to "Christians' participation in the life of God and to the communal life it creates." See also Yves Congar's discussion of the relation of institution and charism in *The Word and the Spirit* (San Francisco: Harper & Row, 1986), 58-62.

[17]Congar, *The Word and the Spirit*, 53.

[18]Johnson, *She Who Is*, 132.

[19]Congar, *The Word and the Spirit*, 55.

[20]Johnson, *She Who Is*, 147.

[21]These are verbs highlighted by Johnson to describe Spirit's action in the world (*She Who Is*, 133-39).

[22]Catherine Mowery LaCugna, *God for Us: The Trinity and Christian Life* (San Francisco: HarperSanFrancisco, 1991), 362.

[23]Rosemary Radford Ruether, *Sexism and God-Talk: Toward a Feminist Theology* (Boston: Beacon Press, 1983), 164.

[24]Ibid.

[25]LaCugna, *God for Us*, 299.

[26]Ibid., 274.

[27]Ibid., 300.

[28]This scene is the most unresolved of the film. Spirit seems missing in the unredeemed fate of Serge. I have assigned my students to imagine further scenes not shown in the film for the possibilities of grace for Serge.

[29]Johnson, *She Who Is*, 132-33.

[30]These are three central values that Patricia Wilson-Kastner finds grounded in *perichoresis* (*Faith, Feminism and the Christ* [Philadelphia: Fortress Press, 1983], 131-33), referred to in LaCugna, *God for Us*, 272.

[31]Jürgen Moltmann, *The Source of Life: The Holy Spirit and the Theology of Life* (Minneapolis: Fortress Press, 1997), 136.

[32]K.-J. Kuschel, *Laughter: A Theological Reflection* (London: SCM Press, 1994), 92.

Mass Culture or *Mass* Culture?

The Frankfurt School's Critique of the Culture Industry vs. The Catholic Imagination of Bishop Fulton J. Sheen

Matthew G. Minix

The multimedia activity of Bishop Fulton J. Sheen, perhaps the greatest American Catholic communicator of the twentieth century, can be considered the example *par excellence* of an American Catholic who, acting as an agent of the Catholic Church, used methods of mass communication in order to reach the wider American culture. In his use of the modern media of radio, publishing, and, especially, television, Bishop Sheen opened channels of communication between the Catholic Church and the American population, and ultimately contributed to "the improved image and reputation of the Catholic Church" within American society.[1] Indeed, at least for non-Catholics within the United States, Sheen was arguably "*the* image and *the* authentic voice most closely associated with the Church during the middle decades of the twentieth century."[2] For Catholics of this period, however, Sheen's work can be interpreted as "providing a quite popular and ecclesiastically approved bridge for Catholics wishing to leave behind the 'Catholic ghetto' and move into an affluent culture where religious homogeneity, not difference, assured social acceptance."[3]

The legacy of Bishop Sheen's ministry becomes more complex, however, when the various elements are considered under the light of critical theory. It can be argued, for example, that Sheen fell into many of the traps that early critical theorists, such as Max

Horkheimer and Theodor Adorno, predicted accompany media celebrity. In their view, the price for success in the entertainment industry required the celebrity to be "appropriately pliable" to the demands of the industry and not "too obstinate" about those issues particular to the celebrity's interest.[4]

Evidence for this kind of critique against Sheen can be found in Christopher Owen Lynch's rhetorical analysis of Sheen's most famous television program, *Life Is Worth Living*. Lynch argues that Sheen modified his message, at least when compared to the content of his earlier radio broadcasts, minimizing the uniquely Catholic elements of his presentation in favor of areas of common Judeo-Christian agreement. While seemingly innocuous, and perhaps even positive in one sense, this action can also be explained as Sheen "reconciling" himself to a culture industry where "anyone who resists can only survive by fitting in."[5]

Additional critical examination of Sheen's ministry demonstrates that an adequate evaluation may require even greater nuance. In his book *The Practice of Everyday Life,* French Jesuit Michel de Certeau examined the way that the "everyday practices" of "the dominated element in society" could be seen as forms of resistance to the dominant "systems of 'production.'"[6] Central to this project was de Certeau's concept of *bricolage*, understood as "an artisan-like inventiveness" that allows for an object to be transformed through its use in an unintended manner by an apparently dominated user who, despite the common assumption of those in power, is not necessarily "either passive or docile."[7] Through something as simple as drawing a mustache on a face in the newspaper, users are able to inscribe their own voices and thus make a space for themselves that resists the dominant structure of power.

When analyzed through the insights of de Certeau, Bishop Fulton Sheen may initially appear simply as a collaborator with the systems of production, a figure to be resisted rather than an ally in resistance. Upon further consideration of his ministry, however, even Sheen's seemingly capitalistic endeavors, such as his promotion of the statue of "Our Lady of Television," can be interpreted as a kind of *bricolage*. Rather than being "written off" as merely another slave to the culture industry, Sheen can be interpreted as attempting to supply his own audience with a method of resistance, a way of "writing on" the dominating medium of television. In other words, Sheen's television ministry can be seen as subverting the pressure of the dominant power structures rather than submitting to them.

Dialectic of Enlightenment

In their work *Dialectic of Enlightenment*, Max Horkheimer and Theodor Adorno argue that "mass culture" has brought with it an unparalleled uniformity of expectation and desire, such that "the whole world is made to pass through the filter of the culture industry."[8] This powerful cultural machine, which even renders "political opposites" indistinguishable beneath its promise for progress, sets the terms of societal life and, metaphorically, "presses the same stamp on everything."[9] The effect of this "constant reproduction of the same thing" is an allegedly antagonistic urge for nonconformity, displayed in "never ending talk of ideas, novelty, and surprise," which naturally requires "everything . . . to run incessantly, to keep moving," and so which, in reality, supports the structure of the culture industry.[10] In other words, the cultural monotony gives birth to moments of false innovation that are ultimately reincorporated into a cultural machine whose hunger for novelty remains insatiable.

And so, new technologies, and especially new technological methods of communication such as the telephone, radio, cinema, and television, are constructed and then argued for on the basis of a "consumer's needs," even though it is clear from the fact of human history that such "needs" were not truly felt until the products were created. Instead, the power that they provide "those whose economic hold over society is greatest" allows for a "technological rationale" that is ultimately "the rationale of domination itself."[11] Eventually, technologies such as movies and television begin to shape the reality in which people live to such a degree that they have trouble distinguishing where these media end and their real lives begin.[12] This inability to distinguish reality from fiction, to separate their own life stories from the myths promoted by the mass culture, begins to weaken individuality and destroy the freedom of those so enthralled, so that "not to conform is to be rendered powerless, economically and therefore spiritually."[13] So shaped has their worldview been "by the myth of success," that to keep from becoming completely impotent, the least powerful find themselves arguing on behalf of "the very ideology which enslaves them."[14]

This shaping of reality also leads to the "classifying, organizing, and labeling [of] consumers," who are then expected "to behave (as if spontaneously) in accordance with his [or her] previously determined and indexed level, and choose the category of mass product turned out for his [or her] type."[15] The entertainment industry accomplishes this labeling of reality through the "explicit and implicit, exoteric and esoteric catalogue of the forbidden and the tolerated," forming "its own language, down to its syntax and vocabulary, by use of anathema."[16] And yet some of what appears to be forbidden in this system of classification can, in certain circumstances, be allowed (and even bestowed with honors) in the name of style, because such "departures from the norm are regarded as calculated mutations which serve all the more strongly to confirm the validity of the system."[17] In the end, style itself becomes a positive artistic value, rather than a "negative truth," and "having ceased to be anything but style, it reveals the latter's secret: obedience to the social hierarchy."[18] And so, according to Horkheimer and Adorno, even clever attempts to circumvent the dominant language of the culture industry ultimately fail. Much like the urge for nonconformity against the "constant reproduction of the same thing," such rebellions really only serve to strengthen the system against which they appear to strive.[19]

In the opinion of the founders of critical theory, every attempt at escape appears to be taken over and incorporated into the system of the culture industry, which views all of humanity "merely as customers and employees," and so patterns all aspects of life to conform to that dualism. Even "value judgments" can only be understood as "merely advertising or empty talk," as intended for customers or employees, leisure or labor, to sell something or to pass the time while working.[20] And to pass the time when not working, the concept of "amusement" is promoted, and is offered as an "escape from the mechanized work process," even though it was in reality created to be a further enslavement to that pattern of life.[21] This is demonstrated through the realization that the forms of entertainment offered are merely "afterimages" of the work that is being escaped; in order to be relaxing, the amusement must require minimal effort and so must follow "rigorously in the worn grooves of association."[22] The end result is that the only "liberation which amusement promises is freedom from thought and from negation."[23] Yet even that is a deception; this amusement really exists for the sake of advertisement, in order to fortify "the firm bond between the consumers and the big combines."[24]

The Culture Industry

In what is perhaps his most lucid critique of the medium, the essay "How to Look at Television," Theodor Adorno seeks to name "the socio-psychological implications and mechanisms of television, which often operate under the guise of false realism," in order that "the public at large may be sensitized to the nefarious effect of some of these mechanisms."[25] In this elaboration of the argument from *Dialectic of Enlightenment*, Adorno explains that the present use of television creates a false reality that rather insidiously attempts to look as real as possible, even while television intentionally modifies the world to convey its own ideals. The result is that television transforms its viewers' perceptions of the real world, so that they see the "world" through the lens that television projects for them.

According to Adorno's argument, in television programs "all conflicts are mere sham" that are ultimately resolved, usually through a positive "realism" that demands that one must "adjust oneself at any price" to the societal rules that the industry provides.[26] This need to adjust is actually conveyed through a "multilayered structure," in both "overt" and "hidden" messages that secretly support each other. This subtle support is accomplished either through "hidden messages" that support the status quo or through overtly "off color remarks" that give an outlet to "repressed gratifications" on the "hidden level."[27] Adorno believes that this is done through a kind of "psychoanalysis in reverse," in which television constructs a rather Hegelian synthesis: "allowed gratifications, forbidden gratifications, and reoccurrence of the forbidden in a somewhat modified and deflected form" that is, nonetheless, acceptable.[28]

Adorno also shows that television creates registers of expectation, in which the viewer is intended to understand certain elements of a program through subtle clues, and this "induces him [sic] to look at life as though it and its conflicts could be understood in such terms."[29] The effect of this new way of looking at the world creates a background of lived expectation, so that the hidden assumption of the television show that crime exists around every corner may come "to affect certain spectator groups more deeply than the overt moral of crime and punishment."[30] In a similar way, television lends itself to stereotyping certain types of people into specific roles, eliminating the complexity of human character into easy caricatures.[31] While it could be argued that all forms of mass media do similar things, television is unique in its ability to simulate reality from a distance, so that it is often genuinely unclear what is reality and what is scripted, what is genuine and what is merely fabrication.[32]

Fulton Sheen: Bishop of All Media

From the beginning of his priestly ministry, Fulton J. Sheen appears to have been interested in using every available medium in order to evangelize a wider audience than could otherwise have been reached. Despite Sheen's own intense intellectual training in Europe, his efforts at writing turned popular very quickly, with the decided purpose of appealing to the much broader audience of the literate general public rather than merely neo-Thomist philsosphers.[33] During the nearly twenty-five years that he spent as a professor at the Catholic University of America, from 1926 until 1950, much of his time was consistently occupied with other activities, such as public speaking engagements, spiritual retreats, and catechetical instruction. Sheen ultimately became extremely famous for his numerous successful conversions to the Catholic faith of "such unlikely prospects as Colonel Horace Mann of Tennessee, credited with leading a mudslinging campaign against Catholic Al Smith; Heywood Broun, arch-liberal freethinker; Louis Budenz, managing editor of the Communist *Daily Worker*"; as well as "Author Clare Boothe Luce, Violinist Fritz Kreisler, Broadway Stage Designer Jo Mielziner," and "Motor Scion Henry Ford II."[34] Sheen's access to these figures developed from the fame he acquired in his other major activity during this period: radio broadcasts.

On March 9, 1930, Fulton Sheen appeared for the first time on *The Catholic Hour,* a new radio program sponsored by the Council of Catholic Men, whose original format "included questions and answers, with questions provided by members of a live audience in New York, and responses by several experts including Sheen."[35] Over time, this dialogical format was to change to a monologue, a one-way communication from the speaker to the audience; Sheen, however, appears to have been one of those very rare individuals equally well-suited for both formats, able to connect to his audience with his responses to their spontaneous questions, but also able to hold their attention on subjects about which he was specifically prepared to lecture.

In his very first appearance on *The Catholic Hour*, Sheen began with a talk strongly linked to the subject of his first book, "Man's Search for God," which "had been criticized before the broadcast for being too scholarly." This concern was unfounded, however, for the program "generated hundreds of letters of praise within days of its telecast." It was the first evidence of what would become Sheen's enormous popularity, such that several later programs would receive over a hundred thousand letters requesting transcripts of a specific talk that he had given. [36] Sheen's growing celebrity status also reached outside of the Catholic subculture, as "upward of 30 percent of the mail received regarding his talks came from non-Catholics." [37]

Eventually, Sheen's celebrity status helped him receive two very interesting promotions within the Catholic Church; in 1950, Monsignor Fulton J. Sheen was made the National Director of the Society for the Propagation of the Faith, and in June of the following year, he was consecrated as an auxiliary bishop of New York. The first position put Sheen in charge of raising funds within the United States for "Catholic missions" around the world, and gave him the opportunity to use his flair for mass media on behalf of the Catholic Church. He immediately gave the Society's magazine a more popular name, *Mission*, and designed for sale a ten-letter "God Love You Medal," created to function as a rosary. [38] The second position gave Sheen a new level of institutional authority within the Roman hierarchy; he was now no longer simply a scholarly priest giving his opinions on church teaching, but was himself one of the authoritative teachers of the doctrines of the church.

This new level of authority fit well with the unexpected job offer that Sheen received shortly thereafter. Only a few months after he was consecrated bishop, the DuMont Television Network decided to donate airtime to the Catholic Church in order to fulfill a government requirement for a "public service broadcast." [39] Almost immediately, Bishop Fulton J. Sheen was chosen to be the host of the program, to be aired in a Tuesday night "obituary" slot opposite Mr. Television himself, Milton Berle. [40]

The DuMont Network's decision to create a television program starring a Catholic bishop came at an interesting time for American Catholics. The decades following the war saw Catholics emerging into the middle class and achieving "greater presence in American politics and society."[41] The American Catholic population was growing at an unprecedented rate, and new seminaries and parochial schools were being created to accommodate this substantial growth.[42] By the 1950s, television celebrities such as Ed Sullivan, Danny Thomas, Jackie Gleason, and Perry Como had become prominent on programs in which their Catholicism went unmentioned, and social critic Will Herberg could proclaim that Catholics had joined mainstream America in his book *Protestant, Catholic, Jew*.[43]

At 8:00 p.m. on Tuesday, February 12, 1952, *Life Is Worth Living*, starring Bishop Fulton J. Sheen, debuted on the DuMont Network with minimal expectations. Against the advice of his producers, "Sheen appeared in full Episcopal regalia, including a black cassock with purple piping, a purple ferraiolo (cape), purple zucchetto (skull cap), and on his chest the large gold pectoral cross given to him by Pius XII at his consecration."[44] On the first show, three "guest" friends asked him "canned questions," to which Sheen responded. Within a few weeks, however, that changed, and from then on "the program featured only Sheen," who "each week spoke for about twenty-seven minutes and twenty seconds, without notes or a Teleprompter."[45]

The response to the program "surpassed almost all reasonable expectations of DuMont executives, and *Life Is Worth Living* would become the DuMont Network's most-watched program for three TV seasons— outdrawing even DuMont's prime entertainment weekly event, *The Jackie Gleason Show*."[46] By 1955, after the Network had folded and *Life Is Worth Living* had moved to ABC, Sheen had gained "an estimated audience of thirty million viewers."[47]

From the beginning of *Life Is Worth Living*, "Sheen spoke on general themes such as alienation in modern civilization, character building, freedom, war and peace, and suffering, plus a wide assortment of practical topics including what to do about fatigue, how to handle teenagers, and dealing with boring work."[48] Only a few months into the program, *Time* magazine would explain in its cover story on Sheen that his talks were "Christian in outlook but not specifically Roman Catholic . . . designed to appeal to listeners of all faiths."[49]

In other words, *Life Is Worth Living* was always substantially different in style than the radio program *The Catholic Hour*, which Sheen quit shortly after beginning his television career. Even with the noticeable shift in focus toward ecumenism that Sheen began to display in his later radio broadcasts, a Catholic organization always sponsored the aptly named radio show, and so the Catholic faith was always a very clear and direct component of every program. In contrast, the Admiral Corporation, "a maker of televisions and electronic appliances," sponsored *Life Is Worth Living*, and so the type of presentation was dramatically altered, even if much of the content was subtly similar.[50]

Despite the apparent popularity of the television show, *Life Is Worth Living* ceased production in 1957.[51] Sheen continued on as National Director of the Society for the Propagation of the Faith for another nine years, until 1966. During that time, he attended the Second Vatican Council and for a few years did a smaller, local version of his television show called *The Fulton Sheen Program*, with later episodes in color. Eventually, however, perhaps due to confrontations with the Archbishop of New York, Francis Cardinal Spellman, over the money that Sheen controlled as head of the Society, Sheen was transferred to the Diocese of Rochester, where he served as bishop only three years before retiring and returning to New York City.

Sheen's speedy retirement from Rochester was due to several administrative failures that he had made during his brief tenure as a diocesan bishop, most notably a donation in 1967 to the U.S. government of "the property of an inner-city parish on which to erect housing for the poor."[52] The government negotiators wanted to keep the arrangement silent until it was substantially underway, but the fact that he did not consult with the parishioners caused real problems for his governance of the diocese.[53] It was also during this time that Sheen, the resilient enemy of Communism, became heavily involved in the issue of peace. On July 20, 1967, Bishop Fulton J. Sheen of Rochester became the first American bishop to issue an "unequivocal antiwar statement," and publicly begged the president "to withdraw all our forces immediately from southern Vietnam."[54]

By the time of his retirement from Rochester, Sheen's days of intense media exposure were at an end. For the next decade, there were occasional appearances and interviews, but his health was slowly failing. He died on December 9, 1979, while keeping his daily holy hour in front of the Blessed Sacrament.

Selling Catholicism to the Culture Industry?

In the early 1950s, *Life Is Worth Living* appeared on Tuesday nights as something of a "novelty" among "sameness," as a "new" product that had not yet been completely "stamped" or "filtered" by the culture industry.[55] Sheen's program found success as the type of "commodity" that could surprise people through its peculiarity and that was capable of success as long as it softened its distinctive edge in "appropriate" places. Under this interpretation, for Sheen to achieve success in the television business, he first had to demonstrate "his superiority by well-planned originality."[56]

This kind of "superiority," which some might view as the more negative side of Sheen's television ministry, is studied in some depth in Christopher Owen Lynch's rhetorical analysis *Selling Catholicism: Bishop Sheen and the Power of Television*. Although this work does not evoke Horkheimer and Adorno explicitly, there are a number of points in which Lynch's interpretation of the television career of Bishop Sheen appears directly connected to concerns that many critical theorists would undoubtedly articulate. Lynch interprets Sheen as a "medieval" figure who uses the power of television to promote his own belief "that the spirit of America is, at root, Roman Catholic," but whose message is necessarily altered through his use of the medium of television.[57]

Among the first observations that Lynch makes concerning Sheen's first and greatest television program, *Life Is Worth Living*, is that the initial format was a deviation from Sheen's original idea for the sake of the studio's convenience. Sheen's initial plan was to record his catechetical instruction from a different parish every week, and to spend the last few minutes of every program taking questions and responding to the audience.[58] Eventually, this plan was rejected due to the cost it would incur, for most parishes were simply not adequately constructed for a television broadcast. Additionally, the studio had some real concerns about the difficulties that could result from such truly "spontaneous" television. Rather than an interactive format, in which Sheen would be directly engaged with a live studio audience (and, by implication, with the concerns of all his viewers), the bishop would instead present the program as a one-way communication toward those who were watching him, which would in turn highlight his own personality.[59]

Eventually, Sheen himself jettisoned the planned instruction in the Catholic faith, choosing instead to make the program "about moral living that related to all religious groups." According to Lynch, "When criticized by fellow clergy for not being more explicit in his propagation of the Catholic faith, he [Sheen] said, 'If the seed falls they have 52,000 branch offices of the Catholic Church where they can get instructions.' "[60] This statement provides two interesting ways of interpreting Sheen's decision that the program be more "general" in focus, both of which probably contain much truth, and both of which also fall neatly into the Frankfort School's criticisms of television.

In the first interpretation, Fulton Sheen's decision to focus *Life Is Worth Living* on more "general" topics, instead of those dealing directly with "Catholicism," can be reasonably viewed as movement toward acceptability for his program. If this is the case, and it almost certainly is, at least in part, then it falls beneath the Frankfurt School's warning that such moves are necessary in order to be accepted on television. As long as Sheen was not "too obstinate" about his "own concerns," as long as he was willing to be "appropriately pliable" when it mattered, then he could be "reconciled" to the culture industry.[61] And, if Sheen wanted to succeed, if he wanted an audience of people other than Catholics, then leaving behind catechetical instruction would appear to be a move that the culture industry demanded from him.

While it can be convincingly argued that Sheen "sold out" much of his Catholic identity on the program for the sake of success, the second interpretation made possible through the lens of critical theory is one that many Catholics may find more pleasing, but which is in many ways far more sinister and troubling. The truth is that Catholicism is always in the background of *Life Is Worth Living*, for Sheen is always clearly a Catholic bishop, and even though there are no "heavy handed" attempts at the evangelization of viewers, that does not mean the program itself was not a "secret" way for Sheen to continue his day job and "propagate the faith." In other words, to use the language of critical theory, Sheen appears to be harnessing the "multilayered structure" of television in order to control the attitudes of his viewers toward the Catholic Church, and to subtly push them toward conversion. While Sheen quite willingly discards the more "overt" attempts at proselytization that might normally be expected of someone in his position, he does not discard the possibility of conversion, as evidenced by the statement Lynch quotes about the "52,000 branch offices of the Catholic Church." Furthermore, Sheen's formal episcopal attire, his references to his "angel who cleans the blackboard," and especially his inscribing of "JMJ" on the top of the blackboard each and every time he writes upon it, all speak "covertly" about his real agenda. In his every action, Sheen provides an example (or, some might even say, a "witness") of what it means to be a Catholic in the United States. Under this interpretation, the bishop's actions convey to the viewers of *Life Is Worth Living* the "hidden message" that was clearly central to the living of Sheen's own life: that all non-Catholics (and even some baptized Catholics who have not been to church in a while) ought to repent of their sins and convert to the Catholic faith.

Lynch presents a number of other subtle ways that Sheen uses the medium of television to persuade his audience to agree with his point of view. Lynch explains that Sheen's personal anecdotes often emphasize his priesthood, even as the usually self-deprecating punch lines are intended to reinforce his priestly humility for his audience.[62] Yet such humility obscures the fact that the format of the program creates a hierarchy, with Sheen at the top as the teacher, and allows him to impose his own hierarchical (Catholic) worldview in subtle ways upon his viewers. Additionally, his corny jokes allow his audience to view him as unthreatening and endearing, and allow him to "illustrate his humanity and his ability to laugh at himself." His humor also "serves to remind the audience that he is a celebrity," and so they listen with rapt attention, easily accepting the philosophy that he proclaims.[63]

Lynch also points out that, although "Sheen never became a salesperson for Admiral directly," he eventually found himself inserting his advertiser, the Admiral Corporation, into his program.[64] Sheen would tell little jokes, such as one with a little girl who responded to her mother that the first two people were "Admiral and Eve."[65] Other times, he makes favorable statements, explaining that Admiral has been "a cordial and genial sponsor," and that he trusts his audience "will continue to support it," if they, too, are grateful for his program.[66]

Sadly, Sheen's willingness to endorse Admiral, even if only in specific moments of humor or thanks, makes him a clear party to the capitalistic use of his name and image. As such, it seems that the Frankfurt School's concern about addiction to the culture industry held some truth in Sheen's case. Apparently, "once his particular brand of deviation" was accepted, Sheen "belongs to it as does the land-reformer to capitalism," for the spotlight of television seemed to have grown to a place of genuine importance in his personal identity such that the bishop was ultimately willing to play the role, at least occasionally, of an advertiser for a commercial product.[67]

Looking at *Life Is Worth Living* through the Lens of Michel de Certeau

Despite Bishop Sheen's clear alliance with the culture industry in the production of his television show, there are at least a few ways that his actions can be said to aid those who oppose the dominant structures of the mass culture, in the sense that he can be seen to provide tools for *bricolage* ("making do") that subvert the mass culture rather than to give in to the culture industry. In particular, de Certeau's understanding of subversion through unintended use, through "procedures of 'consumption,' " can be used to build an account of Sheen's television appearances that allow him some freedom from Horkheimer and Adorno's more general condemnation of television and the entire culture industry.[68]

In *The Practice of Everyday Life*, Michel de Certeau explains that conquered peoples find ways to make "creative use" of the tools of their oppressors, often in ways their oppressors would not approve, therefore creating small areas of resistance to that oppression. Instead of assuming such people are naïve victims of insurmountable forces, de Certeau emphasizes the agency and the cleverness that lies behind even their most ordinary activities. The primary example that he gives of this practice is belief in subversive miracles in Latin America, by which the oppressed triumph over their oppressors. Without the approval of church hierarchy, these miracle stories use the teachings of Christianity itself against those who have conquered the native peoples and transmitted Christianity to them. This use of their conquerors' own system in a way contrary to the conquerors' purposes modifies the system itself into a means of resisting additional levels of conquest in the future.[69]

The most basic use of the system that de Certeau describes is *la perruque*, "the worker's own work disguised as work for his employer."[70] Such resistance "can be as simple a matter as a secretary's writing a love letter on 'company time' or as complex as a cabinet maker's 'borrowing' a lathe to make a piece of furniture for his living room."[71] The important aspect of the resistance is that the worker is spending time that technically "belongs" to his or her employer for an end that does not serve the interests of that employer. This activity is not seen as "stealing" anything material, but merely as reclaiming the worker's right to his or her own time.[72]

A closely related form of resistance, or at least a way resistance can be taught, is through fantastic tales, which are actually a kind of "apprenticeship in tactics." "Moves, not truth, are recounted" in these tales, which offer hope as well as methods of resisting oppression, for they "frequently reverse the relationships of power" and "ensure the victory of the unfortunate in a fabulous, utopian space," even as much of their purpose involves hinting at other methods of subversion and ultimate victory.[73] De Certeau provides examples of ordinary games, such as cards or even chess, that are later recounted as stories of great success against insurmountable odds.[74] The games themselves teach a kind of logic for dealing with new situations and the stories surrounding them instill hope that success is possible.[75]

Finally, when de Certeau speaks of television, there is an extremely critical edge to his writing. He sees it as different from the medium of the printed word, noting that "the child still scrawls and daubs on his schoolbooks; even if he is punished for his crime, he has made a space for himself and signs his existence as an author on it." And then he laments that "The television viewer cannot write anything on the screen of his set. He has been dislodged from the product; he plays no role in its apparition. He loses his author's rights and becomes, or so it seems, a pure receiver, the mirror of a multiform and narcissistic actor."[76] Unlike other methods of domination that the culture industry is able to impose, the television appears immune to being written on or to having a space made upon it.

De Certeau's observations can be related to the way that critical theorists might describe Fulton Sheen in at least three very interesting ways. With regard to *la perruque*, and apart from the fact that his program itself could be seen as a distraction from work, Sheen often advised that prayer could be practiced in any location when a free moment could be found, and was necessary to cultivate good habits and guard against spiritual laziness.[77]

In the second instance, those "fantastic tales" that reverse power relationships, which de Certeau speaks of as "apprenticeship in tactics," are immediately reminiscent of Sheen. On both his radio and television programs, he regularly told quite fantastic tales of hope and salvation, often ones in which he played a minor role in bringing a soul to Christ. While this type of feature was more prominent on *The Catholic Hour* than *Life Is Worth Living*, the fact remains that Sheen was quite famous for telling stories in which an unlikely person came out best. The hero of such tales is rarely Sheen himself, but is more clearly the person who finds salvation, apparently through his efforts, but ultimately through the grace of God.[78] And, in truth, Sheen is trying to teach tactics and offer hope to an audience that has been overpowered by a powerful enemy; it just may not be the enemy that de Certeau would have most closely in mind. From Sheen's own perspective, of course, he is creating exactly the form of resistance that he should be trying to create. After all, it was not the powers of the culture industry that Sheen was trying to oppose with his ministry as much as the powers of sin with which the culture industry was so often allied.

The third way that de Certeau can aid our analysis of Fulton Sheen is significantly more powerful than the first two. This assistance involves *bricolage*, and requires the mention of "Our Lady of Television," a statue that Sheen had created for the "Christianization" of the medium. He chose the Blessed Virgin Mary as the patroness of television because she "was the first to give the Divine Word to the world" and television now seeks to bestow "the human word to the world." During his later broadcasts, a large statue of Our Lady of Television could often be seen behind him, elevating his program to Christ.[79] The interesting development in terms of *bricolage*, however, is that Sheen had a miniature version of this statue created, which people could purchase via postal mail for three dollars. A smaller version, with a suction cup on the bottom "for cars," was also available for one dollar.[80] The interesting question that results, concerning the concept of *bricolage*, is "What exactly did people do with the larger statues after they had them?"

In the official literature about the statues of Our Lady of Television, no instructions are given concerning "what to do" with the statue. That is not particularly important, however, because, as de Certeau himself remarks, "the presence and circulation of a representation (taught by preachers, educators, and popularizers as the key to socioeconomic advancement) tells us nothing about what it is for its users."[81] Some families would have placed the statue in an area of their home with related Catholic items. Noticing the shape, other Catholics would have kept the statue of Our Lady of Television, the arms of which are described as "spiritual antennas which bring us to Truth and Love," close to the television set.[82] An article in the *LaCrosse Register* mentions in passing that the statues are to be placed "on your home TV set."[83]

If this were actually done; if the statues of "Our Lady of Television," after being purchased from the Society for the Propagation of the Faith, were really placed on television sets across the country, whether on the advice of Bishop Sheen or not, it would be a fascinating instance of the object called the "television set" being transformed. In other words, "scrawling upon" the television, creating a space for the oppressed (which de Certeau did not think was possible), was, in some sense, realized. Through distributing these statues, Sheen gave Catholics who, like the native peoples of Latin America, *believe* the subversive, the ability to turn the weapons of their society against it, in a creative act of defiance.

And this, of course, was what Sheen was trying to do with the statues. It may not have been mass culture, particularly, that he was aiming at. Nevertheless, he intended the statues to "elevate the tone of television that it may fulfill its high destiny of sending forth ideas that are as so many scattered letters of the Word Divine."[84] Sheen's plan was always to alter fundamentally the nature of television: he sought to Christianize it.

Conclusion: Mass Culture or *Mass* Culture

It would seem in the final analysis that several important things can be said about the application of the principles of critical theory to Fulton J. Sheen. Many of the criticisms that the Frankfurt School levied against television seem to hit the mark in his case. Sheen was a trained orator who used the medium of television very effectively to manipulate his viewers. He enjoyed being on television and seems to have been willing to sacrifice a few of his principles, in the areas of advertising and more "overt" forms of proselytizing, for the sake of remaining there.

At the same time, Sheen's presence on television led to forms of resistance to mass culture that the Frankfurt School might not have recognized, even if they had seen them. Through his encouragement, and through the *bricolage* of those who adopted such symbols as Our Lady of Television, Sheen helped to transform the medium, at least in part, into a tool for evangelization, and thereby caused it to be used for a purpose very different than that which the culture industry had originally intended.

Notes

[1]Mark S. Massa, *Catholics and American Culture: Fulton Sheen, Dorothy Day, and the Notre Dame Football Team* (New York: Crossroads, 1999), 90.

[2]Kathleen L. Riley, *Fulton J. Sheen: An American Catholic Response to the Twentieth Century* (New York: Alba House, 2004), 314-15.

[3]Massa, *Catholics and American Culture*, 101.

[4]Max Horkheimer and Theodor W. Adorno, *Dialectic of Enlightenment* (New York: Continuum, 1944), 132.

[5]Ibid.

[6]Michel de Certeau, *The Practice of Everyday Life* (Berkeley: University of California Press, 1984), xi-xii.

[7]Ibid., xii.

[8]Horkheimer and Adorno, *Dialectic of Enlightenment*, 126.

[9]Ibid., 120. One need only look at the three or four different versions of both *Law and Order* and *CSI* to see this intense similarity, with minor variation, happening at an even greater level today.

[10]Ibid., 134.

[11]Ibid., 121.

[12]Ibid., 126.

[13]Ibid., 133.

[14]Ibid., 134.

[15]Ibid., 123.

[16]Ibid., 128.

[17]Ibid., 129.

[18]Ibid., 130-31.

[19]Ibid., 134.

[20]Ibid., 147.

[21]Ibid., 137.

[22]Ibid.

[23]Ibid., 144.

[24]Ibid., 162.

[25]Theodor Adorno, *The Culture Industry: Selected Essays on Mass Culture*, ed. J. M. Bernstein (London and New York: Routledge, 1991), 158.

[26]Ibid., 163-64.

[27]Ibid., 165.

[28]Ibid., 166. Adorno attributes the concept of "psychoanalysis in reverse" to Leo Lowenthal.

[29]Ibid., 170.

[30]Ibid.

[31]Ibid., 174-75.

³²Ibid., 170.

³³Sheen's intellectual gifts are evidenced in his Ph.D. from the University of Louvain by his grade of "Very Highest Distinction" when he became the first American to receive the agrégé from that university, and when he became that decade's winner of Louvain's Cardinal Mercier International Philosophy Award (Fulton J. Sheen, *Treasure in Clay: The Autobiography of Fulton J. Sheen* [Garden City, NY: Doubleday, 1980] 26-28); Thomas C. Reeves, *America's Bishop: The Life and Times of Fulton J. Sheen* [San Francisco: Encounter Books, 2001], 53). His interest in communicating to the wider culture is evidenced in many of his books from the early 1930s as well as in interviews where he explained that properly taught philosophy could help lay people to "eliminate present-day deafness and blindness to the really important things of life" (*The Queen's Work* 23, no. 7 [April 1, 1931: 1]).

³⁴*Time*, April 14, 1952, 73. The strange capitalizations of common, descriptive nouns seem to be the style of the magazine at that point, and so were left in the quotation.

³⁵Reeves, *America's Bishop*, 80.

³⁶Massa, *Catholics and American Culture*, 89.

³⁷Ibid., 90.

³⁸Reeves, *America's Bishop*, 221.

³⁹In my sources, Dumont is often spelled "DuMont," but, as it was unclear which was the proper spelling, I have settled on this one, primarily because that is the way it appears in a few quotations I am using.

⁴⁰Reeves, *America's Bishop*, 224.

⁴¹Anthony Burke Smith, "Prime-time Catholicism in 1950s America: Fulton J. Sheen and 'Life Is Worth Living,' " *U.S. Catholic Historian* 15, no. 3 (Summer 1997): 62.

⁴²Martin E. Marty, *A Short History of American Catholicism* (Allen, TX: Thomas More, 1995), 170.

⁴³James T. Fisher. *Communion of Immigrants* (New York: Oxford University Press, 2002), 124, 127.

⁴⁴Ibid., 225.

⁴⁵Ibid., 226. There are a few different ways to look at this change. On one hand, the program becomes more centered on Sheen as a result, and the nature of dialogue is replaced with monologue. On the other hand, it was a fake dialogue to begin with, as the questions were predetermined, and so having Sheen merely "give a lecture" to his audience is, in many ways, far closer to "reality" than the alternative.

⁴⁶Massa, *Catholics and American Culture*, 93.

⁴⁷Ibid., 94.

⁴⁸Reeves, *America's Bishop*, 226; *Priest* (December 1954), 1058.

⁴⁹*Time*, April 14, 1952, 72.

⁵⁰Christopher Owen Lynch, *Selling Catholicism: Bishop Sheen and the Power of Television* (Lexington: University Press of Kentucky, 1998), 26.

⁵¹*Time*, October 28, 1957, 47.

⁵²Reeves, *America's Bishop*, 315

[53]Ibid., 320.

[54]Ibid., 309.

[55]Horkheimer and Adorno, *Dialectic of Enlightenment*, 120, 126.

[56]Ibid., 132.

[57]Lynch, *Selling Catholicism*, 59-60.

[58]Ibid., 24. Also alluded to in "Apostolate of the Airwaves," *Priest* (December 1954), 1058.

[59]Ibid., 9. Of course, as has already been stated, the first few programs had "guests" who asked prearranged questions before the "one-man show" format was decided upon.

[60]Ibid., 24. Lynch received this quote in an interview with Bishop Broderick, who first suggested Sheen for *Life Is Worth Living*. According to the article in *Priest*, however, it was the DuMont Network that "wanted to keep the program as non-denominational as possible" (*Priest* [December 1954], 1058).

[61]Horkheimer and Adorno, *Dialectic of Enlightenment*, 132.

[62]Lynch, *Selling Catholicism*, 127. Additionally, Lynch sees Sheen's refusal to acknowledge applause as a way of showing humility that "further ingratiates him in the role definition of priest."

[63]To give an example in support of this aspect of Lynch's rhetorical analysis: a color episode that I have watched many times (entitled "Superman and Christmas") begins with Sheen telling a story of a child who has just turned on the television, and mistakes Sheen for Superman (presumably, because of his cape)! Lynch's analysis is correct in seeing this as a subtle reference to Sheen's own fame.

[64]There were also numerous occasions, especially in his early episodes, when Sheen clearly refrained from mentioning his sponsor's name. For example, in an hour-long (commercial free) black and white episode (entitled "Good Friday"), Sheen opens his monologue by stating the program would air for a full hour without commercial interruption. He then suggests that, for those viewers who are unaware of who the sponsor is, "it might be worthwhile finding out." On that occasion, it appears Progresso Italian Quality Foods, rather than Admiral, was the sponsor.

[65]Lynch, *Selling Catholicism*, 137.

[66]Ibid., 135.

[67]Horkheimer and Adorno, *Dialectic of Enlightenment*, 132.

[68]de Certeau, *The Practice of Everyday Life*, xiii.

[69]Ibid., 17. See Damian Costello's *Black Elk: Colonialism and Lakota Catholicism* (Maryknoll, NY: Orbis Books, 2005) for a more in-depth treatment. Costello shows how Black Elk sought to use Christian principles against the white oppressors of his people.

[70]de Certeau, *The Practice of Everyday Life*, 25.

[71]Ibid.

[72]Perhaps due to the influence of programs such as *Friends*, *Seinfeld*, and *The Office*, conversation among employees during working hours about their lives and interests is the most prevalent example of *la perruque* in present culture.

[73]de Certeau, *The Practice of Everyday Life*, 23. See also Costello's explanation in *Black Elk* in which the practice of the Ghost Dance utilizes "the Christian narrative to provide an ethical framework to engulf and judge colonialism" (173).

[74]Ibid., 22-23. In our own culture, games can certainly function in this way. Bobby Fischer's victory in the 1972 World Chess Championship became legendary as a tale of an individual mind succeeding against the Communist machine. More recently, the unexpected triumph of poker amateur Chris Moneymaker at the 2003 World Series of Poker Main Event functioned for many people as a story of hope for the underdog in a field of professionals. This story is often credited with increasing the general public's interest in poker, and has led to record-setting entrance figures in subsequent World Series of Poker tournaments.

[75]The game of poker can be seen as teaching various behaviors (bluffing, observation, prudence, etc.), the acquisition of which can help one to function better in American society.

[76]de Certeau, *The Practice of Everyday Life*, 31.

[77]Fulton Sheen, *Life Is Worth Living: Fourth Series* (New York: McGraw-Hill, 1956), 60 and 172. See also the audio tape "The Rosary by Fulton Sheen" (St. Joseph Communications) for a greater exposition from Sheen about how prayer can be accomplished in nearly any situation. Available through www.archbishopsheencause.org/sheen_audiotapes.html.

[78]In the previously mentioned episode, "Superman and Christmas," Sheen tells the story of an unnamed actress whom he brought back to her Catholic roots by pushing her into the confessional. The story concludes with Sheen recounting that she later entered a convent and is still a practicing nun.

[79]Sheen describes the statue in this way: "Television is the projection of the human word to the world. This is represented by the statue of the Madonna who, by giving birth to the Divine Word, gave Him to the world. The world is surmounted by a cross symbolizing our World Mission Society for the Propagation of the Faith. The hand of the Word Incarnate Christ and the hand of His Blessed Mother both touching the world indicate the divine and human influence with which it is hoped television will elevate its moral tone and lift it to God" (*St. Louis Register*, January 14, 1955).

[80]This smaller version presumably functioned as an "Our Lady of the Radio" in automobiles.

[81]de Certeau, *The Practice of Everyday Life*, xiii.

[82]*Mission* (March-April 1962). See the information on "Our Lady of Television" in the archive at The Marian Library/International Research Institute located at the University of Dayton in Dayton, Ohio.

[83]*LaCrosse Register*, January 7, 1955. I would like to thank Anthony Burke Smith, who first pointed out this practice to me, and Kelly S. Johnson, who pointed me to the idea of *bricolage*, for their help with this particular idea.

[84]*Our Sunday Visitor*, November 7, 1954.

If These Walls Could Talk

God's Grandeur amidst Urban Blight[1]

Maureen H. O'Connell

On the side of a traditional South Philadelphia row house at the corner of Dickinson and Bouvier Streets, a stunning image looms large. A woman laughs with a gurgling upheld child who reaches out to her. Both are silhouetted against a spectacular, African-inspired orange sky. The life of Christ, depicted as renaissance stained-glass windows, frames the scene. The nativity, crucifixion, and Mary are prominently featured. The mural is nothing if not unexpected and interruptive; it undoubtedly proclaims God's grandeur as understood by this particular inner-city community. *Born Again* (Cliff Eubanks, 2000), as the mural is titled, provocatively pulls its viewers off the street and into the scene. The onlooker experiences the simple joy of the figures' embrace, their end-of-the-day gratitude for the gift of new life, and the promise of their blossoming relationship. The mural also invites the passerby to make a connection between the life of those portrayed in the foreground and those in the frame. To that end, this public art is undoubtedly a locus of theological and ethical reflection.

Born Again prophetically announces the self-understanding of a forgotten neighborhood of South Philadelphia long dismissed by wider civil society as a haven for gang violence, and a quagmire of chronic underemployment and addiction. The mural's images of love, family, and hope for the future—literally framed by the life, death, and resurrection of Jesus of Nazareth—serve as transformative symbols for anyone who encounters them. First these symbols speak to those *in* this community whose experiences have not always been consonant with the spirit of this mural, and yet who continue to resist a future that does not reflect a God of hope. It reminds the community that its members are more than the dominant culture's estimation of them. It proclaims that their spirit cannot be trampled by generations of social, economic, and political marginalization. It recalls a God who knows their struggles as crucified peoples and whose resurrection kindles in them a stubborn hope. Moreover, in an ironic twist, *Born Again* also prophetically reminds those *outside* of this neighborhood of the many structural impediments to this woman and child flourishing, given its location in one of Philadelphia's marginalized neighborhoods.

To some extent, there is no need to wonder what this wall would proclaim if it could talk. As one of more than 2,700 murals created by Philadelphia's nationally recognized Mural Arts Program, the voice of the community who participated in its creation is clearly amplified here.[2] At the same time, however, a theological and ethical exploration of *Born Again* and several other murals like it throughout Philadelphia suggests that these walls have several things to say to those of us attempting "to do theology" within the North American context with a particular attention to "urban America's core problem" of concentrated poverty.[3]

At the very least these murals serve as an uncomfortable reminder of the dearth of theological and ethical reflection on the social suffering of hyper-segregated communities in contemporary urban America. Certainly, central documents of Catholic social teaching and various theologians highlight urban areas as centers of structural sin as well as social injustice.[4] However, theologians and ethicists have yet to fully turn and face concentrated poverty. This lacuna indicates a moral blindness in "reading the signs of the times" which James Cone suggests is nothing short of institutional racism.[5] M. Shawn Copeland suggests that a failure to be interrupted by this reality indicates a preference for more distant and therefore comfortable contexts of suffering in whose causes we might be less implicated.[6] Finally, our refusal to turn and face the reality of urban poverty challenges the relevance of the social message of the gospel as it is understood by communities of privilege. Do we fully understand the imperative of neighbor love, the radical equality of the kingdom of God, or the comprehensiveness of the common good if we do not perceive these concepts from the perspectives of those struggling to survive in the midst of urban blight? These murals suggest that perhaps we do not.

Therefore, I attempt to begin to fill in this sinful gap in our theological dialogue and praxis by presenting a selection of Philadelphia's community-based murals as artistically evocative conversation partners for three aspects of North American theology—black, political, and ethical.[7] To borrow an expression from Richard Viladesau, these murals are "theological texts" that, without words, present the message of faith "in a way that is persuasive and attractive, giving a vision that can lead to moral conversion and action."[8] Moreover, I suggest that these murals reflect what Viladesau has identified as a paradigm shift or "new way of seeing" in both theology and art that is characterized by an attention to the environment, the voices of neglected persons, and a spirit of ecumenism.[9] Therefore, consonant with Katie Cannon's exploration of "critical truism" in the work of black women writers, I attempt to unearth the wisdom of "Black folk who respectfully yearn to actualize the deepest possibilities of human existence" and do so on the walls of Philadelphia.[10] First I suggest that these examples of public art provide an important contextualization of black theology and spirituality, as well as possible contemporary developments of its identity and praxis, given their origins and primary audience. Second, I propose that these murals also uniquely express a North American political theology that turns and faces those suffering in neighborhoods of concentrated poverty, given the communal process of their creation and the various layers of their prophetic content. And, finally, I suggest that these murals give "moral teeth" to the sometimes abstract principles of Catholic social teaching, which many agree have yet to be effectively applied to the reality of concentrated poverty and race. These walls are indeed talking and our own "God talk" can be sharpened through them.

The History and Significance of Murals as Public Art

We have long gained insight into the lives, beliefs, and worldviews of those unknown to us by examining their self-expression on walls. This phenomenon is increasingly true when we consider art on the walls of communities made invisible by social isolation and marginalization or denied a voice in the public life of our communities. To that end, contemporary American muralism reflects an important trajectory in art history and a constructive intersection of public and activist art.[11] The roots of Philadelphia's murals can be traced to the Depression Era's Works Progress Administration (WPA), which created public art in a variety of civic spaces with the intention of lifting the national spirit as well as the employment rate. WPA murals represented a shift from the influence of European modernists toward a more regional focus on American history, landscapes, and workers. They were certainly influenced by the famous Mexican muralists José Clemente Orozco, Diego Rivera, and David Alfaro Siqueiros, whose work frequently reflected the spirit of the Mexican revolution; in fact, the latter two painted several murals throughout the United States and their influence continues to shape vibrant Latino community murals. Depression- and World War II-era murals in the U.S. reflect "social realism" or a "politically neutral but compassionate stance" that unflinchingly depicts "real life."[12] The "ordinariness" of these murals, their easily identifiable subjects and popular themes, as well as their locations outside of the mainstream of the "art industry," raised significant debate regarding their artistic integrity. This conflict was only exacerbated by the explosion of visual images in media and billboard advertising that fed an emerging consumerism and social conformity in the 1950s.[13]

In many ways, the contemporary mural movement, as well as graffiti art, which increasingly became associated with urban violence and blight in the 1980s, responded to the tensions in postwar America that eventually boiled over in the 1960s. The Civil Rights Movement, community organizing, and political activism, and a growing suspicion of institutionalism and authority in the American creative spirit instilled within artists a desire to move beyond the museum audience and connect with people in the streets. Conceptualism, which sought to expand aesthetic boundaries beyond museums and the artistic elite and to emphasize ideas and context rather than the visual or physical form of autonomous objects, was reflected in a variety of expressions of public art, particularly murals. We might consider, for example, the *Wall of Respect*, a mural depicting black heroes, completed in 1967 in Chicago; a variety of political murals in San Francisco's Mission District done by *Mujeres Muralistas* in the early 1970s; and Judith Francisca Baca's half-mile long *The Great Wall of Los Angeles*, begun in 1976 and completed in 1983.

Throughout the 1970s, with the help of the feminist art movement and its emphasis on "collaboration, dialogue, a constant questioning of aesthetic and social assumptions, and a new respect for audience,"[14] an emerging activist art gained a momentum that carried it through the 1980s. This movement not only questioned "dominant cultural representations" and "configurations of power," but more importantly highlighted the communal and participatory process of public art.[15] Feshin notes that public art and activist art converge on the notion of "public"—the focus is not necessarily on where art is located as much as what it is able to do in terms of social change via "engaged and participatory citizens." To that extent, murals rooted in activist art reflect a sharp distinction from their Depression-era predecessors. By the 1990s, several cities across the country, most notably Philadelphia and Los Angeles, began to institutionalize mural arts as an effective means of youth outreach, community development, and urban renewal. According to muralist Jane Golden, the Director of Philadelphia's Mural Arts Program, muralism increasingly represents "the merging of art and social justice—it's a nexus of public art, and economic and political development."[16]

Contemporary murals can generally be categorized into two groups. Urban environmentalist murals are usually commissioned by a municipal authority or corporate sponsor with the goal of beautification and physical restoration of public space or architectural eyesores. They are primarily aesthetic in purpose and can often (unintentionally or intentionally) camouflage the social problems that lie just below their visual surface. Community-based murals, however, are usually initiated, designed, and often painted by the communities in which they are located, and to that end proclaim these communities' distinctive identities, memories, and visions for the future. Community-based murals can be found on busy public thoroughfares as well as in the very heart of marginalized communities, as is the case with *Born Again*.

Moreover, community-based murals spring from relationships of mutuality, interdependence, and intellectual and lived solidarity among the various parties needed to create authentic, wall-sized communal art. Unlike graffiti "tags" or "spray can art," which tend to reflect individualistic or sectarian self-expression, community-based murals depict the identity, values, and vision of the neighborhoods where they are proudly exhibited. While tags or impromptu wall-memorials frequently experience a short life-span, relatively few community-murals are painted over or defaced. Therefore, these artistic expressions serve as touchstones of community pride and community transformation. According to Golden, "a mural is so much more than a painting on a wall. A mural becomes a catalyst for positive change in a community."[17]

The transformation of city walls and neighborhoods in Philadelphia began in the mid-1980s via an anti-graffiti initiative.[18] Mayor Wilson Goode offered graffiti "taggers" amnesty for their criminal defacing of public buildings and space if they would participate in various mural projects around the city. Soon, taggers began to identify with their mural art, rather than their graffittied signatures, largely because the project's artists incorporated these young people, and eventually their communities, in every stage of the mural process—from brainstorming designs and prepping walls to judging the authenticity of images and organizing dedication ceremonies. Today the city's Mural Arts Program has a $2.5 million budget (the majority of which comes from private and corporate supporters) and involves more than 3,500 Philadelphians every year—from neighborhood block captains and public school students to corporate responsibility departments and incarcerated felons.[19] The city's murals "show alternatives to the often difficult daily round of urban life, especially in poor parts of town," and the process of creating them "suggests how to build those alternatives."[20] This humble and collaborative process has earned Philadelphia a reputation as having the pre-eminent civic mural program in the U.S. and the singular moniker as the "mural capital of the world." More than 2,700 murals now decorate the City of Philadelphia and have become a source of neighborhood and city pride.[21]

Art for the Neighborhood: Murals and Black Theology

I would suggest that several of Philadelphia's community-based murals contextualize central elements of black theology and spirituality. They do so in a way that echoes the insights of leading black theologians and simultaneously suggests new directions for theological reflection and ecclesial praxis. First, the types of murals black communities create and the images they use to express their values and visions reflect the particular challenges faced by Philadelphia's African-American communities in articulating a sense of identity, a notion of God rooted in that struggle, and theological principles that arise from the community's experience as black persons. To some extent, this is the very praxis of black theology.

Its distinctive characteristics clearly surface when comparing murals from different communities throughout the city. For example, many community murals in historic districts or ethnically western European neighborhoods reflect aspects of Philadelphia's colonial and immigrant history. The images and symbols of these murals reinforce an unequivocal identity rooted in a shared national or ethnic history, a patriotic recollection of figures and events, and a confident vision for a future rooted in this triumphant past. Moreover, the very style of these murals reflects the unity of past, present, and future in these communities. Many portray symmetrical, clean, linear, and unambiguous depictions of events or persons with little need for interpretation and relatively little potential for self-reflective pause on the part of the passerby.

Certainly, many black community murals reflect a similar model, particularly in proclaiming national and local black leaders, both past and present. However, many others also reflect the contradictions of a history shaped by cultural genocide, a history imposed by a dominant culture, and a history of searching for authentic self-expression. This dynamic gives rise to symbolically rich and evocative visual arts that clearly resist what Cassidy calls "simplistic attributions" for suffering caused by a history of oppression and present conditions of concentrated poverty.[22] Many of these murals integrate a variety of seemingly disparate images and symbols that passionately pull the viewer into the tumultuous, conflicted, and evolving sense of community identity. Consider *Lincoln Legacy* (Sarantitis, 2005), a 10,000-square-foot mural combining paint and Venetian glass, in the Center City district. While the piece was commissioned by the city and supported by a private foundation, its design emerged from a series of community meetings at the National Constitution Center regarding Lincoln and slavery, as well as the creative input of children from five Philadelphia middle schools that examined these topics through public art incorporated in their curriculum. The end result is an arresting image that explores the history of slavery and abolition, rather than Lincoln himself, whose image appears only in one of three small medallions hanging around the neck of a young African-American girl who is the focal point of the mural. The child, actually one of the many students who participated in laying the tiles for the mosaic component of the mural, separates swirling images of a violent and turbulent past—the African continent, broken planks of a slave ship, shackles, and a skeletal mask—and an im-

Josh Sarantitis, *Lincoln Legacy*. 2005. A 10,000-square-foot mural combining paint and Venetian glass, in the Center City district, Philadelphia. Mural Arts Program, Philadelphia.

age of the future, a woman who appears in the midst of a blue flame arising from a larger West African medallion, which the child holds in her hand. A ribbon of words describing the historic struggle between the principles of right and wrong encircles the girl's outstretched arm, while the stripes of the American flag behind her bleed into the planks of the ship to her right. Vibrant and swirling colors, the specter of the past in the present, and a symbolic reaching for the future reflect the ambiguity and complexity of the thick multiculturalism of the African Diaspora and a resilient spirit that refuses to be consumed by poverty and violence.

These murals reflect the black community's ongoing struggle to resist what theologian Jamie Phelps calls the "continued institutionalized oppression, internalized self-hatred, and nihilistic despair" that often shape black identity.[23] To that extent, the murals amplify the experiences and wisdom of the contemporary community in overcoming these obstacles to individual and communal flourishing. Therefore, they become a new locus of theological reflection and social action for those in the academy, those leading the congregation, and those in the neighborhood. Black scholars and ministers increasingly suggest the community as the optimal starting point for a public discourse that necessarily integrates and then educates the academy, churches, and community in addressing the reality of urban African Americans. In many ways the murals embody the observations of Warren Dennis, an urban minister and theologian: "The very fact that black people still exist in America is an example of unyielding faith in a power greater than humankind. It means, moreover, that hope for the African American lies in reclaiming these beliefs and values as instruction arising out of the community itself."[24]

Certainly, Philadelphia's community-based murals represent an educative art that reclaims beliefs and values. More important, they offer a visual expression of what Kelly Brown Douglas defines as the "harmonious relationality" that epitomizes the theological beliefs and values that arise from the black community.[25] To that end, in their very attempt to articulate an identity and envision a future within the reality of concentrated poverty these murals form a visual dialogue between black theology and political theology in the North American context. These two fundamental theologies merge via an emphasis upon community empowerment, social critique, and social responsibility. Reflection on *Born Again* enables theologians in the academy and ministers in the churches to "walk out from behind the stained-glass windows of [the] sanctuary, and reach into and embrace communities and the residents of those communities to affirm Black life. . . ."[26]

Second, many black community murals reflect what Copeland calls the critical, commemorative and celebratory praxis of black theology,[27] as found in *Steppers* (Cavin Jones, 1996) located at the center of a formerly poverty-entrenched community of North Philadelphia. Like many others, the location itself is prophetic. *Steppers* is displayed on the wall of a former Catholic convent adjacent to the lot where St. Elizabeth's Catholic Church, once the anchor of this community, used to stand. The former church dominates the background of the piece. Interspersed in its peaks and spires are images of three neighbors engaged in everyday tasks: an adult man writing, an elderly woman petting a cat, and a young boy working in a garden filled with sunflowers. At the base of the mural, three young women march staunchly, in bright red and white tasseled uniforms—they are clearly the mural's namesake and project forward-moving energy as they dramatically fill the scene. One could interpret the mural's *critical* message regarding any false or stereotypical connotations of this community or of blackness itself on the part of outsiders. One might also note a critical reflection upon the failure of the Catholic Church to remain a physical and spiritual presence in neighborhoods most in need. At the same time, the depiction of the church, as well as an elderly woman at its highest peak, *commemorates* the various persons who have been the bedrock, memory, and caretakers of the community. Finally, the mural *celebrates* its namesake, The North Philadelphia Foot Stompers, a regionally acclaimed drum corps from the St. Elizabeth's neighborhood, who are clearly portrayed as marching resolutely into a hopeful future. To that end, the mural serves as a new expression of what Cone has identified as a central goal of black theology: creating "a religious value system that encourages us to love blackness passionately and without compromise."[28]

Third, these community murals publicly reflect aspects of black spirituality that visually thicken traditional worship, symbols, and music. *It Takes a Village* (Cavin Jones, 1997) embodies three distinct horizons layered upon each other—the city's skyline most distant, the tops of a block of traditional Philadelphia row homes in the middle, and a low green bush and a semi-circle of thatched huts in the foreground. The focal point of the piece is an enlarged sphere with an infant held aloft by several hands under an arched representation of the mural's title. To some extent the mural reflects aspects of what Phelps calls the "African world-view" that undergirds black spirituality.[29] It emphasizes the role of the community—that of the city, the neighborhood, and the family—in articulating identity and ensuring survival, and a celebration of what Phelps calls a "central life-force or power" that preserves and strengthens the community.

Many of Philadelphia's murals embody and deepen the unique expressions of black spirituality that have arisen from the African-American experience: the unity of the secular and the sacred; an emphasis upon individual sufferings that are gathered into the community and collectively resisted; a focus upon scripture and a dialogical experience with the Word; depictions of an immanent God who is experienced in people's lives through bodily engagement with the Spirit; a sense that worship and the sacred cannot be contained in the physical church but rather in the corporeal body of Christ; and hope in a powerfully transcendent God who seeks liberation for suffering people.[30]

Finally, many of Philadelphia's community murals suggest new directions for black theology and spirituality when rooted in contemporary experiences of urban poverty. Unlike traditional African spirituality that focuses upon the present, most of Philadelphia's murals incorporate futuristic themes epitomized by children reaching beyond boundaries or limitations, young people in various stages of physical and spiritual transformation, or the transformative power of a child's imagination. *Songs of Hope* (Gensler, 2002) is a three-story mural painted on the side of the Give to Heaven Church. It portrays a young boy in an oversized, white basketball jersey gazing at and walking toward the horizon behind the viewer, with three other children engaged in various activities in the background. The prevalence of murals such as this one, that privilege both the imaginative and transformative capabilities of children, might suggest an emerging sacramentality of youth within black urban spirituality. The murals clearly depict young people as members of the community who most effectively embody God's active presence in the neighborhood as well as God's active desire for the community's future. They represent confidence in and a commitment to breaking through the dehumanizing barriers of urban poverty. In addition, the murals' futuristic orientations compellingly proclaim an embodied virtue of hope. They suggest hope not as a simplistic attribution that anesthetizes the community to its suffering reality, but rather as a disposition, imaginative capacity, and communal practice of active resistance against the assumed inevitability of poverty.

Art for Passersby: Murals and North American Political Theology

Murals are intended not only for the community by whom they are created. More than six thousand people take guided mural tours through various Philadelphia neighborhoods each year. Therefore, this art also shapes a type of theological reflection necessary for those *not* trapped in communities of concentrated poverty. In other words, these murals have something to say to God-talk rooted in political theology. Here I am influenced by Johann Baptist Metz, who suggests that as a fundamental theology, political theology resists reducing "the heart of the Christian message and the practical exercise of faith to the decision of the individual standing apart from the world" and formulates "the eschatological message of Christianity in the conditions of present-day society."[31] I do not think it is a coincidence that community art and political theology emerged at the same time in the late 1960s. Each responds to similar questions of relevance, concerns about social suffering, the accurate articulation of communal memory, and commitments to social change. The murals reinforce the objective of political theology. They do more than merely articulate what is going on in a particular reality. Rather, they interpret that reality in light of experiences of urban poverty and a relationship with an immanent God of suffering, hope, and liberation. There are several points of intersection that are important for those of us reflecting upon these murals as "passersby."

First, community-based murals underscore the moral authority of suffering in accurately reading and responding to the signs of the times. Metz suggests that the experiences of suffering persons create a "moral awareness" within traditions—in this case faith traditions and civic traditions—by privileging a perspective of suffering on the social reality.[32] This perspective frequently reveals the connection between prevailing values and visions and the dehumanizing aspects of our culture, in this instance attitudes regarding race, poverty, and the urban poor. Therefore, in a way that is essential for North American political theology, Philadelphia's community murals proclaim an expression of suffering that has been frequently ignored by the theological academy, namely the suffering of urban poverty. Moreover, they do so in a way that avoids "the spiritualization of evil and suffering" in order to "remember, retell, resist and redeem."[33] To that end, the murals empower those who create them. They enable communities to move beyond despair and self-loathing, to reflect upon aspects of their identity and dreams, and then to resist the dehumanization of poverty by prophetically proclaiming these identities and visions.

Perhaps most important, the harmonious relationality of the process and content of these murals echoes Metz's claim that the moral authority of suffering brings passersby to an important stance of self- and social-criticism. This communal art interrupts. Josh Sarantitis, the lead muralist behind *Lincoln Legacy*, says, "I want the murals to create a dialogue so people who pass by will think and question—and even question their own beliefs—whether they pass by ten times or a hundred times. . . ."[34] The murals "ruthlessly unmask the myths of self-exculpation and the mechanisms of trivialization" that we frequently rely on to navigate our difficult encounters with those who suffer.[35] They interrupt conventional notions of everything from art to community development to reveal how the world really works, to remind people of the "struggle against all odds" just to survive, let alone flourish, in these forgotten neighborhoods, and to resist the amnesia of those living in isolated pockets of urban privilege or the sprawling expanse of Philadelphia's suburbs. The murals create conflict, radical questioning, and reflection upon conditions of privilege and structural sin, which create concentrated poverty. They can become the touchstone for self-critical reflection, liberating guilt, and active social responsibility that is equally transformative for flourishing communities within the City of Brotherly Love.

Second, community-based murals offer new constructs for political theology's central categories of memory and narrative. Metz understands memory as a transformative expression of human freedom, an emancipatory act of social criticism, and an essential component of human reason.[36] Certainly, Philadelphia's murals meet these criteria in a visually evocative format. Painters and viewers are transformed as they articulate and interpret memories of forgotten communities. But more important, the murals transform the social reality of the neighborhood and the city. They publicly share narratives of the lived experiences of individuals and communities long denied access to Philadelphia's public square and civil society, and in so doing re-direct public memory and dialogue. The memories of the black community in Philadelphia are not just dangerous; they are, as Diana Hayes claims, "subversive."[37] They speak not only to a future that has yet to be achieved, but to a past that has yet to be accurately remembered. As subversive memories, these murals heal the selective recollection of the city's dominant culture. This is particularly important for Philadelphia, the birthplace of a democracy that denied human rights to a significant portion of the inhabitants of the colonies. Community-based murals subvert notions of blackness, definitions of racism, analyses of poverty, theological anthropologies, and approaches to God that do not incorporate the wisdom of communities of suffering. The subversive memories of the murals heal the imagination of a city grappling to address crippling social injustices by privileging the wisdom of the marginalized and demanding responsibility. A muralist working with truant students on a mural addressing the importance of education, notes: "The fact that we're doing this mural just as you enter the Financial District says that truancy is everyone's problem. It cannot be ignored."[38]

Third, Philadelphia's murals underscore the importance of active and expressive participation and empowerment as essential for protecting individual and communal subjecthood. They enable marginalized persons and communities to become creative agents in social transformation. They suggest that actively expressing memories in art itself is a method of resistance and empowerment. According to Feshin, "individuals are empowered through such creative expression, as they acquire a voice, visibility, and an awareness that they are part of a greater whole."[39]

Moreover, the murals serve as larger-than-life proclamations of what it means to be a human person, frequently the foundational point of justice theories. In a way that is consistent with ideas of black theology and spirituality, the murals emphasize a social and communal nature of persons that is often lost in the rationalism and individualism of Western and liberal anthropologies. They offer a departure from the unencumbered cost-benefit approach to development that frequently shapes models of social-analysis theories of justice. The murals visually ask the "tragic questions" regarding unjust suffering.[40] These questions challenge an individualistic approach to the causes of, and solutions for, concentrated poverty and focus attention on the socially constructed factors of suffering that lie beyond individual control.

In addition, these murals incorporate imagination, emotions and symbols to envision a future that has yet to be achieved, reinforcing the importance of these social capacities in moral reasoning and development. Their very creation suggests a practical and tangible solidarity among disparate city dwellers—one uniting artists, neighbors, and private donors in a dialogical and creative relationship that is restorative and transformative for all involved. Says Golden, "There's something about doing a mural that's different from other art; you have to be in people's homes, getting paint, using their water, developing relationships. I think murals

have an interesting power to transcend hostility and racial barriers. I don't want to sugarcoat it, but it is an interesting dynamic."[41]

Art for Building the City of God: Murals
and Catholic Social Ethics

In her Madeleva Lecture in 2006, ethicist Susan Ross suggested
that beauty is integrally connected to justice when we consider
beauty as an authentic expression of care of self, an expression of
generosity toward, and respect for, others, and an expression of
participation in the transformative work of God.[42] In an article on
the aesthetics of race, Copeland suggests that "beauty is the *living
up to and living out* the love and summons of creation to our
particularity and specificity as God's human creatures."[43]

There are clear connections between these theologians and
muralist Golden on beauty: "When you introduce beauty," says
Golden, "it makes people feel that they have a voice, that they can
be part of the system of change, that there's potential, that redemption is possible."[44] In the spirit of these comments I shall
conclude by briefly suggesting that community-based expressions
of beauty amplify several principles of Catholic social teaching so
that the tradition—whose very origins lie in addressing the suffering of the urban poor—might be more effective in building the
City of God with persons struggling in concentrated poverty.[45]

First, the very "bottom-up" process of creating these wall-sized
subversive memories contextualizes the principle of subsidiarity,
defined in *Quadragesimo Anno* as the imperative of those at higher
levels of civil society to empower those affected by social problems in devising solutions to them.[46] Neighbors are the leaders in
the creation of these murals—from submitting the initial application to the Mural Arts Program, and participating in multiple neighborhood meetings with the muralists to arrive at a shared artistic
vision, to planning dedication celebrations. In addition, the Mural
Arts Program "demonstrates respect for people who are largely
excluded from government and traditional vehicles of public expression," a commitment that not only accounts for the integrity
and authenticity of their art, but also for the growing desire of
communities to invite the program and its muralists into their neighborhoods.[47]

The dialogically creative procedure of each mural is not without conflicts. Golden notes that this type of public art demands an

awareness of the tension among the often perfunctory vision of supporting institutions, the artistically trained vision of the muralist, and the frequently more evocative vision of the community. Together they work toward an organic, over-lapping consensus about the central values of a community, the pivotal memories that shape their self-understanding, and their shared vision for the future. The final product publicly expresses themes of participation and empowerment, which trigger other subtle and substantial changes in the neighborhoods where they are painted. Community organizing grows alongside community gardens; social awareness deepens as social relationships expand; and visual expressions of the future spark actual expressions of it in the present. For example, neighbors in a racially divided community in the Gray's Ferry section of southwest Philadelphia came together to create *Peace Wall* (Golden, Adonis and Pagast, 1997), a top-down view of eleven sets of hands—five black and six white—layered upon each other in the center of a human huddle, with a proclamation about peacemakers from the Sermon on the Mount just to the right. This mural reflects an organic, relational, and practical attempt to respond to racially motivated violence in the neighborhood.

Second, the murals thicken the fundamental principle of the common good, or "the sum total of those conditions of social living whereby [people] are enabled more fully and more readily to achieve their own perfection."[48] The murals expand urban understandings of the term "community." The physical location of this art raises an awareness of neighborhoods that have long been forgotten in Philadelphia's memory and marginalized from Philadelphia's civil society. As a result of these public and subversive memories, the center of political—and theological—reflection in the city has shifted toward the margins in order to explore more effectively what is going on in these places and to embrace urban interconnectivity.

These murals also expand notions of civic space. Whereas public libraries, municipal administration buildings, or public squares were once deemed the appropriate space for public art—implicitly underscoring their significance as centers for civic activity—today community murals call our attention to forgotten spaces of the *polis* where such activity is slowly being restored. The vibrancy of the St. Elizabeth's neighborhood in North Philadelphia, where *Steppers* rises above the street, attests to the transformative power of this public art. In the spirit of black theology, the murals themselves celebrate the importance of life in community as the locus for personal and social transformation. They challenge approaches to the common good that individualize either the causes of poverty or responses to it, and visually underscore the importance of empowerment and participation in revitalizing the common good. As suggested earlier, the mural process creates relationships among previously alienated communities within the city to create a provocative unity that demands the attention and response of others.

Finally, Philadelphia's murals cultivate an approach to compassion that I argue is increasingly necessary if Catholic social ethics is to respond effectively to concentrated poverty. Via this community art suffering communities caught in the cycle of urban poverty make provocative demands on those of us who are privileged to tour the neighborhoods from which they cry out. The murals underscore the claim that an effective response to this social suffering cannot focus solely upon transforming those below the threshold of flourishing. Rather, this response should examine those above the threshold, who participate in the factors that "push" privileged persons out of particular urban areas, "pull" them into communities of self-segregation, and leave behind the economically immobile.[49] These murals can cultivate self- and socially-critical values and visions in the dominant culture by giving "voice to the experiences of groups in our society that we urgently need to understand."[50] This understanding only amplifies the central mission of Catholic social teaching, namely embracing the "responsibilities of resistance and engagement."[51]

Philadelphia's murals offer visual proof that compassionately addressing concentrated poverty demands a rich complement of capabilities best sustained by a variety of institutional actors in civil society and through a humble willingness to be directed by the prophetic narrative art of those who are marginalized. If compassion involves truly entering into the suffering of another in order to effectively resist it, then I suggest these murals enable us to do so in a way that is public rather than private, communal rather than individual, socially critical rather than uncritically sentimental, and oriented toward justice rather than charity. The murals demand that we examine our social and theological ignorance regarding the intersecting variables that create conditions of urban poverty, that we acknowledge our participation in the structural sin of race and "unshared power," and that we participate in social change by privileging the perspective of those who proclaim their visions of our shared future on the walls of our cities.

Notes

[1] I am grateful for the generous support of a Henry Luce Foundation Faculty Fellowship, awarded through the Society for the Arts in Religious and Theological Studies, which makes my continued research in this area possible.

[2] According *to Born Again*'s lead muralist, Cliff Eubanks, the community requested "positive images reflecting care for children and hope for the future." He identifies three themes: expectation of the resurrection, the possibility of renewing and rebuilding communities, and "opportunities that are born anew with each generation." See Jane Golden et al., *Philadelphia Murals and the Stories They Tell* (Philadelphia: Temple University Press, 2002), 150-51.

[3] Concentrated poverty is frequently described in terms of economic and racial "hyper-segregation." See Douglas Massey, *American Apartheid: Segregation and the Making of the Underclass* (Cambridge: Harvard University Press, 1993). David Rusk characterizes neighborhoods of concentrated poverty as having a significant number of residents struggling to survive below the poverty line with minimal access to the common good with a high percentage of abandoned properties and low property values and rents. See "Social Change Strategies for the Future of Metropolitan Areas," in *Living the Catholic Social Tradition: Cases and Commentary*, ed. Kathleen Maas Weigert (New York: Sheed & Ward, 2005), 13-19. In its analysis of 2000 Census data, the Brookings Institution reports that while Philadelphia boasts the second highest percentage of homeownership among the nation's "living cities" (a group of twenty-three identified by the National Community Development Initiative for close examination by the Brookings Institution), Philadelphia's median household income ranks in the bottom quarter of large U.S. cities. In addition, 38 percent of families with children live at or under the poverty line, and "in several neighborhoods more than 40 percent of residents live in poverty." Moreover, at least 100,000 Philadelphians "have incomes low enough that they pay more than 30 percent of their income on housing." African Americans are concentrated in the city's western neighborhoods while Hispanics are concentrated in its northern neighborhoods. See *Philadelphia in Focus: A Profile from Census 2000*, The Brookings Institution, November 2003. Retrieved from http://www.brookings.edu/es/urban/livingcities/ Philadelphia.htm on 27 November 2006.

[4] The dehumanizing impacts of urban poverty and race are sporadically addressed in the central documents of Catholic social teaching. For example, *Pacem et Terris* §94 addresses the discrimination of ethnic minorities within the international community; *Gaudium et Spes* §29 condemns discrimination rooted in gender, ethnicity, or race; and the *Compendium of the Social Doctrine of the Church* §433 reinforces these statements but fails in §477 to include race among the causes of poverty. The U.S. Conference of Catholic Bishops reflects a tradition of examining race and poverty, exemplified in

Economic Justice for All §15 as well as the 1979 statement, "Brothers and Sisters to Us," and its twenty-fifth anniversary document. See also the *Journal of Catholic Social Thought* 3, no. 1 (2006) for several articles examining the issue of race in Catholic social ethics as well as a comprehensive bibliography of Catholic social teaching on racism. This article also incorporates the insights of several scholars whose work considers the intersection of urban poverty and theology. They include Laurie Cassidy, James Cone, M. Shawn Copeland, and Thomas Massaro, among others.

[5]James Cone, "Black Liberation Theology and Black Catholics: A Critical Conversion," *Theological Studies* 61 (2000): 731-47.

[6]M. Shawn Copeland, "Presidential Address: Political Theology as Interruptive," *Proceedings of the Catholic Theological Society of America* 59 (2004): 71-82.

[7]Given the limitations of this article, as well as a dearth of scholarship in this particular area, I intentionally focus my examination here on murals located in Philadelphia's black communities or those created through various urban justice initiatives spearheaded by Philadelphia's Mural Arts Program. Certainly a more comprehensive study would include an examination of the abundant community art located in the city's vibrant Latino and Caribbean neighborhoods, particularly given that Philadelphia boasts the second highest Hispanic poverty rates of the nation's "living cities" and the highest in segregation between whites and Hispanics according to 2000 Census data. See the Brookings Institution's *Philadelphia in Focus: A Profile from Census 2000*. Ana Maria Pineda offers a resourceful theological exploration of murals and *retablos* that decorate and commemorate various Latino immigration roots and neighborhoods. Her work has been influential in shaping my examination of black community art. See, for example, "The Murals: *Rostros del Pueblo*," *Journal of Hispanic and Liberation Theology* 8, no. 2 (2000): 5-17, as well as "Imagenes de Dios en El Camino: Retablos, Ex-Votos, Milagritos, and Murals," *Theological Studies* 65 (2004): 364-79.

[8]Richard Viladesau, *Theology and the Arts: Encountering God through Music, Art and Rhetoric* (New York: Paulist Press, 2000), 124.

[9]Ibid, 114-18. In fact, Viladesau goes so far as to say, "In light of our increased awareness of the symbolic nature of all discourse, and especially religious discourse, it is perhaps not unreasonable to project that the theology of the future . . . will at least in part be modeled more on art and on the humanities than on an ideal of objective evidence and material progress" (118).

[10]Katie Geneva Cannon, "Diaspora Ethics: 'The Hinges upon Which the Future Swings,' " in *Africentric Approaches to Christian Ministry: Strengthening Urban Congregations in African American Communities*, ed. Ronald Edward Peters and Marsha Snulligan Haney (Lanham, MD: University Press of America, 2006), 141-50, at 142. See also *Black Womanist Ethics* (Atlanta: Scholars Press, 1988).

[11]I incorporate a variety of sources in articulating this thesis: Nina Feshin,

But Is It Art?: The Spirit of Art as Activism (Seattle: Bay Press, 1995); Martha Cooper and Joseph Sciorra, *R.I.P.: Memorial Wall Art* (New York: Henry Holt & Co., 1994); Eva Cockcroft, John Pitman, and James Cockcroft, eds., *Towards a People's Art: The Contemporary Mural Movement* (Albuquerque: University of New Mexico Press, 1998); Jane Golden, Robin Rice, and Natalie Pompilio, *More Philadelphia Murals and the Stories They Tell* (Philadelphia: Temple University Press, 2006).

    [12]Golden et al., *More Philadelphia Murals and the Stories They Tell*, 20-21.

    [13]Murals were frequently disregarded as "kitsch" or conventional, popular, and superficial; critics continue to consider them "minority art" or "poor art for poor people." See Golden's overview of this debate in *More Philadelphia Murals and the Stories They Tell*, 16-18, and the "Introduction" of *Towards a People's Art*, xxi-xxii.

    [14]Feshin, *But Is It Art?*, 18.

    [15]Ibid., 26.

    [16]Jane Golden, "More Philadelphia Murals: 'Table Talk,' " at the White Dog Café, Philadelphia, October 22, 2006.

    [17]Kathryn Levy Feldman, "The Big Picture," *University of Pennsylvania Gazette* [updated 28 February 2002; cited 27 May 2006]. Available from http://www.upenn.edu/gazette/0302/feldman2.html.

    [18]For a full history of Philadelphia's murals, see *Philadelphia Murals and the Stories They Tell*.

    [19]In addition to partnering with one hundred communities throughout the city each year to create neighborhood murals, the Mural Arts Program also integrates murals into four social justice initiatives that focus upon resisting concentrated poverty: 1) the Big Picture program, an after-school program offered in conjunction with the School District of Philadelphia for 2,500 students ages 10-18; 2) the Mural Corps program, an intensive artistic training and mentoring program for at-risk youth ages 14-22; 3) the ArtWORKS! after-school program for delinquent or truant students; and 4) the Healing Walls program, which brings together victims and perpetrators of violent crimes in the creative and restorative process of mural-making.

    [20]Golden, *Philadelphia Murals and the Stories They Tell*, 9.

    [21]A full online catalogue of Philadelphia's more than 2,700 murals can be accessed through the University of Pennsylvania's Cartographic Modeling Lab at http://cml.upenn.edu/murals/.

    [22]Laurie Cassidy, "Affirming *Imago Dei*: Implications of the Black Congress Movement's Reception of *Rerum Novarum* no. 32 for Moral Reasoning in Suffering," *Journal of Catholic Social Thought* 3, no. 1 (Winter 2006): 41-46. By this phrase Cassidy means background theories, or linguistic "tropes," that people rely upon to make sense of suffering or injustice.

    [23]Jamie Phelps, "Inculturating Jesus," in *Taking Down Our Harps: Black Catholics in the United States*, ed. Diana Hayes and Cyprian Davis (Maryknoll, NY: Orbis Books, 1998), 73.

[24]Warren L. Dennis, "The Challenges of Africentric Ministry for Urban Theological Education," in *Africentric Approaches to Christian Ministry: Strengthening Urban Congregations in African American Communities*, ed. Ronald Edward Peters and Marsha Snulligan Haney (Lanham, MD: University Press of America, 2006), 131-39, at 132.

[25]Kelly Brown Douglas, *What's Faith Got to Do with It?: Black Bodies/ Christian Souls* (Maryknoll, NY: Orbis Books, 2005), 202. Douglas argues that this relationality pulls together justice, hope, and love, which James Cone identifies as the central theological principles of black theology. She cites his "Calling the Oppressors to Account: Justice, Love and Hope in Black Religion," in *The Courage to Hope: From Black Suffering to Human Redemption*, ed. Quinton Hosford Dixie and Cornel West (Boston: Beacon Press, 1999).

[26]Jonnie Monroe, "Building an Africentric Bridge from Inside Stained-Glass Windows to the Community Outside," in *Africentric Approaches to Christian Ministry: Strengthening Urban Congregations in African American Communities*, ed. Ronald Edward Peters and Marsha Snulligan Haney (Lanham, MD: University Press of America, 2006), 97-107, at 99. Monroe, pastor of Grace Memorial Presbyterian Church in Pittsburgh, suggests four essential "planks" for building a bridge between the church of the academy and the church of the community. I suggest that all four are embodied in the process of community-based murals: prayer, listening, collaboration, and community concept.

[27]M. Shawn Copeland, "Method in Emerging Black Catholic Theology," in *Taking Down Our Harps: Black Catholics in the United States*, ed. Diana Hayes and Cyprian Davis (Maryknoll, NY: Orbis Books, 1998), 120-44.

[28]Cone, "Black Liberation Theologies and Black Catholics," 742.

[29]Jamie Phelps, "Black Spirituality," in *Taking Down Our Harps: Black Catholics in the United States*, ed. Diana Hayes and Cyprian Davis (Maryknoll, NY: Orbis Books, 1998), 183. See also the chapter titled, "African American Spirituality as Survival" in Lee H. Butler's *Liberating Our Dignity, Saving Our Souls* (St. Louis: Chalice Press, 2006).

[30]Ibid.

[31]Johann Baptist Metz, "Political Theology," in *Sacramentum Mundi: An Encyclopedia of Theology*, ed. Karl Rahner (New York: Herder & Herder, 1968), 1239.

[32]See Metz's argument for the development of a moral awareness of tradition in Jewish-Christian ecumenism in "Christians and Jews after Auschwitz," in *The Emergent Church: The Future of Christianity in a Postbourgeois World* (New York: Crossroad, 1981), 17-33.

[33]M. Shawn Copeland, "Wading Through Many Sorrows: Toward a Theology of Suffering in Womanist Perspective," in *Moral Evil and Redemptive Suffering: A History of Theodicy in African-American Religious Thought*, ed. Anthony B. Pinn (Gainesville: University of Florida Press, 2002), 315-38, at 331.

[34]Golden, *More Philadelphia Murals*, 77.

[35]Metz, *The Emergent Church*, 21.

[36]See *Faith in History and Society: Toward a Practical Fundamental Theology* (New York: Seabury Press, 1979).

[37]Diana Hayes, "And When We Speak: To Be Catholic and Womanist," in *Taking Down Our Harps: Black Catholics in the United States*, ed. Diana Hayes and Cyprian Davis (Maryknoll, NY: Orbis Books, 1998), 112.

[38]Catherine Fredman, "Walls Can Talk," *Steelcase 360* [updated September 2004; cited 27 May 2006]. Available from http://www.steelcase.com/na/files/50abbc44d0d6452e9014c5d5f5f9ef20/PhiladelphiasMur.pdf.

[39]Feshin, *But Is It Art?*, 12.

[40]See Martha Nussbaum, "The Costs of Tragedy: Some Moral Limits to Cost-Benefit Analysis," *Journal of Legal Studies* 29 (2001): 1005-36.

[41]Golden et al., *Philadelphia Murals*, 36.

[42]Susan Ross, "For the Beauty of the Earth: Women, Sacramentality and Justice" (paper presented at the Annual Madeleva Lecture, St. Mary's College, South Bend, IN, April 20, 2006).

[43]M. Shawn Copeland, "Disturbing Aesthetics of Race," *Journal of Catholic Social Thought* 3, no. 1 (2006): 19.

[44]As quoted in Fredman, "Walls Can Talk."

[45]Thomas Massaro suggests, "The encyclical tradition is tied inextricably to the reality of the modern urban setting. Indeed, there would be no tradition of modern Catholic social teaching if it were not for urbanization" ("From Industrialization to Globalization: Church and Social Ministry," in *Living the Catholic Tradition: Cases and Commentary*, ed. Kathleen Maas Weigert [New York: Sheed & Ward, 2005], 51).

[46]*Quadragesimo Anno*, §80.

[47]Golden continues, "MAP's greatest strength is in knowing how to listen at sometimes raucous community meetings, derive unifying kernels from often vaguely stated wishes, and turn them into positive visual images worthy of wall-scale public expression" (*Philadelphia Murals*, 8).

[48]*Mater et Magistra*, §65.

[49]Rusk, "Social Change Strategies for the Future of Metropolitan Areas," 13-19.

[50]Martha Nussbaum, *Cultivating Humanity: A Classical Defense of Reform in Liberal Education* (Cambridge: Harvard University Press, 1997), 97-100. I argue that community murals can be applied to Nussbaum's commentary on the transformative power of literature: "A central role of art is to challenge conventional wisdom and values. . . . Literary understanding is a form of imaginative and emotional receptivity that can seem profoundly threatening to the sort of person who would demonize other groups. To allow inside one's mind people who seem alien and frightening is to show a capacity for openness and responsiveness that goes against the grain of many cultural stereotypes of self-sufficiency."

[51]Copeland, "Disturbing Aesthetics of Race," 25.

Contributors

Susie Paulik Babka is currently visiting assistant professor of theology at the University of Notre Dame. She has also taught at Catholic Theological Union, Dominican University, and Goshen College. She completed her Ph.D. at Notre Dame; her dissertation, "Karl Rahner and Jürgen Moltmann on Whether God Is Immutable in Jesus Christ," explores some of the foundational metaphysics toward understanding the relationship between God and suffering. She is working on a book that combines Moltmann's theology of the cross with the theological implications of the *Gnadenstuhl* motif.

Sandra Bowden is a painter and printmaker living in Chatham, Massachusetts. She is president of Christians in the Visual Arts and has championed the renewal of the visual arts in the life of the church. Bowden's art is a complex meditation on time. Her work, which explores the relationship between seeing and reading, image and text, by incorporating biblical archaeological references and ancient texts, is found in collections throughout North America, Europe, and Israel. A book of her art, *The Art of Sandra Bowden* (Square Halo Books), was published in 2005.

James F. Caccamo is assistant professor of social ethics in the Theology Department at Saint Joseph's University, Philadelphia. A former choir director and computer programmer, Caccamo focuses his work on how various cultural and religious modes of communication affect the formation and practice of the moral life. His current research investigates the role of liturgical music in the moral life and the implications of computing and information technologies on spiritual and moral practices. He recently published "Been There, Sung That: How the Music of Worship Shapes People of God," *Liturgy* 22, no. 1 (December 2006).

Ki Joo Choi is an assistant professor in the Department of Religious Studies at Seton Hall University in South Orange, New Jersey. He holds a Ph.D. in theological ethics from Boston College. His research interests include the role of art and material culture in moral discourse, social ethics, political theory, and ecumenical dialogue (particularly between Catholic and Reformed thought).

William J. Collinge received a Ph.D. in philosophy from Yale University. Since 1980, he has taught at Mount Saint Mary's University in Emmitsburg, Maryland, where he holds the Knott Professorship in Theology and a joint appointment to the philosophy department. He is the author of *The A to Z of Catholicism* (Scarecrow, 2001) and "What Story Are We In? The Use of Tolkien in John Dunne's Recent Work," *Horizons* 30 (2003): 208-26.

Colleen Carpenter Cullinan is an assistant professor of theology at the College of St. Catherine in St. Paul, Minnesota. Her current research is divided between her ecofeminist interests and a project involving a theological approach to the problem of fistula, a devastating injury of childbirth common in Africa. She is author of *Redeeming the Story: Women, Suffering, and Christ* (Continuum, 2004) and several articles on spirituality and ecology. She received a Ph.D. in religion and literature from the University of Chicago Divinity School.

Frances M. Leap is associate professor of religious studies at Seton Hill University in Greensburg, Pennsylvania. She is a founding representative of the Consortium for Educational Resources in Islamic Studies (CERIS), and served as a visiting scholar at South Valley University in Egypt in December 2003

Thomas M. Lucas, S.J., is professor of art and design and former chair of the Visual Arts Department at the University of San Francisco, where he also serves as director of USF's Thacher Gallery. Lucas holds a doctorate in theology and the arts from the Graduate Theological Union, Berkeley. He designed and directed the restoration of the rooms of St. Ignatius in Rome. His book *Landmarking: City, Church and Jesuit Strategy* won an Association of Jesuit Colleges and Universities book prize in

2000. A nationally recognized liturgical designer, his work at St. Ignatius Church, San Francisco, has won awards from the American Institute of Architecture. His most recent project is the collaborative design process for stained-glass windows at Shanghai's St. Ignatius Cathedral.

Matthew G. Minix is a Ph.D. student in the University of Dayton's theology program in the U.S. Catholic Experience. Matthew received a B.A. in religious studies and in philosophy from Indiana University, and an M.A. from the St. Meinrad School of Theology. He has presented papers on Archbishop Fulton J. Sheen to both the Midwest American Academy of Religion and the College Theology Society in 2006. He is a contributor to Terrence W. Tilley's *Religious Diversity and the American Experience: A Theological Approach* (Continuum, 2007).

Maureen H. O'Connell is an assistant professor of theology at Fordham University. She holds a Ph.D. from Boston College in theological ethics and is currently a Luce Faculty Fellow through the Society for the Arts in Religious and Theological Studies.

David C. Robinson, S.J., is assistant professor of interdisciplinary studies and director of Educational Mission and Spirituality of Learning in the College of Professional Studies at the University of San Francisco. He holds a Ph.D. in theology and the arts from the Graduate Theological Union in Berkeley and has worked extensively on the contemporary intersection of spirituality, pedagogy, and technology. He works closely with the deans of adult and continuing education in Jesuit universities and the national on-line learning consortium, JesuitNET. He has also presented a CTSA plenary address ("Beyond the Gutenberg Hologram") on the twenty-first-century profile of the theological personality.

Randall S. Rosenberg, a Ph.D. candidate in systematic theology at Boston College, holds a B.A. in philosophy from Saint Louis University and an M.A. in theology from the Aquinas Institute of Theology. He is currently writing his dissertation on the thought of Bernard Lonergan and Hans Urs von Balthasar. His writings and book reviews have appeared in *America*, *Review for Religious*, and *Heythrop Journal*. His forthcoming articles on John Henry Newman and Thomas Aquinas will appear in *The Newman Studies Journal* and *Angelicum*. His interests include the relationship between theoretical and aesthetic-dramatic categories for systematic theology; the mystery of evil, suffering, and death in relation to the cross; and political theology.

Julie Hanlon Rubio is currently associate professor of Christian ethics at St. Louis University, where she has taught courses in marriage, religion and society, and social justice since 1999. She earned her M.T.S. from Harvard Divinity School and her Ph.D. in religion and social ethics from the University of Southern California. Her articles on family ethics have appeared in *Theological Studies*, the *Journal of the Society of Christian Ethics*, *Horizons*, *INTAMS (International Academy for Marital Spirituality) Review*, and *The Living Light*. Her *A Christian Theology of Marriage and Family* (Paulist Press, 2003) received a Catholic Press Association book award.

Don E. Saliers is the William R. Cannon Distinguished Professor of Theology and Worship at Emory University. He received both his M.Div. and Ph.D. degrees from Yale. He has served as president of the North American Academy of Liturgy and the Society for the Study of Christian Spirituality, and is on the editorial board of *Spiritus*, *Weavings*, and *Worship* journals. Among his publications are *Worship as Theology: Foretaste of Glory Divine* (1994), *Worship Come to Its Senses* (1996), The *Soul in Paraphrase* (1991), and most recently *A Song to Sing, A Life to Live* (2005), co-authored with daughter Emily Saliers. He is an active composer and serves as organist and choirmaster at Emory University's Cannon Chapel.

Jennifer Elisa Veninga holds an M.T.S. from Harvard Divinity School and is currently a doctoral student in theology and philosophy at the Graduate Theological Union in Berkeley. She was named a 2006 Summer Fellow for Research in Residence at the Howard V. and Edna H. Hong Kierkegaard Library at St. Olaf College in Northfield, Minnesota, and has studied in Copenhagen. In addition to Kierkegaard, her research focuses on the concept of social imagination, with particular attention to the role of religion and media in the public sphere.

Kimberly Vrudny teaches in the theology department at the University of St. Thomas in St. Paul, Minnesota. She co-edited, with Wilson Yates, *Arts, Theology, and the Church: New Intersections* (Pilgrim Press, 2005), which includes her essay, "Spirit Standing Still: Documenting Beauty in Theology." She is also the editor of the academic journal *ARTS: The Arts in Religious and Theological Studies*. She completed her Ph.D. in 2001 at Luther Seminary and currently serves as the interim faculty coordinator of service learning at St. Thomas.